Patents, Registered Designs, Trade Marks & Copyright
FOR DUMMIES®

by **John Grant, Charlie Ashworth, and Henri Charmasson**

With forewords by

Robin Webb
Director of Innovation, UK Intellectual Property Office

and

Trevor Baylis, OBE
Founder of Trevor Baylis Brands plc

John Wiley & Sons, Ltd

Patents, Registered Designs, Trade Marks & Copyright For Dummies®

Published by
John Wiley & Sons, Ltd
The Atrium
Southern Gate
Chichester
West Sussex
PO19 8SQ
England

E-mail (for orders and customer service enquires): cs-books@wiley.co.uk

Visit our Home Page on www.wiley.com

Copyright © 2008 John Wiley & Sons, Ltd, Chichester, West Sussex, England

Published by John Wiley & Sons, Ltd, Chichester, West Sussex

Wiley also publishes its books in a variety of electronic formats. Some content that appears in print may not be available in electronic books.

British Library Cataloguing in Publication Data: A catalogue record for this book is available from the British Library.

ISBN: 978-0-470-51997-4

10 9 8 7 6 5 4 3 2 1

WILEY

About the Authors

John Grant is a UK and European Patent and Trade Mark Attorney with over 35 years' experience in the prosecution, management, and licensing of Intellectual Property Rights (IPRs) for Redland PLC, now Lafarge SA, until early retirement in 1998.

For the last five years, while remaining as an IP consultant to Lafarge and others, John has provided IP services to Trevor Baylis Brands plc and has personally advised several hundred inventors concerning their innovations; some good, and some very good. Alas, however, some inventors have re-invented an old idea. In such cases, John's philosophy has been to let them down as gently as possible and to ensure that they're not too deflated but move quickly on to their next project that may prove to be more fruitful with the thought that 'if you don't roll the dice, you can't get a six'!

Charlie Ashworth is an Associate of the Chartered Institute of Patent Attorneys. Having graduated with a Bachelor of Science in Industrial Design and Manufacture in 2002, she went on to work for a leading product design consultancy in their IP team. Charlie completed both a Certificate and Masters in Intellectual Property Law and Management in 2006, and has worked as the Intellectual Property Manager for Trevor Baylis Brands plc, for whom she continues to act.

Charlie has over five years' experience in IP searching and the appraisal of new ideas and inventions, considering both the commercial and protectable aspects. She also works as a consultant to Stanleys, an established intellectual property practice, with offices in the UK and the Channel Islands.

Henri Charmasson is an attorney who specialises in intellectual property cases, and a product-branding consultant to major corporations. He's also an entrepreneur and inventor with his name on a dozen patents. In a distant life, he was an electrical engineer who designed aerospace and computer hardware.

Henri has authored several books and articles on patent, copyright, and trade mark topics, including an authoritative treatise about the art of naming companies and branding products.

Dedication

To innovators, young and not so young, whose ingenuity is a credit to each one of them and a bonus to us all.

Authors' Acknowledgements

We're most grateful to Henri Charmasson for his work that has enabled us to address the re-editing of this book, which we've found to be a most enjoyable and rewarding experience.

In addition we wish to thank the following for their help and encouragement. Miles Rees and his colleagues at the UK-IPO who kindly reviewed our final draft and kept us on the straight and narrow. Paul Leonard of the Intellectual Property Institute (IPI) and the Intellectual Property Network (IPAN). The Chartered Institute of Patent Attorneys (CIPA). Kevin Mooney and others of Simmons & Simmons. Derek Gambell of Graham Watt & Co LLP. Peter Jackson and Philip Robinson, the co-editors of the sister book *Inventing For Dummies*, for their assistance and advice in avoiding inconsistencies and anomalies between the two works.

JG and CA

Publisher's Acknowledgements

We're proud of this book; please send us your comments through our Dummies online registration form located at www.dummies.com/register/.

Some of the people who helped bring this book to market include the following:

Acquisitions, Editorial, and Media Development

Project Editor: Rachael Chilvers

Content Editor: Nicole Burnett

Development Editor: Colette Holden

Copy Editor: Martin Key

Proofreader: Anne O'Rorke

Technical Editor: UK Intellectual Property Office

Publisher: Jason Dunne

Executive Editor: Samantha Spickernell

Executive Project Editor: Daniel Mersey

Cover Photo: © Getty Images/John Foxx

Cartoons: Ed McLachlan

Special Help: Rev Mengle

Composition Services

Project Coordinator: Erin Smith

Layout and Graphics: Reuben W. Davis, Alissa D. Ellet, Joyce Haughey

Proofreader: David Faust

Indexer: Cheryl Duksta

Contents at a Glance

Table of Contents

Forewords

T he United Kingdom has never been short of creative people. It leads Europe in knowledge-based and high-tech businesses such as Formula 1 technology, computer gaming, and pharmaceuticals.

Industries such as these place great emphasis on the value of intellectual assets. Intellectual Property (IP) underpins businesses and helps stimulate innovation, allowing substantial returns on research and design investments.

IP rights are not influenced by the size of the company or the popularity of an individual but are based on the quality of the invention or, in the case of copyright, the creative work. The result of this is that IP rewards an inventor in his garden shed or the composer in her bedroom as much as a big automotive company or a pop superstar.

Ideas – the creations of the mind – are found across every aspect of our lives: ideas like a bagless vacuum cleaner, a clockwork radio, a vaccine against polio, a distinctive shape of a perfume bottle, an attractive brand name, a catchy tune, or the adventures of a boy wizard.

A similarly wide range of rights exists to protect the results of those ideas. The title of this book gives an indication of how widely those rights extend: patents for the way an invention works or how it is made; design rights in a product's appearance; trade marks for a company's logo or branding; or copyright in artistic, literary, or musical works. Some, like copyright, arise automatically, but others have to be requested.

Not surprisingly, many creative people remain unaware of the benefits of such a potentially complex field. Even the language of the rights can be daunting, with terms not always carrying the meanings used in everyday life. For example, to many people an assignment is a task undertaken for an employer, but to the IP lawyer an assignment is a formal document transferring legal rights from one person to another.

The aim of this book is to provide a readable guide to the rights protecting creative works; to help the people who generate good ideas to safeguard them and avoid the pitfalls of not looking after them. Its authors are experienced professionals in intellectual law who are well versed in meeting and helping creative people to define, protect, and develop their ideas.

And if we can help to ensure that a reasonable share of the benefits from new products and services go to reward the people who created them, we may bring forward even more good ideas and may all enjoy the better lifestyle they offer.

Robin Webb
Director of Innovation
UK Intellectual Property Office

Many of us have an inventive idea within us but lack the information needed to protect it and to gain its deserved rewards. All too often inventors fall prey to cowboys who give them misinformation and turn them over like a proverbial turkey.

Our society depends on creativity and must acknowledge, help and reward the people who provide it. They are amazing people and they have the ability to change all our lives, both commercially and socially. UK plc is good at inventing but appalling when it comes to looking after its inventors and inventions. Frustratingly in this country we spend more money on art than on invention. As they say, art is pleasure, invention is treasure, and this nation has got to recognise that. If it can spend a fortune on dead sheep and formaldehyde, then it can spend a bit more of that money on inventors whose ideas represent our future.

Society must guide you so your invention doesn't get stolen. It must help you record the invention. No one will pay you for just an idea, but they may pay you for that official piece of paper which shows you have an idea with some rights attached to it. That official piece of paper also gives you the chance of a day in court to defend yourself against the sharks. But remember that to be an inventor you need an ego the size of a truck and have to be prepared for a rough ride. Invention is frequently one per cent inspiration and 99 per cent litigation.

I am very pleased to add my name to this book. It is a great step into meeting the need to educate inventors and their facilitators on how to secure that all-important official piece of paper. It aims to guide you in making sure that the inventive idea gets official protection to provide a firm basis for a successful product bringing respect, rewards, and recognition.

Read, enjoy, and learn from this book, and keep it by you to refresh and encourage you through all your innovation efforts.

May all your dreams be patentable.

Trevor Baylis, OBE

Introduction

∴∴

*H*ave you always thought you might be the next Thomas Edison or perhaps another Danielle Steele? Has your company recently developed a bold new corporate logo or eye-catching trade mark? Perhaps you're thinking of a new concept in software, one that can revolutionise the entire manufacturing process. Or maybe you've just dreamed up the latest in 'latest things' – something to rival the zippy little scooters flying around your neighbourhood.

If so, you've come to the right place because having the great idea, creating the magnificent work of art, or coming up with the next fad is only the first step to cashing in on your creativity and hard work. Next up is protecting your intellectual property.

But, obviously, you know that. You've been enticed to pick up this book (and buy it, we hope) by a bunch of words that make up intellectual property rights: patents, registered designs, trade marks, and copyright. We're guessing you want to find out more about these matters. Well, you're about to find out everything you need to know (but were afraid to even think about). You're entering the exciting world of intellectual property rights (IPRs). Well, maybe the term *exciting* is pushing the envelope a bit, but we try to make it as painless as possible – Welcome to the World of Intellectual Property! We'll try to make your visit as pleasant and enlightening as we can.

About This Book

The book you now hold in your hands explains, in layman's terms, the basic nature, function, and application of intellectual property (IP) rights, including how you can acquire those rights, wield them effectively against your competitors, or exploit them lucratively through licensing agreements and other rewarding schemes.

To make this book effective for anyone interested in intellectual property, each of the main types of IP protection – patents, registered designs, trade marks, and copyright – is covered in its own complete part.

After checking out the information presented in each part, you'll have a solid grasp of the processes involved in acquiring, registering, maintaining, and protecting the intellectual property rights due to you and/or your company. You can then make informed decisions and speak confidently with the IP attorneys and other experts you meet along the way. And you'll have the tools and knowledge to take care of much of the work involved in the various research and registration processes.

However, this book is no substitute for legal advice from a specialised professional. When you deal with intellectual property and IP rights, you face many complex legal issues. Remember that there's only one definite answer to any legal question. 'It depends.' So make sure that you have a competent IP attorney to guide you through what can be a legal monster.

Conventions Used in This Book

We use the following conventions throughout the text to make things consistent and easy to understand.

- ✔ New terms appear in *italic*, closely followed by an easy-to-understand definition.

- ✔ **Bold** highlights the action parts of the numbered steps.

- ✔ Actual trade marks and service marks will appear in all caps when they're used as such, in keeping with legal usage.

- ✔ Sidebars, containing text enclosed in a shaded grey box, include information that's interesting to know but not necessarily critical to your understanding of the chapter or section topic.

- ✔ We regularly use the abbreviation IP to refer to intellectual property.

- ✔ Throughout the book, we provide *estimates* of fees you may run into in your quest to sew up your intellectual property. Fees are paid to the UK Intellectual Property Office once a year. Some charges can be substantial. The fee estimates we give are based on the most recent published fee schedule at the time of writing. Failure to pay the full applicable fee can result in a missed deadline and lapse of your application, patent, registered design, or trade mark registration. Always check the current fee schedule on the UK-IPO website before sending a payment.

- ✔ When we use the term *you*, we're, of course, referring to you the reader. But for those tasks, jobs, and other assorted legal hoops where we advise you to consult an IP attorney – and there are many of them – *you* often refers to both you and your support team, which may include one or more of these handy attorneys.

Foolish Assumptions

In order to channel the sea of IP information into a single book that's helpful to you, we make a few assumptions about you, the reader. See whether one or more of these shoes fit:

- ✔ You've a penchant for entrepreneurial adventure.
- ✔ You're running a business. Even the smallest commercial enterprise, such as an ice cream van, can benefit by making intelligent use of IP – creating an inspiring business name, for example.
- ✔ You're a budding or accomplished sculptor, painter, playwright, choreographer, musician, or songwriter, or you're involved in some other type of artistic activity.
- ✔ You're a writer, publisher, or computer programmer, or you're in another profession that takes advantage of the products of your creative mind.
- ✔ You're a scientist, engineer, or an inventor.
- ✔ You were born on a day ending in the letter *y*.
- ✔ You're a student who's considering a career in the field of IP law.
- ✔ You're a business lawyer, an executive, or are in middle management and wish to understand certain aspects of IP rights.

If we've hit the mark with any of the previous descriptions, this book is for you.

How This Book Is Organised

Patents, Registered Designs, Trade Marks & Copyright For Dummies is organised so that you can easily access the information that you need. We've organised the material into six parts, each with several chapters related to a common theme. We now give you a preview of coming attractions with a brief statement about each section. Projector, please.

Part 1: Covering Your Assets: Intellectual Property Basics

Part I talks about intellectual property and briefly describes how patents, registered designs, trade marks, copyright, trade secrets, and other IP tools protect your IP assets. We also include the basics of dealing with the experts, such as IP attorneys, and UK-IPO examiners.

Part II: Patenting Your Product

Part II deals with perhaps the most complex type of IP protection – the patent. Here, we explore what types of inventions qualify for a patent and whether you should patent your invention based on costs and other considerations.

We show you how to better your odds of getting your patent by doing a search to see whether your invention is really new. We then explain, in detail, how to go about getting that patent – getting professional help, preparing your patent application, following up on your paperwork, and dealing with the patent examiner.

Throughout Part II, we also show you how to protect your invention during that perilous period when your application is active (and somewhat public) but not yet protected by a patent. All that for the price of admission!

Part III: Knowing Your Copyright

Part III talks about the wide variety of creative works, from symphonies to software, that are protected by copyright. And we give you some good news and bad news. The good news is that you may already have exclusive rights to some of your works; you just need to make sure to keep them. The bad news is that if you created something original while employed by someone else, that person may have exclusive rights. But we help you manoeuvre that maze here in Part III. We also look at the world of designs, which can encompass anything from a block of chocolate, or new design for wallpaper patterns, right through to the distinctive shape of an item of furniture, or your latest sculpture. We delve deeper into what can be protected by a registered design and help you to decide whether to file. Would a registered design be a useful addition to your IP portfolio? Hopefully Part III provides the answer, and of course the ins and outs of how to go about doing so.

Part IV: Making Your Mark: Protecting Your Brand Identity

Part IV gives you the lowdown on trade marks and service marks – basically, the process of putting an exclusive brand on your goods and services. We define the various types of marks (such as trade marks and service marks), show what makes a good mark (and what should be avoided), and talk about how a good brand name, logo, or product name can give you a leg up on the competition. We also show you how to search to make sure that your mark is new and how to register and use your trade mark or service mark.

Part V: Exploiting and Enforcing Your IP Rights

Part V gets into what you can do after you've acquired your UK patent, registered design, trade mark, or copyright. We tell you how to protect your IP overseas, how to employ your IP to the greatest possible advantage to make some money, and how (and when) to go after those who infringe your rights – the baddies.

Part VI: The Part of Tens

The icing on your IP cake, the Part of Tens contains valuable information that you absolutely need in convenient top-ten packaging. What kind of valuable info, you ask? Good question. Here's a good answer: Things not to do in a patent application, frequently asked copyright questions, blunders to avoid when selecting a business name, and some great IP resources. The Appendix has a sample Patent application for you to peruse.

Icons Used in This Book

The bull's eye marks tips and tricks that you can put to use to make your life easier while you're protecting and profiting by your IP.

This icon highlights something you need to keep in mind while working on your patent, registered design, trade mark, or copyright.

The Warning icon alerts you to common mistakes that can trip you up and to other factors that may prove hazardous to your market image or your financial or legal health.

This icon tells you that the info is a bit more complex than most of the fine and fascinating points we raise throughout the book. Although technical information is still interesting, you can skip it if you want and not miss out on any need-to-know advice.

Where to Go from Here

One good thing (of the many good things) about a *For Dummies* book is that you don't need to read it from beginning to end to access the information you need. This book is designed to let you get in and get out, only focusing on the information you need. Simply turn to the part, chapter, or section that contains the info you want to know. Only interested in creating a catchy new product name? Turn to Chapter 15. Want the scoop on copyright? Turn to Part III. It's easy – you won't need a compass to get around. Of course, you can read the entire book (and truthfully, we'd be thrilled if you did).

We do suggest that, if you have questions about which IP tool can best meet your needs, you read Chapter 1, which provides an overview of the main IP components. After that, let the index at the back and table of contents at the front of the book be your guide. And then just follow the signs, which in this case consist of headings and those handy little icons.

A final thought. HM Treasury requested an independent review of the IP framework in the UK, the results of which launched in late 2006. A chap called Andrew Gowers conducted the review, and here's an inspiring extract from that very report:

> *'For many citizens, Intellectual Property is an obscure and distant domain – its laws shrouded in jargon and technical mystery, its applications relevant only to a specialist audience. And yet IP is everywhere. Even a simple coffee jar relies on a range of IP rights – from patents to copyright, designs to trade marks.*
>
> *In the modern world, knowledge capital, more than physical capital, drives the UK economy. Against the backdrop of the increasing importance of ideas, IP rights, which protect their value, are more vital than ever.'*

Part I
Covering Your Assets: Intellectual Property Basics

'Well, you've certainly got something there, but I've no idea what it is either.'

In this part . . .

1f you're currently reading this page, you probably have an invention, a creative work, a trade mark, or some other piece of intellectual property that you want to guard against all the copycats out there. Well, you've come to the right place. In this part, we give you an overview of intellectual property (IP) in all its glory and tell you why protecting these assets is important. We map out each IP instrument – patents, designs, copyright, and trade marks – showing how they each protect a different type of IP asset. We also talk about ways to treat your IP as a trade secret, by restricting access to information, using confidentiality agreements, and taking advantage of other tools at your disposal. And we top things off with info on hiring an IP attorney (when, why, and how), working effectively with them, and estimating how much the whole process can set you back.

Chapter 1

Examining the Tools in Your IP Box

In This Chapter

▶ Understanding the difference between IP assets and IP rights

▶ Sharing some trade secrets

▶ Making money with your IP rights

▶ Enforcing your IP rights in court

· ·

*W*elcome to the world of intellectual property rights (IPRs). If you've created, invented, or named something that you're selling, you already have intellectual property (IP). And that property may be quite valuable. What if you invented the Dyson vacuum cleaner or wrote the first *For Dummies* book? Wouldn't you like to be able to cash in on it? Exploiting your IP assets for your own financial gain and at the same time pursuing people bent on infringing your precious but fragile rights to those assets is what this chapter and, in general, this book is all about.

Buying into Intellectual Property

We've encountered many true and effective definitions of IP, including information with a commercial value, proprietary product of the mind, and things protected by patents, registered designs, copyright, and trade marks, but none of the definitions is quite complete. Here's the definition we like best:

Intellectual property is intangible creations of the mind that can be legally protected. Because IP has no physical form, we give you a better idea of what it is in the following comparative examples:

> ✔ IP is not the new and wondrous machine that you developed in your garage, but the invention embodied in that machine.

> ✔ IP is not the marvellously efficient cholesterol-reducing pill you see advertised on TV, but the formula and the process used in manufacturing that pill.

✔ IP is not the portrait that an artist made of you, but the aesthetic expression of the artist's talent reflected by the painting.

✔ IP is not the lawnmower that you reluctantly start up every Saturday, but the brand name that embodies the reputation of the product and its manufacturer.

Now we want to expand on our definition. IP comprises two components:

✔ **Assets:** IP assets are intangible creations, such as the invention, the formula and process, the expression of artist's talents as reflected in a painting, and the brand name.

✔ **Rights:** IP rights consist of the legal protections that secure each IP asset against its unauthorised use by others. One or more of the following legal protections can be used to secure IP rights:

- **Copyright:** Holding a copyright shields artistic expression against copying by others.

- **Patents:** Obtaining a patent protects the invention from outright thievery.

- **Registered Designs:** Registering your design(s) protects them from being copied by an infringer.

- **Trade Marks:** Adopting a trade mark as a brand name keeps it and its market reputation yours and yours alone.

- **Trade secrets:** Keeping a formula or manufacturing process confidential safeguards it against imitators.

Some IP rights – copyright, design rights, and trade mark rights, in particular – attach themselves automatically upon the creation or use of the IP assets without you ever having to lift a finger or spend a cent. Obtaining other IP rights – patents, registered designs, and registered trade marks – requires you to put up a pretty good fight and spend plenty of money.

An unprotected IP asset is up for grabs – anyone can copy it, steal it, or change it for the worse (possibly damaging your good reputation). The bottom line is that your unprotected IP fattens the bad guy's bottom line.

But there's more to IP assets and rights than mere talk of patents, registered designs, copyright, and trade marks, and that's what this chapter is all about. You first must verify that you own that IP asset you want to protect, make sure that it's original, and know how to secure all the IP rights that can apply to it. And last but not least, you have to know how to get the professional advice that you need.

A little IP history

Although the first letters patent (an archaic meaning of patent) was granted by King Henry VI to John of Utynam in 1449 for the manufacture of stained glass, it was not until 1852 that the United Kingdom Patent Office was set up to act as the sole authority for the granting of patents.

The Patent Office, renamed as the UK Intellectual Property Office on 2 April 2007, now deals with all manner of IP, including patents, registered designs, and trade marks.

Exploring the Patent Process

The most well-known – although not the most practical – form of IP protection is a patent. A *patent* is a temporary legal right granted by the government as a reward for a unique invention, giving you – the inventor – a way to keep others from stealing the fruits of your labour – the invention.

Patent law defines an *invention* as a technological advancement that's useful, new, and isn't obvious to a person with ordinary skill in the field of technology. Inventions can take many forms, from a machine or device to a method or process, from a new composition to a new use of an old product.

If you're wondering whether your latest and greatest invention actually fits the invention bill, check out Chapter 4, which details the types of patents and the inventions covered by each.

Obtaining the grant of a patent

You file an detailed application that completely describes your invention in order to get a patent from the UK Intellectual Property Office (UK-IPO). We cover the nuts and bolts of a patent application in Chapter 7. The UK-IPO rigorously examines your application (see Chapters 8 and 9 for all the gory details). If you satisfy the patent examiner that your invention meets all the requirements, the examiner grants you the patent. This procedure may last up to four and a half years; however, if your commercial interests may be compromised by an infringer, provision exists to speed up the procedure. We're aware of one inventor who gained a full patent in less than ten months.

We make no bones about it: The patent process is costly in terms of both time and money. If you think that you may want to head down the patent road, be sure that it's the best path for protecting your IP. Check out Chapter 5, which provides you with other options and an exercise to help you decide whether a patent's the right choice for you. The first stop in your journey is probably to conduct a patent search before pouring a great deal of money into a doubtful application – in Chapter 6 we provide a road map for that side trip.

Putting a patent to good use

Emblazoned with fancy lettering and signed by the Comptroller General of Patents, a framed patent makes an impressive conversation piece on your living room or office wall.

You can also use your granted patent against people who infringe any rights granted to you. However, before entering an action for infringement take legal advice from a patent attorney; and if your attorney recommends seeking the advice of a Queen's Counsel, do so. You may consider other courses; for example, the UK-IPO provides a non-binding mediation service. Alternatively, you can approach the infringer with a view to granting them a licence on terms to be agreed. The latter course may be attractive if your own business aspirations are limited by cash flow or other factors that can't be readily resolved. (You can find more about these legal processes in Chapter 20.)

You may resort to defending your patent rights by entering an infringement action, but we earnestly advise against such activity unless no other avenue is available and then only if you've sufficient funds to do so. Such funds may be provided by having IP insurance; however, as with any insurance policy, make sure that the policy gives you the cover you may require. Lastly, don't make any threats against an alleged infringer unless you're prepared to enter into an infringement action. The reason is that the Patents Act 1977 makes provision for an alleged infringer to pursue an action against you for groundless threats. Responding to a threats action can be costly and time consuming. Find out what else you can do with your patent in the section 'Putting Your IP to Work at Home and Abroad' at the end of this chapter.

A patent has teeth, but those teeth come at great expense. We suggest you also look at your other IP rights too. You can also obtain insurance policies that cover some of your litigation costs. We discuss insurance issues in detail in Chapter 20.

Considering Copyright

Copyright is a temporary right giving a creative person exclusive control over the use of an original work of their authorship (OWA). An *original work of authorship* is a textual, graphic, plastic, musical, dramatic, audio, or visual creation that you created. A few examples of original works of authorship include (for the complete scoop, turn to Chapter 11):

✔ Any writing, including a computer program.

✔ A drawing, painting, or computer-generated image.

✔ A sculpture.

✔ An architectural design.

✔ A song, symphony, or opera.

✔ A play.

✔ A video or audio production, including a movie, video game, television or radio broadcast, or recording on cassette, CD, or DVD.

Even if the same thing's been done before, copyright is created if your work wasn't copied from or influenced by the pre-existing work. For example, think of how many books have recanted the life stories of Winston Churchill and Lawrence of Arabia. Copyright protects the form in which an idea or concept is expressed, not the idea or the concept itself. So the 'form' is the particular book whereas the 'idea' is the life history of Churchill or Lawrence of Arabia.

Copyright doesn't extend to abstractions or to technical or functional things. For example, an idea for a new TV programme isn't protected by copyright, but the way the idea for the show is developed and played out is protected. Many film and TV dramas depict factual and fictional episodes based on the miners' strikes in the 1970s and 1980s, but each film and drama was from a different perspective, although set in the same time frame. The copyright on a cookbook prevents anyone from copying the way the various recipes are expressed in words and images, selected, and arranged. The cookbook's copyright doesn't prevent you from using the same recipes and incorporating them step by step into your own cookbook (because the steps are actually a technical process), as long as you don't express them in the same style, compile them in the same order, or arrange them in the same format. We go over this idea/expression distinction in great detail in Chapter 12.

Copyright in computer programs

Copyright law is always lagging behind developments in technology, especially in the area of computer programs. Computer programs are now copyright-protectable writings, which gives programmers, and the entire software industry, an effective security tool. In a computer program, the choice of words or lines of computer code and their respective positions in an instruction represent the creative portion of the program and form a critical element to its operation. The fact that others can't copy this specific language greatly expands the scope of copyright protection for software. Recent decisions in the UK-IPO and the European Patent Office (EPO) indicate that patent protection for computer programs *per se* is not likely. However, a recent count decision means that claims for computer software will be allowed if, but only if, the program implements a patentable invention.

Copyright attaches automatically, without the need for any formality, as soon as a work appears in a perceptible and reproducible form. So, as soon as you print out your great novel, your story is automatically the subject of copyright. This is a big advantage over patents. If, however, you want to sue someone for infringement – or, worse, someone sues you – you need to prove that the novel's actually your original work. Therefore, we suggest you make the copyright official – see Chapter 12 for more on this topic.

You can use your copyright in much the same way you use a patent – to pressure and sue an infringer; but, be warned that entering an action for copyright infringement can be as expensive as any patent infringement action.

Claiming Your Identity: Trade Marks and Other Commercial Handles

Trade marks are only one species within a class of IP assets called *commercial identifiers* that you use to distinguish your company, product, or services from others. The three basic types of commercial identifiers, which we cover in more detail in Chapter 14, are:

- **Company identifiers:** A company is identified by its legal name (for example, British Petroleum) and often by the logo that adorns its buildings and letterhead ('BP' or the familiar green and yellow livery of its fuel outlets).

✔ **Product identifiers:** Trade marks (brand names) are the most familiar product identifiers and can also take the form of a single letter, or a mere design or symbol, such as the 'swoosh' mark on a popular brand of athletic gear.

Any fanciful and non-functional characteristic of a product or package can act as a product identifier – for example, the ribbed bottle of a large soft-drinks company. Non-functional characteristics often are referred to as *design marks*, or *trade get up*, which, like trade marks, can be registered at the UK-IPO and/or the Office for Harmonisation within the Internal Market (OHIM) for member states of the European Union. OHIM is based in Alicante, Spain, and receives trade mark applications from applicants in all the countries of the European Community. When registered, the trade marks become effective throughout all 27 member states of the European Community. OHIM is also the Office for receiving Community registered design applications (see Chapter 11)

✔ **Service identifiers:** The services that a company offers to the public – such as automotive-maintenance or fast-food restaurant services – are usually identified by a trade mark. It can be a word or phrase ('McDonald's'), logo (the arched 'M' on those fast-food chains), or the shape and decoration of a building (the KFC brand of restaurant service outlets).

Commercial identifiers constitute the IP rights that we consider to be most neglected, misunderstood, and underestimated by entrepreneurs in their new industrial, commercial, educational, or scientific ventures. Watching as new businesses spend their money on chancy patent applications always puzzles us when they're obviously neglecting the wondrous marketing tools provided by good commercial identifiers.

Company image, product fame, or a reputation for providing quality service form critical aspects of a business that can be greatly enhanced by, and benefit from, the right choice and use of motivating identifiers, logos, and distinctive packaging. However, coming up with an identifier that's a hit with customers isn't easy, so we devote the whole of Chapter 15 to providing an insight into making such a selection.

We detail all you need to know about the ins and outs of developing marks and names that the courts protect, and explain how the degree of protection awarded to company identifiers and other commercial names depends mainly upon the distinctiveness of the name, all in Chapter 14.

A great name can be the most valuable asset of a company and deserves a lot of attention and appropriate protective measures, such as registration and proper usage. But a great commercial identifier won't do you any good if it duplicates an existing identifier, so before you begin the registration process, discussed in Chapter 17, we suggest you do a search to make sure that no one else is using your brainchild – or even something close to it. We explain trade mark searches in Chapter 16.

Keeping Quiet: Trade Secrets

Kiss and tell only on a need-to-know basis. The best way to keep a commercially advantageous piece of information such as a manufacturing method or customer list away from your competitors is to take advantage of laws that protect *trade secrets*, a very important and inexpensive IP right. Don't let anyone in on a trade secret other than the people who necessarily need to know about the secret. For example, you may have developed a new formulation for a polymer-based coating for a concrete roof tile. Although you may file an application for patent protection, it's more advantageous not to and to keep the details secret, especially if reverse engineering of the formulation and process steps is a remote possibility.

Not every type of commercially advantageous material can be safely and practically kept under lock and key. Whenever that happens to be the case, and you can't keep certain information as a trade secret, you need to rely on other types of IP rights – patents, registered designs, copyright, or trade marks – for protection.

In Chapter 2 we explain how to implement a trade-secret strategy and how the law provides for enforcement of trade secrets in case of negligent or intentional disclosures. We also discuss the trade-offs between patents and a trade-secret policy.

Putting Things in Writing: Looking at Contractual IP Rights

A category of legal contracts, which we explain in Chapter 19, deals specifically with IP rights. The contracts provide contractual IP rights to all parties. For instance, a company may acquire the contractual right to manufacture a patented product while the inventor obtains rights to a percentage of the sales proceeds called *royalties*. Even if you're not an inventor or computer programmer, you may acquire contractual rights to inventions or software that you can exploit in place of, or in addition to, their creators.

Similarly, after you acquire your patent, registered design, copyright, or commercial identifier, you can profitably sell or lease it to others. You can transfer your IP rights through an *assignment* (the outright purchase or sale of the IP right) or a *licence* (an agreement allowing another individual or business to use your IP rights). For example, if you want to publish an author's book, you must buy the copyright from the author using an assignment, or obtain the author's permission to publish the work under a licence.

When you commission independent contractors to do a job for you, you can enter into written and signed agreements stating that any technological advancement or original work of authorship that results from the commission belongs to you. See Chapter 12 for information on assigning and licensing copyright and Chapter 14 for information about commercial identifiers. In relation to employees, the Patents Act 1977 sets out the ownership of rights in inventions made by an employee while in your employ.

Any contract with a commissioned contractor should always be in writing and be signed by all parties to the agreement.

You can also acquire contractual rights to intellectual property by buying a *franchise* for a specific type of business – fast-food and dry-cleaning franchises are common examples in the UK. In Chapter 19, we explain how a franchise constitutes a classic and convenient way of exploiting a bundle of IP assets and related IP rights.

Putting Your IP to Work at Home and Abroad

You can use IP assets and rights in many ways. Developing and protecting your intellectual property assets and rights can give you an edge over the competition by discouraging unscrupulous competitors, developing new revenue sources, and increasing the value of your company. (We talk about each of these aspects in detail in Chapter 2.)

But because IP rights are rare exceptions to antimonopoly and antitrust laws and regulations, their use is strictly limited. (The limitation became very apparent in relation to Microsoft, who incurred the wrath of the European Commission over its monopolistic position in regard to its own software, which it won't share with its competitors. Microsoft's competitors and their customers find themselves forced to only use Microsoft software for access to other Microsoft features.)

The European Commission enforces EU competition rules on restrictive practices and abuses of monopoly power for the whole of the European Union when cross-border trade and competition are affected.

When you misuse your teddy bear – even though it belongs to you – to beat your little sister, the bear is confiscated. The rules haven't changed with regard to IP rights. The usual penalty for an abusive misuse of an IP right is forfeiture.

When you take advantage of your IP assets within the confines of your own company – basically exploiting your own invention – you face little risk of running foul of the law. However, when you use your IP rights against others outside of your company who infringe upon them, you need to be more careful. Trust your IP litigation attorney to know how to stay within the bounds of the law. Check out Chapter 3 to find out how to select and work with an IP Attorney. IP Attorneys are bound by strict confidentiality obligations and are subject to discipline and loss of their right to practise if they breach their obligations under the Rules of Conduct set by the Chartered Institute of Patent Attorneys (CIPA). Therefore, you can reveal your most sensitive knowledge or information to your attorney. There's no need to make them sign a confidentiality or non-disclosure agreement because they're already bound by rules of conduct set down by their professional body to complete discretion.

Most industrialised countries have IP laws roughly parallel to those in the UK. Because acquiring a copyright doesn't require any application or other formality, you can readily defend and exploit your copyright all across the planet; however, take note of our comments in Chapter 3 relating to the likely costs of such activity.

By contrast, patents, registered designs, and trade marks require local applications and examinations in almost every foreign land, which we explain in Chapter 18. Costs tend to be even higher abroad than they are in the UK, and proceedings can drag on for years. Establishing a foreign patent portfolio is not for the fainthearted and requires substantial financial resources.

Chapter 2

Protecting Your Intellectual Property

*I*n any serious endeavour, logic and pragmatism pay off. You can be logical by following a well-defined plan. You need to be pragmatic by using your resources efficiently and remaining within budget. Although you may not yet be involved in any kind of business activity, the minute you start dealing with intellectual property (IP), you have assets that may be financially valuable. Therefore, developing an IP acquisition and protection strategy is a must for a business venture of any size. Briefly, your IP strategy should include evaluating your IP assets, deciding what type of IP rights would best protect them, doing a search to make sure that you can protect your assets, and going for every form of IP protection available to you, for example patents, registered designs, trade marks, and copyright.

Examining Your Motives

When you implement an IP programme, it's easy to make the mistakes of getting carried away and spending cash beyond your needs and means. One of the biggest errors is chasing a patent when a registered design, trade mark, copyright, or trade-secret policy would better serve your needs – for less money. If your motivation is pride, and your goal is displaying a patent on the wall behind your desk, perhaps you need an easier ticket for your ego trip.

We know of only three good reasons for developing and protecting an IP asset:

✔ Gaining an edge over your competitors

✔ Creating a revenue source

✔ Enhancing the value of your business

IP rights can be aptly compared with an interest in property. You can keep people off your lawn; you can sell, lease, or otherwise share a piece of your land with others; and you can count your plot as an asset. Likewise, someone who buys a house simply to look at the deed or brag about it to others probably isn't the shrewdest property mogul.

Keeping your competitors at bay

Almost every IP right gives you a way to exclude others from doing something that interferes with, or competes against, a vital part of your business. If you can tolerate competition and still maintain a reasonable income, you can forget about IP protection and spend your resources on marketing or some other more productive and lucrative activity.

Try to think of a business that wouldn't benefit from acquiring at least a few IP rights. At a minimum, your business can capitalise on the protection afforded by a trade-secret programme, which can prevent, or at least deter, former associates or employees from using any of your manufacturing or marketing methods or stealing your customer list. At most, acquiring a patent, registered design, or trade mark, or relying on any copyright that may attach to a development, may give you a huge competitive advantage in the market place with considerable legal clout to stifle copycats.

Developing a new revenue source

After you acquire IP rights, you can generate income with those rights by licensing someone to manufacture your product or by leasing your commercial identifier to another organisation to market products under your brand name using your trade mark. You can also franchise other folks to manufacture or sell your goods and services under your guidelines. Under any of these arrangements, you make money each time someone makes, sells, or uses your goods or services.

Finding manufacturing ventures that close down after securing solid protection for a product or technology and then license the IP rights to others isn't unusual. The business may even license those rights to former competitors.

Licensing IP rights is like renting out a property: You maintain title to the property (the IP assets and IP rights) and collect rent on a regular basis in the form of royalties. One typical situation is when an entrepreneur launches a new line of sporting garments, enhances the product line with an attractive brand name and logo, and then licenses the brand to other clothing manufacturers as soon as the brand is established. The entrepreneur then gets out of the business except, of course, for opening envelopes containing the quarterly royalty cheques and laughing all the way to the bank. When you plan and market IP rights well, those rights can be an essential part of your product line.

If you don't want to get out of the business completely, you can maintain the right to continue manufacturing your product by granting only non-exclusive licences to one or more manufacturers. However, the royalty rate is lower than for an exclusive licence. We cover this approach in Chapter 19.

Adding value to your business

When the time comes to sell your business, you can get more for it if your:

- ✔ Products are protected by patents.
- ✔ Proprietary computer programs are covered by copyright.
- ✔ Brand names (trade marks) are unique and can be a deterrent to blatant copying by competitors.
- ✔ Goodwill is transferable to the buyer under your business name.

But you don't have to sell your business merely to capitalise on its IP-enhanced value. If you need to raise more capital or borrow money, your IP can provide a nice boost to your net worth, making your stock more attractive to investors and offering added collateral security for the lender to consider.

Implementing an IP Programme

Developing an IP acquisition and protection strategy is a must for business ventures of all sizes. Although such a strategy probably is more elaborate for a major corporation than for a small business, the recommendations that we make in the sections here apply to all commercial and professional enterprises, regardless of size. The two components – taking stock of your IP assets and mapping out a strategy for protecting those assets – comprise the essential part of an effective IP acquisition and protection programme. (By *acquisition,* we mean developing and safeguarding your own IP assets and IP rights and only occasionally acquiring IP rights from someone else.)

Business people are often unaware that they use IP assets already developed or created by themselves, their employees, associates, or contractors, including inventions and other technological advances, computer programs, and other original works of authorship. Because these assets go unrecognised (and unprotected), they often remain in the hands of their developers and creators or fall into the public domain. Nothing is more frustrating than discovering that an asset you thought you owned is being used by a former employee or contributor who becomes your toughest competitor.

In relation to employee inventors, the provisions of the Patents Act 1977 (Sections 39 to 43) set out the ownership of employee inventions. Normally, where a person (the employee) is employed in a position where he or she is expected to develop new technology, devise a new method(s) of operation of an apparatus and/or formulate new recipes and compositions, the rights in those developments automatically belong to the employer. Exceptions exist, notably where an employee holds a post in which he or she has no responsibilities in relation to the business interests of the employer; for example, a shop-floor labourer is not regarded as an employee whose inventions automatically belong to an employer. For example, if the employer has an interest in woodworking routers and the shop-floor labourer devises an improved attachment for a woodworking router, he may offer it to the employer for agreed terms; say, a lump sum or royalties. If, however, an employee who develops new technology devises the improved attachment for a woodworking router, the rights automatically belong to the employer.

However, in relation to associates and/or contractors with the proper preventative measures packaged as a well-planned IP programme, you can ensure that you own the IPRs relating to anything that's devised by the associates and/or contractors. The first step in such a programme is preparing proper written agreements to be routinely signed by your associates and contractors. The second step is defining and applying a trade-secret protocol. Finally, you must look at each IP asset and protect it by going for every applicable IP right available.

Taking stock of your IP assets

To implement an IP protection programme, first take an inventory of the intellectual property you already own. Begin with the following steps:

1. **Identify all the innovations in products and manufacturing methods that you, your associates, and your employees have developed during the past couple of years that have not been made public – older technology may have already fallen into the public domain.**

   Identifying every development, gives you a list of all your assets that may benefit by patent or trade-secret protection.

2. **Gather all the software, instructional manuals, and promotional litera-ture developed or published under your direction or authority for the past five or six years.**

    These items, assuming they're original, are automatically protected by copyright.

3. **Look at all your commercial names and logos, including business identities and product brands.**

    This shows all your assets that can be protected by a registered trade mark.

Once you've gathered this information, you have at your fingertips an inventory of the IP assets that you can protect with a variety of IP rights.

Before you invest in protecting what you already have, or acquiring more IP assets, make sure that your assets are the best they can be. You can always improve inventions and processes, and you can often boost the marketing and legal strengths of commercial names with some adjustments and selec-tive use (see the section 'Preserving company identity and brand names' later in this chapter). Likewise, before investing your hard-earned cash in acquiring IP asset protection, make sure that your widgets, assembly lines, and logos are in the best shape possible. Copyrightable material – such as manuals, books, graphics, and computer programs – is the exception here. Copyright protection, for a limited period, is automatically applied as soon as the work is put on paper (or saved to disk). Nevertheless, make sure that you revise and update all documents to include any improvements you've made to the assets they represent. By updating any document, you automatically extend the period of copyright in the revised work. (See Chapter 12 for the periods that apply to copyright.)

Identifying trade secrets

After you take stock of your IP assets, you need to define and apply a trade-secret protocol. You may think that you don't have any trade secrets because you and your staff always appear open, candid, trusting, and trustworthy, but you may have information that isn't readily available to the public that gives your company a competitive edge.

We don't mean cloak-and-dagger scenarios and those skeletons in your filing cabinets, but consider, for example, your customer list: How would you feel if one of your former associates, or perhaps the employee who maintained that list, jumped ship, hooked up with your closest competitor, and started using that list to solicit your largest customers? Other examples include someone revealing the identity of your supplier of a hard-to-find component, the para-meters of a tricky manufacturing process, the way you allocate your financial resources, and the details of your next marketing campaign. See the section

'Protecting technological advances' later in this chapter for more tips about determining whether you need to take the trade-secret route, go with a patent, or rely on registered designs or copyrights.

You can maintain and enforce the confidentiality of this type of information only by establishing a *trade-secret protection policy*. Such a policy may involve:

✔ Getting all members of your staff, your contractors, outside consultants and advisers, your critical suppliers, and anyone else who may be exposed to any sensitive information to sign a confidentiality agreement. You may even be wise to add some customers and casual visitors to the list of folks signing a confidentiality agreement.

✔ Restricting access to certain areas of your place of business such as research departments, laboratories, the design office, and the IT department where innovations may be devised and recorded.

✔ Marking particular documents with a confidential legend.

✔ Limiting the circulation of confidential documents.

✔ Locking away sensitive material.

✔ Including appropriate warnings and directives in your employee manual.

You don't necessarily need these measures, but you do need to exercise reasonable precautions. You need to ensure that any leak that may occur can only be the result of gross negligence or breach of duty for which you can get legal remedy. No breach of duty can occur when your rules aren't clearly set out and understood.

Courts enforce reasonably drafted and implemented trade-secret protection policies by issuing restraining orders or injunctions against anyone breaching policy and against the beneficiaries of the indiscretion.

Devising a trade-secret policy involves no application, no registration, no long wait, and no expensive filing fee. You just need advance planning, discipline, and a bit of legal work by your IP attorney to draft a few confidentiality agreements.

Managing third-party contributions

A common business mistake is thinking that you automatically have the rights to property you obtain through the labours of others, including that of all of your employees. Some employees don't fall into the category of those whose employment comes under the provisions of the Patents Act 1977 (Sections 39 to 43), as explained earlier in this section. Acquiring an asset and obtaining the IP right that attaches to that asset are two different things. You must take some precautions and legal steps to get all the rights to what you acquire from others.

Company or contractor: Who owns the copyright?

A common distressing scenario occurs when a freelance computer programmer (not an employee, but an independent contractor) contributes a substantial and critical piece of software without a proper contractual arrangement. The company commissioning the programmer may then be unable to make lucrative use of the software because the programmer refuses to co-operate. Worse yet, the company may find itself on the receiving end of an infringement complaint filed by the programmer if the company unknowingly or unwisely does something restricted by the programmer's copyright.

One way to prevent such a disastrous situation is to use a well-drafted agreement signed by anyone you ask to contribute any type of IP component to your projects. In Chapter 13, we give detailed information about using this type of agreement in connection with copyrights.

In the UK there's no formal copyright registration system, unlike in the US.

Some public companies provide services that include assistance in defending the copyrights you may own. We list the details of such companies in Chapter 24.

The law distinguishes between objects that embody their underlying IP asset and the IP rights protecting that asset. For example, if you hire a painter or a photographer to produce a portrait of you, and you pay for those professional services and for copies of the artwork, you don't acquire all rights to the use of those materials, to make copies, to distribute those copies to your fans, and to draw a moustache and devil horns on some of the copies. Those acts are restricted by the copyright that automatically attached to the artwork the minute it was put in a perceptible or reproducible form, in this case a canvas or photographic film. Unless you specifically acquire the copyright, in most cases the artist or photographer retains control over how the material can be used, including, in some cases, making any alterations.

We tell you much more about copyright in Part III. For now, we just want to let you know that what you think you acquire isn't always what you get.

If you're the contributing third party (that is, the cameraman or set designer for example), insist upon retaining some rights to use the material that you contributed, otherwise you may paint yourself into a corner. One day, you may need to incorporate part of that material into another project, only to find that you no longer have the rights to what you created because all aspects of your art have been assigned to your former customers. Under those circumstances, you have to adopt a new style and develop a new stock of frequently needed material.

Protecting technological advances

As a means of promoting inventiveness and other forms of technological breakthrough, a company needs to ensure the protection and encouragement of all valuable contributions by:

- ✔ Implementing a record-keeping system to document all new developments.
- ✔ Devising a reward programme for its creative employees.

Preparing complete written disclosure of potential inventions and submitting them to a patent attorney is important. The attorney helps you determine on a case-by-case basis whether you need to file a patent application or treat the breakthrough as a trade secret. Your decision is extremely critical in further helping you achieve your desired scope of protection within the constraints of your company's budget.

In general, whenever you know that your inventions can't be readily reverse-engineered – your competitors can't figure out what's going on by breaking it down or analysing it – you can keep the inventions confidential and thus protected by a tight trade-secret policy. Chemical compositions are prime candidates for the reverse-engineering treatment. Someone may be able to detect every chemical element in a new plastic material or eyedrop medicine, but is unlikely to determine the amount of each element or the mixing process with any level of practical precision. In many cases, keeping the formulae, dosage, and mixing parameters as a trade secret insures protection against imitators.

The main advantages of treating an invention as a trade secret are:

- ✔ The invention need not be disclosed to the public in a patent application.
- ✔ The life of a trade secret isn't limited to the 20 years normally associated with a patent.
- ✔ The costs for preserving a trade secret are relatively insignificant compared with the amounts involved in obtaining and maintaining a patent.

With trade secrets, you run a substantial risk that another party may independently discover the same thing and even secure a patent for it.

The only major disadvantage of not seeking patent protection for an invention, for example a new composition and/or a new process for the manufacture of a product, is that any third party may formulate the same composition or define a new process that's the same or similar to that for which you could have sought protection. Thus, they may seek and obtain valid patent protection for the same developments because you maintained a veil of secrecy over your developments, which were not placed in the public domain and were not the subjects of earlier patent applications. However, the Patents Act 1977 provides for the continued use of your developments; that is, the composition and process.

Your use of developments is restricted to the use you established at the priority date of the patent application filed by the third party. You can continue, but not expand by creating other manufacturing facilities to grow your business.

Although computer software is protected by copyright, no patent protection can be obtained through the UK-IPO or the European Patent Office (EPO) (refer to Chapter 1).

Preserving company identity and brand names

Commercial names, specifically a company's business name and logo and more significantly its brand names, determine how a company is perceived in the marketplace. Such commercial names often provide the vehicles upon which all of a company's marketing programmes ride.

Few brand names that you see every day strike you as outstanding. We'd go so far as to say that many seem downright mediocre. At worst, some brand names are counterproductive because they impede rather than bolster the promotion of the goods and services they identify. Do you have gems in your commercial-name jewel box or merely lumps of coal in your stocking? We suggest you find out and act accordingly (see Chapters 16, 17, and 24 for advice on how to create a good brand name and how to conduct a search to see if it's available).

If budgetary constraints force you to choose between protecting your product and polishing your commercial image, we recommend favouring the latter. Establishing a good brand-name programme is cheaper than obtaining patent protection, and you get much more return for your money. (Check out Chapters 15 and 16 for the scoop on creating effective commercial identifiers and avoiding bad ones.)

Screening commercial names

Be methodical in assessing your commercial names:

1. Take a hard look at all your current commercial names and logotypes.

2. Rate their promotional value according to the criteria defined in Chapter 16.

3. Phase out the names that don't make the grade and replace them with more judiciously selected identifiers.

Registering commercial names

Registering your company names on the Companies House Register greatly enhances your chances of proving ownership of your brand name if it's the same as your company name when you have to weed out copycats. The Companies House Register is the Official Register for all limited companies in the United Kingdom.

Keeping a watching brief on the registration of new company names that may give rise to a conflict of interests is easy. From personal experience, we know that the Company Secretary of Redland PLC, now Lafarge SA, was responsible for checking the register at least once a week and initiating action for redress of any situation that was likely to impact upon the company's business interests. You can see the details of all registrations free of charge on the Companies House Web site at www.companieshouse.co.uk.

Also, we strongly recommend that you consider registering the following:

- ✔ All your brand names and logos as trade marks.
- ✔ Service marks. These are the marks used in relation to any service you provide. For example, if you own a string of restaurants, you may register your brand name as a service mark at the UK-IPO Trade Marks Registry.

Protecting distinctive product and package configurations

Don't overlook the fact that an attractive and non-functional product shape, or ornamentation – such as the unique shape of a bar of soap or a whimsical design on the side of an athletic shoe – can be recognised as source identifiers and registered as a trade mark, just like a brand name. For example, the fanciful shape of a perfume vial and the bright stripes across a pesticide package are distinctive packaging that can be registered as trade marks.

Even the recognisable sound of a motorcycle exhaust and the springy feel of a textile product can influence a buyer and so can be deemed registrable, non-visual marks.

The Trade Marks Act 1994 had provision that protection can be obtained for the unique smell of a perfume or any product having a distinctive aroma. However, because of the difficulty inrepresenting a smell, the UK-IPO and the Office for Harmonization in the Internal Market (OHIM) aren't inclined to receive applications for the smell of a product, because they're difficult to represent graphically.

If you don't have such unique identifiers for your product line, put your designer to the task of creating them. The more unique and distinctive you make your product, the easier it becomes for you to prevent your competitors from copying it.

Developing contractual procedures

Contractual engagements with your associates, employees, contractors, advisers, and eventually visitors, which are essential for implementing your IP protection strategy, always need to be secured in writing. You need to consider contractual agreements with:

- ✔ Potential inventors, excluding those employees covered by the Patents Act 1977 (Sections 39 to 43) and others who contribute to your techno-logical assets. Agreements with these people ensure your ownership of their work products.

- ✔ Computer programmers, writers, artists, photographers, music writers, producers of audio-visual works and sound recordings, microcircuit mask designers, choreographers, architects, and others who contribute copyright works to your business. Contractual agreements:

    - • Make you or your company the legal author and copyright owner when contributors' creations come to life; and,

    - • Obligate those contributors to transfer any copyright they acquire to you or your company.

 For contractual agreements to be effective, a competent IP attorney must draft them. Don't rely on a personal-injury or criminal law practitioner or even a business lawyer or solicitor because they may not know the latest developments in IP law. Well-meaning but often unsuitably qualified lawyers routinely rely on forms plucked from outdated manuals or may even use the wrong form for the job altogether.

An IP attorney can save you money and keep you out of trouble when draft-ing agreements to implement IP programmes by:

- ✔ Combining necessary contractual agreements into a single document.

- ✔ Ensuring that the contractual agreements and terms of employment extend, where necessary to employees and agents of the parties signing them.

- ✔ Forbidding personal use of confidential material by the parties and other similar acts.

- ✔ Making sure that any agreement conforms to legal requirements.

- ✔ Charging a fair fee for actual legal work and not merely for clerical tasks.

The responsibilities of the executives of a company while employed by the company mean that anything devised by them within the business interests of the company belongs to the company. If an executive takes steps to obtain patent, or other, protection in her own name, redress is available, if necessary, through the courts. In such a case it's considered that any invention, or other IPR, is held in trust for the company by such an executive. Therefore, if an action arises concerning the ownership of the invention and/or any other IPRs, the courts most likely order that the rights in anything devised by the wayward executive should be assigned to the company.

Even after an executive leaves a company, she's usually bound by an obligation of confidentiality that would prevent her from using any information relating to the company's business for a defined period after cessation of her tenure of the executive post. Exceptions to this scenario do exist, especially where the executive cannot continue to practice her trade because of unfair conditions imposed on her by the company after she leaves their employment. It's up to the company's legal advisers to ensure that provisions are put in place to safeguard against any eventuality that may have a detrimental impact on the company's business interests but also to ensure that the company is safeguarded against an action brought against it by its former employee for restraint of trade.

Chapter 3

Dealing with Professionals and Picking Up the Tab

In This Chapter

▶ Knowing when you need an accredited IP professional

▶ Finding and selecting a professional at home and abroad

▶ Keeping an eye on the finances

▶ Factoring in costs of foreign professionals

*I*f you're like most people, the idea of hiring a professional probably sends shivers down your spine, puts goose bumps on your arms, and sets your heart palpitating. (The thought even starts us quivering – and we're IP professionals.)

You're almost certain to need an IP professional's services sooner or later. Attorneys *are* expensive – and probably even more so than you think – especially if they specialise in IP cases. But in this chapter we show you ways to mitigate the high cost of professional services. First, though, you have to know what kind of help you need and how to get it.

Getting the Help You Need

When diving into IP waters you have to have professional help because acquiring and using IP rights to protect and exploit IP assets are essentially legal procedures. Laws are characterised by nuances, exceptions, and loop-holes – and IP laws are no exception. Over the past 20 years the huge volume of IP applications and filings, and the necessity to harmonise the UK's IP procedures with those of other industrialised countries, have brought many changes in IP law. These changes require increasingly complex and expensive procedures. The days when a garage inventor could navigate a patent appli-cation through the UK Intellectual Property Office (UK-IPO) with the help of a how-to manual are over.

Law students spend years studying this stuff, bringing a level of expertise to the table that most people can't easily duplicate. By steering you clear of legal pitfalls, your IP professional saves you the time, grief, aggravation, and the expense of having to abandon an application and to refile a new application or other paperwork. More importantly, your IP professional makes sure that you don't miss any critical deadlines and therefore lose the opportunity to acquire the IP protection you require.

This book, helpful as we hope it is for you, is no substitute for engaging the services of a competent IP attorney.

Identifying the right person for the job

Because IP is such a vast and complex field, many professionals limit their practice to narrow specialties, such as patent applications, IP litigation, or entertainment copyright cases. You need to find the professional most qualified to handle your case.

Registered UK patent attorneys

Registered patent attorneys, or Fellows of the Chartered Institute of Patent Attorneys (CIPA), are qualified to represent individuals and companies before the UK-IPO in matters relating to the prosecution of patent applications.

To be registered, patent attorneys have to meet the following criteria:

- ✔ They must have a technical or scientific education or experience (typically an engineering or scientific university degree).

- ✔ They must pass rigorous examinations set by the CIPA concerning all aspects of IP. In addition all members of the CIPA have to attend sufficient conferences and symposiums or deliver appropriate papers on IP in any 12-month period to accumulate adequate Continued Professional Development points to the satisfaction of the CIPA in order to continue in practice.

Any attorney registered as a Fellow of the CIPA may give you legal advice and represent you before judicial or administrative authorities, including the UK-IPO.

Unqualified IP advisers

Some well-intentioned business and corporate lawyers won't hesitate to tackle intellectual property matters, but they're not necessarily competent to handle such issues. Many corporate lawyers are knowledgeable and do their best but are most likely to be out of their league when it comes to the latest developments in IP law.

Be particularly careful if you decide to use a corporate lawyer who's not an IP specialist. Question the legal eagle about his or her IP competence and experience – something you need to do anyway whenever you consult an attorney. Check out the next section, 'Asking the right questions,' for more.

The CEO of a medium-sized company consulted an IP attorney when the company was threatened with an infringement lawsuit for the use of a company and brand name. The CEO thought his business adviser had *cleared* (searched) the name. After appropriate searches the IP attorney discovered that although the business attorney had checked for the availability of the name, his searches weren't thorough. By searching the Companies House Register of business names and the Trade Marks Registers of the UK-IPO and OHIM, the IP attorney discovered that the company and brand name was already used as a trade name elsewhere in the UK. The CEO had to change the name of his company, his company's brand name, letterheads, signs, stickers, labels, and packaging, at significant cost and loss of *goodwill* (business reputation) already accumulated under that name.

If the CEO had consulted an IP attorney, namely a patent attorney who's a Fellow of the Chartered Institute of Patent Attorneys (CIPA), or a trade mark attorney who's on the Register of the Institute of Trade Mark Attorneys (ITMA), the CEO could have sought redress through the respective Institutes if the attorney failed in his duties of care to his client.

Asking the right questions

To ensure that the person you hire is the right one for the job, ask some hard questions before you make your final decision. IP attorneys gladly supply you with references and samples of their work and answer questions such as:

- What is your technical background?
- How long have you been practising in this field of law?
- Are you familiar with my area of technology?
- Have you assisted clients in obtaining patents related to my invention?
- How many patent applications have you handled?
- How many patents have you obtained?
- Do you draft licences and other IP contracts?
- Do you issue infringement opinions?
- Who else, besides you, will be working on my case?

Using unaccredited individuals and companies

Some individuals and companies offer various IP services, such as searches for patent (which we talk about in Chapter 6), registered design (more on this in Chapter 11), copyright (which we discuss in 13), and trade marks (see Chapter 17). Many of these suppliers advertise in local business telephone directories and professional publications. Although they can do some leg-work for you, their services are limited and don't extend to any kind of legal matter. For instance, a company may conduct a trade mark availability search and come up with a list of similar marks and trade names already in use. However, it can't give you a legal opinion as to whether the use of that mark would infringe on the rights, if any, of the users of the uncovered marks and trade names. Like the CEO who relied upon the advice from his business adviser (see the earlier section 'Unqualified IP advisers'), when seeking advice from any service provider, make sure that they're competent in the areas of concern to you.

We recommend that you consult with an IP specialist, namely a patent or trade mark attorney or an IP lawyer, in connection with the kind of search you require and the analysis of the search results. You can have confidence in their opinions.

Finding and Retaining an IP Attorney

The best way to find a competent IP attorney is by referral from someone who's used that professional's services in the past and been satisfied. You do have other options, though, which we list here in our order of preference:

- ✔ Ask for a referral from your solicitor or bank manager who you know and trust.

- ✔ Consult the Chartered Institute of Patent Attorneys (CIPA), which can advise you on patent and/or trade mark practices situated close to your address or business premises. You can locate a member by region, post-code, location, or firm's name at CIPA's Web site `www.cipa.org.uk`.

- ✔ Most UK patent attorneys provide a free half-hour during which you may disclose, in confidence, the outlines of your IP asset in order to receive advice on how you may best secure protection for that IP asset.

- ✔ The UK-IPO runs established 'travelling shows' intended to enlighten inventors from all sectors of the community to encourage them to take steps to protect their IP assets through an IP attorney or direct to the UK-IPO.

Giving up a piece of the action

Fledgling entrepreneurs are usually short of cash and often eager to offer a third party a part of their business, technology, or invention in order to pay for the attorney's services. If you're tempted to do so, and assuming that you can find a third party who's willing to go along with your proposition, here are a few things to think about first:

✔ A part-owner of your company or its assets may have some say about how the business is run. Have a clear, written understanding about these matters to prevent a costly dispute.

✔ You don't yet know what your business or IP is worth, so you may be giving up too much for the services you're trying to secure. Later, you may find yourself without enough remaining assets or ownership of the business to obtain the capital and resources you need. Don't sell yourself short. Wait and see where you're going before making that kind of trade-off.

✔ A part-of-the-action fee arrangement is non-starter for an attorney because the likelihood that a conflict of interest eventually develops is high. Such arrangements place the IP attorney at a disadvantage because of the strict duty of loyalty imposed by the professional codes of ethics. Although it's not your problem if the professional runs into trouble with CIPA, we'd seriously question the prudence, integrity, and professionalism of an attorney who takes such a risk. Get the entire financial arrangement in writing and get a second opinion from another attorney.

When you're ready to retain or hire an IP attorney, insist on an engagement contract or retainer agreement that clearly spells out all the services, terms, and conditions of your professional relationship.

Here's a checklist of some of the most important things to include:

✔ What is the IP attorney going to do for you?

✔ How much, and when, you have to pay for the attorney's services.

✔ The additional costs and fees you may encounter.

✔ How you can terminate the agreement and hire another attorney.

✔ Who the IP attorney represents – you, your associate or partner, your company, the man on the moon. . . .

This last point is particularly important. You must be careful that you don't ask your IP attorney to do something that isn't beneficial to your associate or your company. An eventual conflict of interest that wasn't properly anticipated can lead to a nasty legal fight.

Staying Within Your Meagre Means

Legal services are expensive and eat up the lion's share of the money you spend to protect your intellectual property. We give the low-down in this section on what you might need to spend. But don't panic – we also show you how to keep your IP protection expenses within your budget.

Calculating the costs

Don't be surprised if your IP attorney quotes you an hourly rate somewhere between £300 and £400. Keep in mind that fees and costs, including government charges, often change and may not be the same in all places. Below we offer some sample budgets for common basic services, using attorneys' average rates.

Patents

Before applying for a patent, and after reading Chapter 6, you may decide to conduct a preliminary search to explore what's already been done in your field and to get a professional opinion about whether a patent is right for you. Here's what a search can cost:

Invention preliminary search	£400
Review of search results and attorney's opinion	£500
Total	£900

Assuming you don't encounter any complications, a patent for a simple mechanical invention costs about £2,500. A more complex invention may cost between £5,000 and £10,000. Here's a detailed breakdown for a UK patent application covering an electro-mechanical device of medium complexity:

Preliminary interview and draft of application	£2500
Drawings and filing fee	£500
Review of examiner report with attorney	£500
Answer/amendment	£500
Publication and other miscellaneous fees	£150
Total	£4150

Trade marks and other commercial identifiers

When you select a mark or trade name, you want to make sure that it won't infringe upon a commercial identifier already in use (as we explain in Chapter 16). Here's what each availability search may cost you:

Word mark availability search (no attorney's opinion)	£250
Legal review of search results and attorney's opinion	£300
Total	£550

A trade mark registration can set you back £500–750.

The following table gives the details for registering a trade mark in two classes:

Preliminary interview and draft of application	£350
Filing fees and drawing	£250
Review of examination report with attorney	£250
Answer/amendment	£300
Total	£1,150

Protection abroad

You should budget between £50,000 and £150,000 for overseas patent protection and between £10,000 and £20,000 for trade mark registration. All of which covers only 10 to 20 foreign countries. See Chapter 18 for more on international patents.

Exercising caution with TV invention-development services

Wow, those commercials touting invention-development and marketing companies probably sound pretty enticing, don't they? What a saving they represent compared with the fees we quote in this chapter. Our advice is beware! This industry is riddled with abuses. Many of these companies prey upon the ignorant, the naive, and the elderly, taking inventors' money and never returning a penny to their trusting victims. If you do choose to use their services, be as prudent as you are when selecting an IP attorney. Insist upon proof of prior performances by asking how much money the company has doled out in the past and how many customers have received those disbursements. Ask for references and check them out thoroughly. Interview and compare. And keep in mind that only a licensed IP attorney can give you valid legal advice. Remember that if it sounds too good to be true, it probably is!

Doing it yourself

Throughout this book, we point out various things you may do yourself. However, the savings may be minimal and may not be worth the risk you're taking. An IP attorney would rather start from scratch than try to unravel the tangled mess of an inadequate patent application. The best thing you can do is to carefully prepare the background material, as we explain in Chapter 7.

Managing the expenses

Your IP attorney can help you properly allocate your resources and minimise IP-related expenses. Here's a short list of what your attorney can do for you:

- ✔ Give you short-term and long-term estimates of all fees and costs.
- ✔ Show you how to strategically spread the protective measures over a number of years so you don't have to blow the entire budget all at once.
- ✔ Devise the least expensive approach for protecting your intellectual property – such as relying on copyright, registered design, or by implementing a trade-secret protection programme using confidentiality agreements and other procedures.
- ✔ Give you some peace of mind and a bill for their services – not necessarily in that order.

Paying the piper

You can pay for IP professional services in one of three common ways:

- ✔ An hourly fee
- ✔ A fixed amount for the whole job
- ✔ A combination of the above

If you agree to an hourly fee, request a complete estimate of all the costs over the life of the project, such as filing fees, copying and mailing costs, foreign agent charges, and maintenance fees. You pay *maintenance fees*, also called *annuities*, to patenting authorities during the life of a patent. In some countries, the annuities fall due from the date of filing the application.

If you agree to pay a fixed fee, ask about other expenses, such as government charges, drawing costs, and copying charges that may not be included. In all cases, clarify how and when you must make the payments.

Working with Foreign IP Professionals

You must have a representative in every foreign country in which you file a patent application, a registered design application, or a trade mark application. Most UK patent attorneys maintain working relationships with IP professionals in other industrialised foreign countries. The global network of patent and trade mark attorneys depends upon the size of their practice and their client base. Larger practices have ongoing associations with very many overseas IP professionals in other industrialised countries.

In all cases, you need to pay the foreign IP professionals' fees and government charges. Usually, neither you nor your attorney has any control over these costs, but always ask for a rough estimate when you file overseas. Because foreign costs tend to be substantially higher than in the UK, don't forget to take those expenses into account when preparing your IP budget and laying out your IP protection strategy.

You don't have to worry about searching and selecting attorneys abroad, but on occasion your UK IP professional may ask you to review their reports for any unexpected charges. We encountered an overseas attorney who regularly sent invoices for reviewing the company's portfolio of patents and/or trade mark applications at least once a month! Such attention to detail is neither necessary or requested.

Co-ordinating with Other Professionals

Don't forget to keep your other business advisors informed about your IP programme. We suggest the following strategies:

- ✔ Keep your business or corporate attorney aware of all your IP activities. It's a good idea to give your attorney copies of all your major correspondence with your IP professionals. Your patents and trade marks may be put to good use in distributorship and representative agency agreements.

- ✔ Inform your accountants and other bean counters about your IP expenses. Acquiring a patent, or developing a trade secret, can have important tax implications, and you don't want to miss lucrative amortisation or depreciation deductions. Proceeds from the sale of licensing of an invention may benefit from special taxation rules, and your technological acquisitions and research programme may qualify for tax credits.

- ✔ Make your PR and advertising agency fully aware of the trade marks and logos you acquire and register. Those trade marks and logos can be effectively put to work in your promotional campaigns. As we explain in Chapter 15, your advertising and marketing people can play an important role in selecting your commercial identifiers.

Part II
Patenting Your Product

'Actually, it's a death ray — oops!'

In this part . . .

Getting a patent can be tough; no question about it. But we're here to guide you through the entire process of preparing and filing the patent application. In this part, we introduce the basics of the patenting process, including the legal and practical definitions you need to get a handle on before you enter the world of patents, and the criteria you and your invention must meet to qualify for a patent. At every step of the way, we illustrate how your chief confidant – your IP attorney – can clear obstacles from your path.

Acquiring a patent is probably the most complex, expensive, and time-consuming type of IP protection. Because getting a patent can be so difficult, we help you evaluate whether you should really apply for a patent or use another way to protect your IP.

For similar reasons, making sure that no one else has already come up with your device is the way to go before you start the application process. So we show you how to do a novelty search to see whether your invention is new, original, and useful – because these factors determine whether your invention is really patentable.

We then give you tips on preparing your patent application, help you push it through the UK Intellectual Property Office and deal with the patent examiner, and, finally, show you how to get that coveted piece of paper.

Chapter 4

Understanding Patents and How They Work

A patent is the most common, effective, and valuable of all intellectual property rights (IPRs), but it also happens to be the most misunderstood. In this chapter we untangle, one step at a time, the knotty complexity of patents so that you've no doubts about what a patent is and whether you can get one. In Chapter 5 we delve deeper into whether you really want a patent as part of your IP strategy.

Presenting a Patent Explanation

A *patent* is a temporary legal right granted to an inventor by the government to prevent other people from manufacturing, selling, or using the invention. This is a loaded definition, so try reading it again – the most important words are:

⊳ **Temporary:** A patent doesn't last forever but exists for a specified number of years. Currently, the life of a patent is 20 years, provided that fees are paid annually to the UK-IPO.

⊳ **Right . . . to prevent:** A patent allows its owner to go to court and *ask* a judge to stop someone from doing something. But remember: An inventor isn't immune from the *right to prevent* held by the owner of another patent.

A patent gives its owner the right to manufacture, use, sell, license, or otherwise exploit the invention protected by the patent. It may also be used to prevent others from stepping on your rights. That may require a trip to a High Court or the patents Court and paying huge lawyer fees if the infringer isn't inclined to desist from her infringing activity or enter into a licence agreement.

Seeing what your patent can do for your country

The UK Intellectual Property Office (UK-IPO) is in charge of the UK patent system. This patent system is a bit of an exception to the general free competition and anti-monopolistic principles that underline our body of laws, because it gives one person sole control of a possibly important technological field. Yet, in a roundabout way, patents still ensure fair competition among all citizens. A patent gives an inventor incentive to disclose and use their precious invention and to 'promote the progress of science and useful arts'.

A patent also publishes the nuts and bolts of the invention, giving the public knowledge of the invention very early in the game, even though the inventor gets about a 20-year head start on profiting by the invention.

When the patent expires, anyone can apply the invention or manufacture and sell anything that falls within that previously taboo area of technology – free competition reigns once again and the country is richer for the new technology.

Appreciating what your patent can do for you

A patent can be a powerful legal tool that affords you, as an inventor, businessperson, or entrepreneur, the sole rights to your technology and a competitive edge in the market.

The patent reserves, exclusively for your benefit (but only in the country where you've obtained the patent), an area of technology corresponding roughly to your invention (we explain in Chapter 7 how the scope of a patent is defined). For the life of the patent, you can exclude others from making, selling, or using any machine, device, composition of matter, method, or process that falls within the technological area defined by the claims in your patent so long as your patent remains in force. When the patent is allowed to lapse, or it expires at the end of its twenty-year life, your rights as a patent owner cease and anyone may make use of your invention.

After your patent is granted, you can go into business yourself to make use of your invention, free of competition. You can also license your patent to someone else (a lease that allows another party to exploit your invention). If you've invented something really valuable, potential licensees are going to line up for the opportunity to pay you handsome royalties for the right to profit by your invention.

Or you can sell the patent outright for a bundle, giving the new owner the patent's exclusive benefits for the remaining term of the patent.

Understanding what a patent is and what may be protected

Unlike the US that grants three types of patent depending upon the characteristics of the invention or design, the UK only grants one form of patent. There's no utility, design, or plant patent in the UK; designs are protected by unregistered design right, a registered design, and copyright in the design. Protection of new varieties of plants operates under Plants Breeders Rights, which are overseen by DEFRA (see www.defra.gov.uk/planth/pvs/pbrguide.htm).

A patent protects new inventions and how they work, what they do, how they do it, what they're made of, and how they're made.

To become the subject of a granted patent, your invention must:

- ✔ Be new
- ✔ Have an inventive step
- ✔ Be capable of being made or used in some kind of industry
- ✔ Not be obvious

We go into more detail about these requirements in the later section 'Playing by the Rules: The Four-Part Patentability Test'.

Your invention must not be:

- ✔ A scientific or mathematical discovery, theory, or method.
- ✔ A literary, dramatic, musical, or artistic work.
- ✔ A way of performing a mental act, playing a game, or doing business.
- ✔ The presentation of information or some computer programs.
- ✔ An animal or plant variety.
- ✔ A method of medical treatment or diagnosis.
- ✔ Against public policy or morality.

If your invention satisfies the above criteria, you may obtain patent protection for your invention.

When you obtain a granted patent, you have to pay annuities to the UK-IPO from the fifth to the twentieth year if your invention has a successful commercial life (see Chapter 10 for more on annuities). On average, most patents are allowed to lapse after eight to ten years because the technology has forged ahead and may impact upon the commercial value and sales of a patented invention.

You can't patent a law of nature, such as a mathematical theorem, or a physical phenomenon or property, even if you're the first to discover or articulate it.

Claiming your rights as a patent owner

Under your patent, you can sue anyone who manufactures, sells, markets, or even uses your product without your permission. It doesn't matter that you, as the patent owner, may be excluded from all of those activities yourself under someone else's patent – you can still sue, which can lead to the following conundrum:

Jane has a patent covering a widget. You develop a modification that makes the widget more efficient and cheaper to produce and have been granted a patent covering the improvement. Jane wants to modify her widget according to your invention, but she can't do so without your permission. You, on the other hand, can't make or sell the improved widget without Jane's permission. The solution is to get together and strike a deal. Here are your options:

✔ You give Jane the exclusive right to use your improvement for a fee.

✔ Jane gives you permission, for a fee, to make and sell the improved widgets.

✔ Each of you agrees not to sue the other and goes into business using the other's invention.

Checking Out the Mechanics: Specifications, Claims, Drawings, and Abstracts

A patent doesn't define any particular device, machine, composition, or process but sets aside an area of technology just for you. You can compare a patent to the deeds of your house: The deeds don't spell out the layout of your house and how many bedrooms and bathrooms it has, but it describes the limits of your property by reference to certain landmarks, geographical orientations, and topographical coordinates.

Two primary parts of a patent get most of the job done, the specification and claims:

✔ **Specification:** This is a description of what the inventor considers to be the best way to work the invention, accompanied by drawings if necessary. It must be detailed enough to allow a skilled person to work the invention without undue experimentation.

✔ **Claims:** These constitute the legal component that defines the area of technology, based on the specification, that is reserved to the patent owner. Each claim defines a different scope of coverage.

✔ **Drawings:** Often you need to include drawings of your invention in order to illustrate to a UK-IPO Examiner and to substantiate your claim to have devised a new product, machine, process, or method of operation of a machine. The UK-IPO Examiner appointed to examine your patent application is highly qualified in the discipline in which your invention is placed.

✔ **Abstract:** An abstract is required in order to inform a reader of the nature of the invention, for example, a window cleaner's ladder and stabiliser assembly. Just sufficient detail is required to inform the reader of the patent specification so he can decide if it's of interest. The abstract is printed on the front page of a published patent application and a granted patent.

Playing by the Rules: The Four-Part Patentability Test

The UK Patents Act 1977 requires that the claimed invention complies with a series of elaborate tests in order to meet the four-pronged *patentability test*. It must:

- ✔ Be new
- ✔ Involve an inventive step
- ✔ Be capable of industrial application
- ✔ Not be obvious (see 'Avoiding the obvious' later in this chapter)

The reason for these tests is to guarantee consistency when granting patents. However, the tests are rather complex, with many accommodations for special cases.

In the following sections, we explore each of the hurdles the invention must clear and then provide you with a checklist that you can use to make sure that your invention meets the requirements necessary to receive a patent.

Making yourself useful

The *industrial applicability test* determines whether your invention has any use in the real world. As long as you can dream up some kind of application for your invention, you've no problem passing this test. You don't even have to prove that the invention actually works! However, without adequate description and drawings of how your invention works, a UK-IPO Examiner has just cause to refuse the grant of a patent.

Demonstrating the inventive step

The *inventive step test* determines whether you've developed an original way to solve a problem. Your invention is compared with everything relating to your invention that has been created in the past, which is called the *prior art.* Contrary to what you may think, the inventive step test is rarely insurmountable. Your patent can't be denied unless a prior art device, machine, or process includes *all* the basic components of your invention. For example, if you invent a watercraft with a hull made of plastic sheets heat-welded together, it would be considered new even though you found a similar craft in a prior patent, but with glued components. However, you may have a problem with the next test.

Avoiding the obvious

The *non-obviousness test* is the crux of the matter and also the toughest test. To pass, the difference between your invention and the prior art (which we mentioned in the previous paragraph), it must not be obvious to a person with ordinary skill in the relevant field. The problem with the obviousness test is defining that mythical person with ordinary skill in the field; for example, the person isn't a weekend do-it-yourselfer or a design engineer but a good technician who knows, or has access to, all prior art information in the field of the invention at the time when the patent application is filed at the UK-IPO.

Another way to look at it is to say that your invention is not obvious if it provides a solution to a long-standing problem in an off-beat way or, as the courts like to put it, by *teaching away* from the prior art. The following examples illustrate the two tests.

Stating the obvious

Say you're an artist who moulds statues and other artefacts out of polyester or other types of *thermosetting resin* (the resin hardens with increased temperature, instead of melting). You also sprinkle flakes of aluminium and other metals into your resin in order to create decorative patterns. It's a type of resin commonly used to cast countertops and bathroom vanities, so to an ordinary bathroom fixture builder, there's nothing new or non-obvious in your process.

However, while experimenting with different types and sizes of metal flakes, you realise that by reducing the size and increasing the number of metal particles, you can colour the entire material in various hues, for example, red with copper dust, silvery grey with aluminium, and so on. If you conduct an anticipation search, you won't find your invention in the prior art, but you'd be dead wrong to think that you can get a patent. Even though you've come up with a new product and fabrication process, a patent examiner can probably reject your application for being obvious because a 'person with ordinary skill' would expect a change of colour by scattering large quantities of small metal particles in the resin.

Making the best of a non-obvious situation

Taking our example a little further, you notice that the resin reacts with the metal particles, coating each one with a thin layer of oxidation. You now mix the resin with a metal powder made of extremely fine particles. When the metal particles become almost completely oxidised by reaction with the resin, you discover that you've created a new composite material whose physical properties differ substantially from those of past composites. You also observe that your compound conducts heat more like a metal than a plastic substance but doesn't conduct electricity.

Can you get a patent on your development? Probably. Your results wouldn't be obvious to anyone with ordinary skill in the fields of plastics and electrical insulators. For years, electrical engineers have been looking for a material that insulates electronic components from one another and effectively dissipates the heat the components generate. They've even mixed resins and metal particles to create electrical contact pads. Congratulations! You found an unexpected solution to a longstanding problem in electrical assemblies.

Making a list and checking it twice

Before proceeding to prepare and file a patent application (see Chapters 7 and 8), consider whether your development meets the following 'rules' for being protected by a granted patent.

The 'rules' are, if you will excuse some lawyer-style wording as a warm-up, arcane, recondite, and abstruse. Translation: mysterious, obscure, and foggy. These 'rules' are important and you'll probably refer to them on several occasions. So, turn off the TV, finish your chicken nuggets, and concentrate.

If you're still a little fuzzy after reviewing the above list, don't worry. If you *fully* grasp these concepts, you'll be able to pass the patent exam – and no one is asking you to do that. If you decide to go after a patent, your patent attorney investigates these matters with you. So for now, just be aware of these rules and make an initial analysis of how your invention would score.

> ✔ **Your invention must be useful.** The utility test can be satisfied if you can show that the invention is practical.
>
> A method for growing parsley in your nose may appear totally crazy and useless. Who would want to grow an herb in their nasal cavities? But who's to forbid such an innocent activity? Certainly not the UK-IPO. After all, perhaps you relish the fragrance of fresh parsley. What better way to satisfy your olfactory fetish than to keep a sprig of it in our nose at all times? This argument, as silly it may sound, is enough to establish utility.

✔ **Your invention must have credibility.** If you apply for a patent on a product or process that runs contrary to the laws of physics, you'll be asked to provide persuasive evidence that it actually works. Applications for perpetual motion machines are routinely rejected because of the inventors' failure to convincingly demonstrate that their contraptions work.

✔ **Your invention must be practicable.** You must be able to work the invention with existing components and materials. For example, if your invention requires milling a component down to a micron range, and no equipment is available to do so, your invention is indeed useless.

✔ **Your invention can't have been previously known or used by others anywhere in the world before the date when your patent application is filed at the UK-IPO.** If someone else had possession or knowledge of the invention before you did – and didn't conceal it from the public – you're out of luck. It doesn't matter that you came up with the invention on your own and didn't know about the other person(s).

✔ **Your invention must not have been previously patented, or described in a printed publication, anywhere in the world prior to the date of your patent application.** If a printed description of it is readily available to the public before the date of your patent application, anywhere or in any language, you lose out, even if only one copy, in any language, is freely available to the public in a library in Outer Mongolia.

✔ **The applicant, who may be the inventor(s), must have come up with the invention alone or in collaboration with one or more colleagues.** This means that you and/or they can't have found out about the invention on their last overseas holiday.

✔ **The inventor must be the first to file a patent application in the UK.** Inventors should carefully document the development of their inventions and file their patent application at the most opportune time bearing in mind the many hurdles that may have to be surmounted in finding a route to market for the invention.

✔ **The invention must not be obvious to a person with ordinary skill in the field at the time of the invention.** This is the last and toughest of the rules. Countless court decisions have struggled with the requirement of non-obviousness. Review our comments and examples in the section 'Avoiding the obvious' earlier in this chapter. We go over the point again in Chapter 10.

Chapter 5

Testing the Water Before You Apply for a Patent

· ·

· ·

*P*rotecting a technological breakthrough with one or more patents isn't a trivial undertaking. The complexity, costs, and long delays that accompany such a project necessitate a clear understanding of the process and a thorough exploration of alternative, more practical, and less expensive approaches.

But don't let us scare you – we've no intention of discouraging you from applying for a patent. A patent can be an effective protection tool that provides you with a lucrative source of income. However, we've seen many inventors jump into the patent application fray with no reasonable prospect of seeing through the application to a successful completion. If you've read Chapter 4 and still think that you have a patentable invention, take a deep breath and follow the pre-patent exercises we describe in this chapter.

Assessing What You Have

The first step in attempting to protect an invention or other technological breakthrough is formulating a clear vision of your idea and determining what rights you have to it. Be prepared for some surprises.

Defining the invention in writing

At first glance, preparing a written description of your invention may seem like a childish exercise, but putting the invention on paper is exactly what patent attorneys do before actually drafting an application. To follow their lead, go over your notes, drawings, and models and write down an accurate description of your new device, process, or composition. Try to be as concise as possible without missing any key features that make your invention new and unique. Help yourself by drawing a little sketch of your invention with cross-reference numbers that refer back to the text.

Focus on the nuts and bolts of the invention in your description – how it's made and how it operates – rather than its advantages and commercial applications. The description of your invention becomes the cornerstone of the patent application, so make sure that it's technically accurate and complete.

Qualifying the invention

Now you determine whether your invention qualifies for a patent. You don't need to do the detailed analysis of a patent examiner, but you do need to be sure that your invention exceeds the basic patentability threshold. Don't waste your time pursuing a patent process that's already doomed to failure because of an inherent flaw in your invention or idea.

Surpassing the *basic patentability threshold* first means finding out whether your invention fulfils the necessary requirements. Then, pit your invention against the important patentability factors – novelty, inventive step, and industrial application – that make up the first three prongs of the four-part patentability test as we describe in Chapter 4.

Novelty doesn't mean the latest gadget or Christmas stocking filler, but something that's new and has never been done before. Inventive step requires that your invention offers a technical advance over anything that's already out there, and this advance can't be obvious (the fourth part of the patentability test – refer to Chapter 4 for a discussion of what 'obvious' entails). If your invention still looks good, you can double-check your findings against the patentability checklist, which is a bunch of hoops you must jump through to get a patent, as we discuss in Chapter 4.

When you get to the second part of the patentability test – the one about whether your invention is something that would be obvious to someone skilled in that particular area, don't waste too much time pondering: That happens to be the big money question that patent examiners or judges ultimately answer.

Coming up with an inventor

Be brutally honest in assessing whether you alone conceived the invention or whether someone else made suggestions or contributed to the concept. You also need to know whether anyone else refined or improved the device when you built the prototype or model. Maybe a co-worker or your 10-year-old whizz-kid helped you out. Regardless of the circumstances, be sure to acknowledge any helpful outside contributions now. Any contributor may have rights that are equal to yours and therefore must, by law, be listed as an inventor on the patent application.

Determining exactly who came up with your invention is an extremely tricky but critical legal issue that requires the advice of a competent intellectual property (IP) attorney. We help you find an IP attorney in Chapter 3.

Figuring out ownership

Although ownership of an invention and patent is related to the question of who originated the invention, it remains a separate issue. We look at ownership from two perspectives: securing ownership of contributions to the invention by others, and ensuring ownership of your own creations.

Acquiring contributions

Taking care of your invention's ownership issues early in the game reduces the chances of running into problems later. It's not unusual for a former associate, employee, neighbour, or relative to claim a role in a commercially successful invention, so watch out for people giving you advice you don't need! Troublesome people always seem to crawl out of the woodwork at the most difficult times in an entrepreneurial venture.

If anyone contributed to your invention, secure your exclusive ownership through agreements with that contributor, regardless of who's named as inventor on the patent application. You can use the same type of agreement that we discuss in Chapter 13 in connection with copyright. Ask your IP attorney to draft an invention and patent transfer agreement that fits your circumstances.

Claiming your own creation

If you invent something in your role as an employee, chances are you have no right to that invention, even if you invented it entirely on your own. You need to establish that you own your invention, so check through the following sticky points before proceeding with a patent:

> ✔ Employment contracts often include invention-assignment clauses that folks sign without much thought. Even an invention made entirely at home and using your own resources in any technological field may actually belong to your boss.
>
> ✔ Even an unwritten agreement to work together on a project or an advance of funds may give each a claim to ownership. See Chapter 13 for more details.

Don't waste time and money on something that may not be yours. If you have any concerns in this area, consult an IP attorney.

Identifying who should apply

In the UK, the patent application can be signed and filed by the inventor, assignee, or their legal representative. An *assignee* may be the employer(s) of an inventor and, even though they may have a right to the invention and seek patent protection, they still have to obtain an assignment of the IPRs, especially if they're going to file overseas. An assignee is also the person or entity that an inventor may assign his IPRs to.

Identifying the applicant gets a little trickier when inventors can't be found or refuse to co-operate and sign the application. Employee-inventors become frustrated after realising that they don't own their inventions and quit their jobs or refuse to help their employers get a patent. When that's the case, anyone who can show a documented right to the invention, including a co-inventor or employer, can file on behalf of an absent or unwilling inventor. The procedure requires an earnest attempt to notify and offer the missing party the opportunity to join in the application.

Making Sure that a Patent Is Right for You

So you think that you have a patentable invention. You believe that the invention's all yours, and you have the right to file a patent application. Now you get to play doctor and diagnose whether a patent is the right medicine for you.

Comparing the pros and cons of the patent game

Applying for a patent is a lengthy, expensive, and uncertain endeavour. Therefore, we suggest you first understand all the alternative, less-taxing approaches for protecting your invention. You may want to use one or more of those approaches instead of, or in addition to, the patent application.

In our opinion, the advantages of applying for a patent are:

- **Broad scope of protection:** Can extend to a broad field of technology. A particular development may have application in several different areas. For example, a new high-tech control panel may be used in a vehicle assembly plant, a processing plant for manufacturing roof tiles, or a in a still in a brewery. So the best protection that you can obtain may extend to a 'broad field of technology'.

- **Increase in the value of your business:** A patent or IP portfolio is a real advantage if you want to raise capital.

- **Powerful anti-competition tool:** Business people are wary of infringing patents because of high litigation costs and damages awards.

Don't ignore the following disadvantages, however:

- **High costs:** The costs of patenting are extremely high and unpredictable. Patenting is a continuous process and may require multiple applications in several countries to cover all aspects of the invention, eventual improvements, and potential markets outside of the UK.

- **Letting out your secret:** You must bare it all in your application, and once published it's easy for others to use your invention as soon as the patent expires.

- **Long wait for (relatively) short-lived protection:** The protection lasts 20 years, provided you keep up the renewal payments.

Exploring alternative routes

If you decide that the disadvantages outweigh the advantages of applying for a patent, you can still protect your invention. The easier and less expensive approaches that you can follow include the trade secrets and copyright routes.

Looking at trade secrets

You may be dealing with a chemical or process invention, or other improvement that you don't ever have to expose the details of to the general public. You can keep your chemical formulations under wraps and not file a patent application(s). In such an instance, secrecy may be the best approach.

Check out Chapters 1 and 2, where we talk about using a trade-secret strategy. The most serious risk is that someone else independently discovers the invention you're keeping secret, files a patent application, gets a patent, and causes you considerable grief.

In general, keeping an invention a trade secret is a great idea when the useful life of the invention is relatively short, say five or six years. The odds that someone else discovers the same invention and obtains a patent during that period are in your favour. A good example is the formula for Coca Cola. The Coca Cola Corporation has managed to keep its formula a trade secret since its creation. Other companies have attempted to imitate the drink, but the tastes to most people are different. Had its formula been the subject of a patent application, it would have been publicly available within two to three years after the patent application was filed. At present, the period between filing a patent application and publication is only eighteen months.

Using copyright protection

As we explain in Chapter 2, copyright is automatic and should always be part of your IP protection strategy.

Sometimes copyright provides better protection or alternative protection to the other forms of intellectual property available. Here are a few examples:

- **Computer programming:** Relying on copyright protection is particularly effective if you've invented a type of process or method that's implemented with a computer program. But remember, the copyright covers only the written part of the program and not the actual process.

  Say you develop a complex process for shredding recyclable rubber, melting it, and turning it into a paste that can be moulded at room temperature for 24 hours before it cures into a resilient body. The method consists of multiple steps involving precise temperature and timing controls, which must be managed automatically by computer.

  A copyright on the computer program prevents others from copying your specific application but doesn't prevent anyone who's familiar with your process from independently devising essentially the same process and writing an original computer program to achieve the same results. But you can charge anyone who reproduces any part of *your* software while trying to devise such a process with copyright infringement. Along with copyright protection, you need to keep *your process* confidential as a trade secret.

- **Peripheral material:** Manuals, promotional material, packaging, presentations, lectures, and handouts automatically enjoy copyright protection once you've created them. Making sure that you protect peripheral materials properly, by copyright, goes a long way towards substantially stifling your competitors.

- **Style and ornamentation:** Instead of seeking a registered design, and incurring the expense of doing so, to protect the style or ornamentation of your product, you may find that design copyright does the trick (refer to Chapter 11 for more on design copyright).

Because of its inability to cover concepts and processes, copyright doesn't extend to some parts of a manual, mode of operation, or game rules because of their essentially functional aspects (which we explain in Chapter 12).

Going registered design rather than patent

A registered design is intended to cover purely decorative and non-functional aspects of a product – the aesthetics, look, or shape of the product. However, in certain cases a registered design turns out to be a more effective tool than a patent in stopping an infringer. The forms for registration are far easier to complete, and a number of different designs can now be included in one application. The registered design route is also much lighter on the wallet!

The protected appearance of your device may be so striking that a copycat would find marketing a competitive product difficult without using the same look. For instance, look at the distinctive shape and ornamentation of the Jif Lemon juice bottle. Can you imagine yourself picking up a similar product presented in a totally different container? You automatically rely on the look of the product and don't have to read the brand name to know what you're buying.

Recognising the role of corporate branding

All this protection stuff we've been talking about serves only one purpose – to give you an edge over the competition. The same can be said of good *corporate branding*, so don't overlook the marketing power of a good trade mark, or a company name.

Look at all the products around you. Almost every one of them has a trade mark prominently displayed on it. Now see how many patent numbers you can find. Two, one, or none at all? In most cases, the market position of a product or service is enhanced more by a good name than it is by a patent.

For example, do you ever buy fabric fastener strips by asking for anything other than the brand name 'Velcro'? Probably not – the name does the marketing. How about Rolls-Royce? After all, what do many would-be entrepreneurs aspire to drive? The answer is in the name. Check out Chapter 16 to discover how to create powerful names.

Starting Things Off on the Right Foot

The wild blue yonder of patents and patent applications is no place for a learner's first solo flight. However, even though explosive legal issues lurk behind every cloud, you can do some of the work without waiting for professional advice or assistance. You can also use the guidelines that we provide in Chapter 6 and conduct a preliminary search to find out exactly what's been done previously in the area of your invention.

As you develop your product or process, take copious notes that include plenty of illustrative sketches, preferably in a bound notebook with numbered pages. Use a pen, not a pencil, and don't erase but cross out your mistakes; thus avoiding any later difficulty that you amended your notes or sketches. Once in a while, ask a trusted relative or friend, providing of course they've first signed a confidentiality agreement, to review your notes, date, and sign the last written page, stating that on the specified date, she or he read the notes and understood the invention. Also sign and date any sketches or notes you have made and get into the habit of doing so after every new addition.

These precautions are necessary because you need to know how to create a legally admissible document. Many inventors send themselves a description by recorded delivery in the post, and never open the date stamped package after it's arrived, or choose to leave a description with a solicitor or person of similar authority. These actions give you peace of mind more than anything, but are unlikely to stand firm in court if the issue of who invented the product first is ever raised.

Your well-kept notebook, however, has many uses. It can:

✔ **Provide your IP attorney with a complete history and disclosure of the invention.** Your attorney, in turn, may see something in some of your earlier and now discarded designs that deserves a patent.

✔ **Help you organise your thoughts, providing an easy review of your progress and helping you avoid reinventing the wheel.** You may also have a Eureka moment in the process, and find a new element or way of solving a problem you perhaps would not have stumbled across.

Chapter 6

Conducting a Patent Search

. . . .

In This Chapter

▶ Deciding whether you need a preliminary patent search

▶ Developing a search strategy

▶ Understanding your search results

▶ Carrying out other types of patent search

. . . .

*I*magine looking all over the house for your car keys so you can drive to your relative's house for your mandatory monthly visit. If you go, you miss seeing the last ten minutes of an important football match on the TV. Do you really want to find those keys? In the topsy-turvy world of patents, you may find yourself in a similar situation – searching for something you hope you won't find. The last thing you want to find in a patent search is your cherished brainchild plainly described in someone else's patent or in some publication. But you must keep looking.

Preparing and filing a patent application takes a lot of time and a good chunk of money. Pushing your application past the patent examiner at the UK Intellectual Property Office (UK-IPO) may take even more time and money. After shelling out all that cash, think how you might feel, some 12 months down the line, when the examiner says that a complete description of your invention can be found in patent number so and so, granted some 30 years ago.

To find out whether your invention is old hat or is innovative enough to deserve its own patent, you conduct a *novelty search* – a careful study of published patent specifications and other documents relevant to your invention. A novelty search is the most common type of search relating to patents. For info on other types of searches, see the section 'Looking at Other Patent Searches' at the end of this chapter.

No law says that you have to do a novelty search before filing your patent application. But you can save yourself a lot of money and avoid a great deal of embarrassment by first looking at prior patent specifications, as well as technical books and other publications in the area of your invention. An Internet search can also unearth other activities in the area that you're concerned with.

Most inventors don't understand what they can gain or lose by conducting a preliminary patent search, or whether one is even indicated. In this chapter we look at the pros and cons of doing a search, how to conduct a search, and how to interpret what you find.

Deciding Whether to Search or Not to Search

Before plunking down your credit card for an expensive holiday, you probably get lots of information about the places you want to visit. You may study maps, read some guidebooks, talk to someone else who's been there, and even consult a travel agent. If you think of a patent search as a journey to parts unknown, you can see why you want to know a little bit more about where you're heading before you embark on a long voyage.

To search or not to search is a tough question. Probably the best reason to do a search is because you want to know the odds of your patent application being approved. A search can tell you if someone else invented the same machine or process before you. However, because a search delays the filing of your patent application and isn't cheap if conducted by a professional searcher, plus there's no guarantee that you'll get a patent, you shouldn't jump into it without weighing up the pros and cons.

Considering reasons to do a search

If your search uncovers something very close to your invention, you save yourself the cost and aggravation of filing a patent application only to have it rejected after two or three years of futile pursuit. But don't despair – you can possibly use the information gained to improve and refine your invention or to help you draft a more focused and convincing patent application.

Perhaps the best reason to do a search is that a search gives you some peace of mind and confirms that you and your invention are on the right road.

Skipping the search

One downside of doing a thorough patent search is that as you wait for the results before filing your application, someone else may file for a similar invention – and that other person ends up with the patent.

As we explain in the section 'Analysing your search results' later in this chapter, no one can ever safely rely on a search to conclude for certain that your gadget is new and deserves a patent, or that there's absolutely nothing patentable in its construction.

The high cost of a professional search and interpretation, which can set you back by several hundred pounds, is another reason some people avoid doing a search. And extending a search to technical publications may end up costing more than the preparation and filing of the application itself.

Deciding whether a search is right for you

You may wonder why anyone would bother with such a time-consuming and costly procedure instead of just filing the patent application. We think that getting a balance is the best way forward – weighing the peace of mind that a successful search can give you against the high cost in time and money. We suggest a simple, reliable, cost-effective approach – do a preliminary novelty search only if you suspect that your invention may not be new.

A search may be a good idea if your invention meets two or more of the following criteria. Your invention:

- ✔ Is relatively simple.
- ✔ Belongs to a high-tech field.
- ✔ Isn't fully developed.
- ✔ Is marginally useful or practical.
- ✔ Uses very old or obsolete technology.
- ✔ Is just another version of a very common device.
- ✔ Closely resembles something that already exists.

Getting a second opinion

If you're like most inventors, you probably overestimate the importance and novelty of your creation. Before you get carried away, get a second opinion from an expert in the field. Let your technical expert (under a confidentiality agreement) or a patent attorney review the previous section and give you an educated guess as to whether your invention is unique before you do a long and expensive search. Check out Chapter 3 about dealing with patent attorneys.

Conducting a Novelty Search

In the classic film *All About Eve*, Bette Davis's character says, 'Fasten your seat belts – it's going to be a bumpy night.' The same can be said of patent searches, so buckle up on a trip through some arcane, Byzantine, convoluted, disorienting, eccentric, foggy, and obscure legal concepts. When you perform a preliminary patent search, you're trying to predetermine how the patent examiner will deal with your application. Therefore, your search shouldn't be limited to looking through documents for something resembling your invention. You also need to analyse what you find under the rules of patentability to decide if your invention qualifies for a patent. To do so, you must step into the shoes of a patent examiner and:

- ✔ Look for legally admissible information about existing technology in the area of your invention, commonly called the *relevant prior art* (see the 'Looking for relevant prior art' section, later in this chapter).

- ✔ Apply the patentability test to the invention (which we describe in Chapter 4), considering the relevant prior art to draw a conclusion that your invention is or isn't patentable.

The most you can get from a novelty search is to find out that some other chap has already made your widget. In other words, you may obtain a clear indication that your invention is *not* new, but you can never be sure that it *is* new, no matter how long and how deep you search.

Looking for relevant prior art

When rejecting patent applications, examiners have been known to rely upon prior publications as diverse as the writings of the Greek poet Homer, rare doctoral literature of all types and languages, and, of course, domestic and foreign patent specifications.

An examiner once rejected a patent application for a wetsuit because of a drawing of a medieval suit of armour published in an encyclopaedia circa 1900.

Accordingly, prior patents and patent applications aren't the only source of prior art. Any other published document can be used against your application. However, not all prior technology related to your invention is legally admissible against your patent application.

Selecting related patents

The esp@cenet worldwide patent database contains in excess of 60 million patent specifications. A patent examiner can use any of these documents, including expired, cancelled, abandoned, and published patent specifications, as proof that your widget is neither new nor non-obvious. It's almost impossible to sift through such a mountain of documents when doing your own novelty search, but you can make it easier by taking advantage of patent classification indices.

Patent documents are grouped into a number of technological classes, allowing you to limit your search to the fields of technology most related to your invention. Each country tends to have its own system, with its own classification key containing a list of alphanumeric codes and their meanings. Similar but multi-national systems include the European Classification and the International Classification – esp@cenet gives the option of searching through either or both of these.

After you find the class or classes relating to your invention, you can use them to search and retrieve prior patent documents. If your invention is simple and well defined, you may limit the search to just one relevant class. The details revealed for each of the documents are massive: you can inspect not only their descriptions, claims, and drawings but also their owners, inventors, and relevant dates, and whether the rights are still in force. See the next section, 'Examining patent documents' for a quick guide on how to navigate to the bits you want.

You can find the classification keys and lists by logging on to such Web sites as esp@cenet (`http://ep.espacenet.com`) or the UK Intellectual Property Office (`www.ipo.gov.uk`) and looking under Patents.

Examining patent documents

Searching patent documents to see whether someone has already come up with your invention can be as difficult and frustrating as looking for a wayward golf ball in a thorny thicket alongside the fairway. You have to interpret legalese while looking in lots of out-of-the-way places for your idea. Just as you may miss a ball caught in the bushes if you look only at the ground, you have to look at all sections of the patent document, which is not easy to read or understand.

But don't fret – here's a short course in navigating patent specifications. Most patent specifications, whether of a granted patent or a published patent application, can be divided into five sections:

✔ The *reference section,* shown on the front page(s) gives information that identifies the patent. Besides the patent number, title of the invention, names of the inventors, name of the assignee (owner), if any, and filing and publication dates, it includes the classification heading(s) allocated by the official examiner. In some, but not all, specifications this section also includes '*References Cited'.* (But sometimes the cited documents appear as part of the last section – see later in this section.)

The classification headings refer to the standard technological classes in which the subject invention falls. The cited documents consist of prior publications that were presented during the patent application examination because they contain material relevant to the invention. Check out the 'Organising and conducting the search' section later in this chapter to see how to use these cited documents during your search. For now, just remember that although you didn't see your idea in the patent document, it may be disclosed in one of those related prior publications.

✔ The *abstract*, also normally found on the front page, gives you a very concise, but often very narrow, description of the invention, and is usually illustrated by a single figure which is representative of the drawings included in the patent application.

Don't conclude that the patent isn't relevant to your invention simply because you don't recognise your baby in the abstract or the illustration on the cover page. Don't stop now – the info you've found can be very misleading as to the true contents of the document. Look at the whole specification.

The pages of typed text that follow the cover page should give you information as set out below.

- The field and background of the invention.

- A summary meatier than the abstract.

- A brief description of each drawing figure (if there are any).

- A detailed description of the inventor's preferred embodiment of the invention with numerous references to any drawing figures. The description is the meat of the document – go over it with a fine-tooth comb.

✔ In the next section, headed '*Claims*', you find a numbered list of on e-sentence definitions of what the inventor considers to be his or her contribution to the art – in other words, the invention. Don't let the formal and circuitous wording of the claims confuse you. (Refer to Chapter 4 to get an idea how claims must be read.) If necessary, grab a pencil and a sheet of paper, draw a diagram of the described structure or procedure, and add some notes in your own words. Understanding the 'Claims' section is important because it provides you with a very precise picture of what the invention is all about.

✔ The next pages carry the drawing figures with reference numbers that identify the components of the depicted devices. Note that not all specifications have or need drawings. Some chemical patents may instead provide chemical formulae or molecular diagrams. Some process patents include a block diagram of the process or processes) involved and some electrical patents include examples of suitable circuit diagrams.

Finally in some patent specifications, the last pages include a copy of the examiner's search report, listing the documents cited in the official search stage.

Organising and conducting the search

We suggest you map out a search strategy by deciding where and how to search. You can search manually or electronically and do the job yourself, or pay a professional.

Searching manually or electronically

You can conduct preliminary novelty searches in two basic ways: manually and electronically.

You can search manually in a number of libraries, for example in locations such as The British Library's Business and IP Centre in London, or one of the Patent Information Centres (PATLIB) situated in major UK cities. Begin by thumbing through reference manuals, such as the *Classification Key,* for a list of class headings to look at (see the 'Selecting related patents' section, earlier in this chapter). Then, with the serial numbers of those within each class that appear to be of interest, look up the paper copies of those patents, typically arranged in country sections and filed in serial number order. In some libraries the copies are kept on microfilm or microfiche.

You can run electronic searches on the Internet. You can access the full text of published patent applications on the European Patent Office databases by logging on to Esp@cenet (http://ep.espacenet.com). Considering that your patent application can be rejected because of a prior description in any domestic or foreign published document, you need to review patent specifications: published, granted and expired, or abandoned, from anywhere in the world, including published international patent applications such as those under the *Patent Cooperation Treaty* (PCT). Esp@cenet lets you do this. (Check out Chapters 7 and 19 for more information about the PCT.)

Also, most libraries provide computer access to the databases. But, you can't do a keyword search for the actual patent images. You can only do a visual review just like you'd do in a manual.

Searching strategies

Many professional searchers have their own approaches and connections for conducting a novelty search, which they keep very close to their chests, much like trade secrets. But here are effective searching strategies that are often recommended. If these approaches look too complicated, hire a professional.

If you're willing and able (and have plenty of strength and fortitude), you can try to do the search yourself. You have two ways of searching.

Because the best searching strategy is one that's thorough and also saves time and money, here's a shortcut approach that you should try first:

1. **Locate the latest patent or patent application that's most closely related to your invention by conducting an electronic keyword search in the most pertinent class.**

   For example, if you invented a new formula for an epoxy glue, you may want to try searching 'resin adhesive'.

2. **If that patent specification doesn't completely describe the invention, find its mention of '*References Cited*' and any further numbered patent references in its description.**

3. **Check out two or three of the most recent of its mentioned patent specifications.**

4. **Repeat the last two steps, going back in time through the cited references on each newly found patent specification until you have reviewed at least 15 of them.**

Promptly abandon branches that deviate from the invention and concentrate on those that look most promising.

It's not over 'til it's over. A novelty search isn't complete until you find what you don't want to find – an exact description of the widget that you invented. By definition, you can search forever, so it's up to you to decide when to stop searching.

A more elaborate approach is the following multi-step search strategy:

1. **Look at the classification definitions in the *Online Classification Keys* (on the British Library Web site at `www.bl.uk/collections/patents/class.html`) to identify all the classes your invention fits into.**

   You can also get this info by logging on to `www.ipo.gov.uk`.

2. **Browse through the titles of listed patent specifications to help narrow down the class list.**

   Look for keywords related to your invention and then note the corresponding classes.

3. **Retrieve the list of all patent specifications in those corresponding classes.**

4. **For further UK specifications, check the weekly *Patent Official Journal* and add to that list all patents issued during the current week.**

5. **Repeat these steps for all the patent specifications remaining on your list.**

   Review the abstract of each specification, and eliminate those that don't relate to your invention.

Be sure to have plenty of coffee handy: This job takes a few hours!

Don't forget to look at published patent applications as well as granted or issued patents. Even though published applications may not have been granted yet and may never be so, they still form relevant prior art.

A novelty search shouldn't only examine what a patent covers in the claims, which describe what the owner can prevent others from doing. You must look at everything the document discloses, teaches, and even suggests.

You should also consider conducting a registered design search, particularly if your product has an appealing shape or surface features. These might be the subject of someone else's registered design rights (See Chapter 11 for more information about registered designs.)

At some point in your search, you may feel as if you're in way over your head. But you don't need to drown – just call in the lifeguards (in this case, a professional searcher) to help you navigate the patent maze. You can find professional searchers in the Yellow Pages or at `www.yell.com` under Patents, Patent Attorneys, Patent Lawyers, or Patent Searches. The Chartered Institute of Patent Attorneys (CIPA) can also point you in the right direction.

Beware! Search results are always full of holes

Patentability standards are extremely subjective. After you find out what's been done in the past, you must make an educated guess about how a patent examiner applies those findings in assessing the patentability of your invention. The more you know about patent law, the more accurate that guess is going to be. Unfortunately, there's no black-and-white answer. You may want to refer to Chapter 1 to find out what types of things are more patentable.

Most novelty searches only look at patents and published patent applications and overlook a vast volume of prior material such as technical books, and foreign patents not accessible online, as well as scientific articles. Ignoring such material puts you at a big disadvantage compared to the legal eagles and can make for some unpleasant surprises if potential competitors come to light later in the process. Whoops – your educated guess just became a wild goose chase!

Compounding the problem is the fact that patent applications are held in secrecy until they're published, which is mostly not until some 18 months after their filing date. Up to that publication stage the patent application file is open only to the inventor or owner. Therefore, the hundreds of thousands of patent applications filed over the last year and a half won't show up during a search. By the time your application reaches an examiner's desk, many of those pending applications may be published or turned into patents. If one of those pending applications, lurking like a shark underwater, exactly discloses your invention, the patent examiner can cite that document in rejecting your application. You can see now that your educated guess looks more like a shot in the dark. The moral of the story – no matter how thorough your search, the results are always full of holes.

Analysing your search results

If you find a stack of patent specifications and other documents related to your invention, you need to act like a patent examiner and apply the novelty and non-obviousness tests (which we describe in Chapter 4) to your invention in view of the relevant prior art found during the search.

As with all legal concepts, many nuances and exceptions blur the rules about novelty and non-obviousness. The prosecution of a patent application is like a court battle. Patent attorneys and patent examiners often fight like cats and dogs and don't always find common ground.

Only in a clear and blatant case of exact duplication can a lay person safely conclude that the invention is not patentable. Usually, only a competent patent attorney, after a careful analysis of the search results, can provide a reliable opinion of non-patentability.

You can contact a registered UK patent attorney or agent via The Chartered Institute of Patent Attorneys (CIPA). They have a searchable database of members at www.cipa.org.uk.

Don't forget to keep all the prior art you found during the search so that you can save your patent attorney time and yourself money by avoiding duplication of effort in conducting further searches. In addition, you may want to refer back to any pertinent document as your invention evolves and you or your patent attorney can make a better assessment of the prior art.

Looking at Other Patent Searches

A novelty search is the most common type of patent search, but sometimes you may need one of these other types of patent search.

- ✔ **A patent title search** finds out the current owner of a patent. To be fully effective, the sale of an ownership interest in a patent (legally called an *assignment*) must be recorded in the IP registers of the country in which the patent was granted. The IP offices keep a chronological record of all assignments and other recorded transactions related to a patent. For example, for the UK, log on to www.ipo.gov.uk and you can find the current owner of any patent.

- ✔ **A state-of-the-art search** is often conducted as part of a programme of research and development or to gain expertise in a technical field. A state-of-the-art search looks at the latest published patent specifications in a particular field, but has very little to do with getting a patent. In most state-of-the-art searches, inventors review the most recent advances in that field, not just patents – it's a very detailed and technical search of electronic databases and Internet sites. You probably wouldn't do a state-of-the-art search by yourself – it's usually a job for engineers, scientists, and other research and development types.

- ✔ **An infringement search** is a totally different kettle of fish from a novelty search. The most common reason for doing an *infringement search* is if your novelty search reveals an unexpired patent that seems to cover your invention. This information is disappointing, but not fatal. If you've already manufactured and sold your widgets, you may worry that someone will get you for patent infringement. Before you panic, find out from an attorney whether you're really infringing an existing patent. What you see in a patent isn't always what's legally covered. That patent may be very easy to get around.

An infringement search is extremely complex and requires a thorough study and analysis of currently active patents and published patent applications in your field. You can check the status of both European and UK patents and patent applications through the UK-IPO website and for patents elsewhere through the local patent office sites. However if you're investing time and money into the invention, you should consult an experienced patent attorney who's studied hundreds of patent infringement cases. Check Chapter 20 to find out more about patent infringement.

Chapter 7

Preparing Your Patent Application

- -

In This Chapter

▶ Examining the form and function of a patent application

▶ Preparing to file an application

▶ Understanding the mechanics of writing claims

▶ Defending the patentability of your invention

- -

*W*e suggest you let your patent attorney prepare your patent application for you. But your patent attorney can't do a good job without your supportive participation – you came up with the invention, after all. In this chapter, we give you a basic understanding of the purpose, structure, and function of the patent application, so that you can efficiently and effectively assist your patent attorney.

If you want a design registration, you may be able to prepare and file the application yourself, following the guidelines in Chapter 11 and using the information you download from the UK-IPO Web site (www.ipo.gov.uk). Registered design applications don't require the highly legalistic claim drafting of a patent application.

You may also feel that with your writing and drawing skills, you could have a stab at preparing your own patent specification. The guidelines on the UK-IPO website provide a good starting place should you wish to have a stab at drafting your preliminary specification. This chapter, therefore, deals with preparing a patent application.

Knowing Who Can Apply for a Patent

The following people can apply for a patent for your invention:

- ✔ Your employer if you're employed in a position where you're expected to invent
- ✔ You, the inventor, (along with any co-inventors)

✔ Your assignee (the person or company you sell your rights to)

✔ Your patent attorney (your guide along a path full of pitfalls)

Take care when naming the inventors. A patent can be withdrawn if it was granted to a person who was not entitled to it. And if you don't name as inventor someone who feels they should have been named they can apply to be added.

Two or more people who work on an invention together are called *co-inventors* or *joint inventors* and must apply for a patent as such or be individually named as co-inventors. In the absence of an assignment or other agreement, each joint inventor has an equal share in the patent and – if they so choose – can exploit it without reference to the other. You can imagine the disputes that can cause. Make sure that you have agreed with any co-inventors the terms of your joint rights – in writing – and if at all possible, before you file the patent application.

Only people who actually contributed features of the invention are co-inventors. A person who merely provided advice or other assistance – like where to buy, or delivering to you, a special lubricant for the device's gearbox – is not an inventor. Other examples of people who aren't inventors include:

✔ **Financial contributors:** Someone who funds the research and/or development but doesn't do any of the actual work in the intellectual creation of the invention is not an inventor. Listing the name of your financial supporters is a nice thought – but not a good one. Wrongly naming the inventors can lead to problems, although it may be possible to remove the name of an inventor who shouldn't have been so named.

A better way of handling financial backers who want an interest in a patent is to include them as co-applicants. But make sure that you settle and record in writing the respective ownership and other rights of each of the co-applicants. Another way is to establish a company and assign the patent rights to that company. Your backer can make his or her contribution by buying shares in your company and indeed you may wish to open it to other shareholders too. You can get free advice on starting your business and what type of business you want from organisations such as Business Link (www.businesslink.gov.uk).

✔ **Your spouse:** Couples frequently have both names on their cars, houses, and other personal property and may not think twice about listing both names as inventors on a patent application. But unless both parties can legally prove that they're co-inventors, you may run into the problems indicated above. Solutions if a spouse is to be included in some way may again be to add them as co-applicant or form a company in which they can have a defined share.

Understanding the Patent Application

A patent is a legal exclusive right granted by the Government (in the UK by its delegated office, the United Kingdom Intellectual Property Office or UK-IPO) to you, as the inventor of a useful new process, manufacturing method, machine, or other product, for you alone to have the right to make, use or sell the subject of the invention, for as long as the patent is valid.

A patent also gives you the right, in the country where it's granted, to stop others making, using, offering for sale, or importing your invention for a fixed period of time. The patent gives you the right to take court action to sue others for infringing the patent (utilising your patented invention without your permission).

But on the negative side, a patent *does not* guarantee that your invention makes you money. A patent does not show that the product or process is necessarily superior to what was previously known, although it does indicate that the product or process represents an inventive step forward.

Your primary goal when preparing your patent application is to make its associated area of technology as broad as possible – within the scope of your invention. Your patent may eventually cover inventions that are inconceivable today but that fall within the exclusive area covered by your patent.

The strength of your patent depends as much upon the skills of your attorney to persuade the patent examiner to grant legal rights to the broadest area of technology as on the value of your invention. However, the patent examiner's duty is to make certain that your patent doesn't carry more rights than your invention deserves.

Patents aren't granted for the asking. The complex application process often takes unexpected turns. The process breaks down into three major phases:

1. **Preparing the application.**

   For patents, preparation is definitely the key to success, and that's what this chapter is all about.

2. **Filing the application.**

   It's not just lobbing forms in the post. We cover the nuts and bolts of filing in Chapter 8.

3. **Pushing the application through the UK-IPO.**

   Technically, this phase is called the *prosecution*. At this point, your attorney may have to answer communications from the patent examiner. Head to Chapter 9 for the low-down on prosecuting your patent application.

Choosing a Representative

We cover using professional advice in several chapters of this book, but we think that this chapter's a good place to mention it again. If you think that applying for a patent by yourself is a way to save money, we suggest you reconsider and read on.

A good representative helps you draft a patent specification that clearly defines your invention and shows its differences and improvements over anything known before. Your patent needs to be defensible in a court of law. If the invention is really good it may be only a matter of time until you're faced with infringers – people using your invention without your permission. You then have to resort to tough negotiations with them or their lawyers. At best the negotiating procedure leads to them stopping the infringement or agreeing to take a royalty-paying licence. At worst you fail to reach agreement and find yourself in court in a patent infringement action.

So not only do the strength and quality of your patent specification help in getting the patent accepted by the examiners, and have a major bearing on the outcome of the any negotiations or court proceedings, but so do the strength and quality of your representatives. Choose well and prepare well!

A patent attorney is also helpful in writing the patent description, defining your invention in carefully worded claims that distinguish it from what's already known, arguing your corner against official patent examiners who find a variety of objections to granting a patent, and adjusting your claims to overcome the examiners' objections so as to give a granted patent with the maximum available cover. They're also great translators of legal speak, and understanding what is effectively a language all of its own. Long sentences that your English teacher would have taken a red pen to, and words without spacing such as 'therebetween', 'herein', and 'whereinafter' are very often found in patent specifications.

Finding the right attorney for your project

Although an experienced patent attorney doesn't come cheap, hiring a qualified person doesn't cost nearly as much as losing the rights to your invention – especially if you're counting on your invention to provide a source of income. You need to make sure that your patent is as near perfect as possible. Some inventors who've taken on by themselves the task of preparing and filing their own application, have been heard to say that when they take into account the number of hours and days it took, and the earnings they could have made in that time, it would have been cheaper to use a patent attorney anyway.

You may think that your telephone directory is the best place to start looking for a patent attorney. Not necessarily. Patent attorneys tend to specialise, just as physicians do, so look for one who knows the law *and* something about the field of your invention. For example, if you've a mechanical product, look for a patent attorney with an undergraduate degree in engineering; if you invented a better light bulb, look for an electrical background.

You can assist your patent attorney with the application process by providing them with a clear and concise description of your invention. Try to be as broad as possible with many applications and selling advantages. You know your invention much better than the attorney does. If you don't like the way a feature of the invention is worded in the draft description, tell them. Don't make the mistake of the inventors who say 'Well, I didn't agree with the way it had been described but I thought that must be what the rules needed'.

Choose a patent attorney you get along with, someone you can understand and with whom you can have a good rapport. Taking into account the fact that you're going to be working together over several years to get your patent granted, and then possibly defended, you're likely to come into contact quite a lot. Therefore, the ability to work together well is essential. In the words of the UK Court of Appeal judge, Lord Justice Sir Robin Jacob, 'If you can't understand your patent adviser, get another one!'

If your product is successful, chances are high that at some point you end up in some sort of litigation focused on it. Whether you initiate an action over patent infringement or an action is brought against you or your company is irrelevant. No matter what the lawsuit focuses on, one of the very first items to be challenged is likely to be the validity of the patent. If your patent doesn't hold up under scrutiny, you may lose a great deal of money. Paying the price to have your patent done right from the start is the smart way to go.

Going without an attorney

If you simply don't have the money at first to pay for a patent attorney but do have spare time that would otherwise be earning little or nothing, then you can contemplate writing and filing your own patent application, although we repeat that this isn't the recommended route. The filed application gives you an official receipt that confirms your possession of the invention at the date of filing. You're then able to approach third parties: would-be investors, manufacturers, or licensees, safe in the knowledge that, even in the unlikely event of their seeking to exploit the invention without your permission, you can prove that you had it first.

Unless you're unusually proficient in technical writing and patent law, there's a significant risk that a self-prepared patent application may leave unprotected aspects that lets a competitor get around your claims.

To overcome at least a few of the risks in filing your patent application unaided, a common solution is get together with an interested (and asset-rich) third party soon after filing the application and reach an agreement with them under which they take on the responsibility for strengthening and pursuing the patent application, and any equivalents to cover other countries. The deal should include payment to you by such means as a lump sum, ongoing royalties, and ongoing technical consultancy.

Filing a Patent Application

So you've invented a new process or machine and you want to apply for a patent to record and protect your rights. The most common route, and indeed the recommended one, is first to prepare and file an application in your home country. You don't need at this stage to do anything about filings in other countries, although you need to be mindful of where in due course you want to file equivalent applications, as it may have a bearing on the content of your patent description. For example US patent examiners insist that the patent description should include a review of the closest prior patents known to you. If you're intending to file in the US it may be easier to put this information together at the time of preparing the home application.

In the following section we deal with the requirements and procedures of filing a patent application at the UK Intellectual Property Office (UK-IPO). Filing in other countries involves similar activities, but we mention key differences where appropriate.

Defining the patent specification

Before you take the formal steps of filling in forms and paying fees (which we cover in Chapter 8), you need to address the patent specification: Describing and defining your invention.

Preparing the patent specification requires much thought and care and usually quite a lot of time. Ideally your patent attorney prepares the patent specification. In the following sections we explain what the specification contains, which should help you understand some of the questions your attorney may ask you, or even help you prepare the specification yourself, if you really want to go down that route.

The United Kingdom patent specifications conveniently indicates typical contents headings for use in a specification:

- ✔ Title
- ✔ Field of the invention *
- ✔ Background of the invention
- ✔ Description of the prior art
- ✔ Summary of the invention
- ✔ Description of the preferred embodiment *
- ✔ Drawings (if any)
- ✔ Brief description of the drawings (if any) *
- ✔ Examples (if any) *
- ✔ Claims
- ✔ Abstract

Items indicated by * form the patent's *description*. Don't get cross with your attorney if your draft description omits some of these items – different inventions require different treatment to describe and define their key features.

Many US patents retain such headings at the start of the respective parts of the specification. But if you include such headings in the specification for a UK or European application the examiners may well ask you to delete most of them – it's just a requirement from the UK-IPO, listed within their drafting guidelines.

Make sure that you explain the invention fully in your description, because you're not allowed to add information to it later. You can explain certain elements in more detail, and clarify features of the invention, but you can't add new material.

Title

The title should give a short indication of the field of the invention. This title, along with the name of the applicant(s), the official application number, and the filing date, are the only items published in the first official record of the application made available to the public (usually within a week or so of the filing date). It can be – and usually is – about 18 months from the filing date before the full specification is published and made available for public inspection. It's the first time that your competitors can see the full details of your invention.

You'll probably want to choose a title that doesn't give away too much of your invention so soon after filing. 'A vacuum cleaner that retains the collected dirt in a vertical cyclone instead of a collection bag' may have the other vacuum cleaner makers heading for their research labs. A title of 'Vacuum cleaner' would be fine, although even that alerts Hoover Ltd to the fact that you're looking into one of its market areas. But don't try to disguise the invention too much. A title that simply says 'Device' may provoke the formalities examiner to publish as the title much or all of your main claim. Now that really does give it all away before you're ready.

The title should be the heading to the first page of the description. The various parts of the description are as follows.

Field of the invention

The opening paragraph is a single sentence statement of the field of the invention: the general and specific technical or scientific area in which your invention falls. For example, if your patent is to do with a door hinge for motor vehicles, the paragraph may read, 'This invention relates to motor vehicles, specifically to an improved vehicle door hinge'. Don't get into the fine detail of your invention yet.

Background of the invention

The 'background' section is much the same as a description of the prior art. The term *prior art* includes all the published information and knowledge in your field – patent specifications, other publications, a product, or a schematic of a product. So the background section is where you include an informal description of what people have done before in the field of your invention – the place where you review the prior patent specifications that have made similar proposals to yours. Importantly the background section also gives the opportunity to point out disadvantages with the prior proposals and explain what you have done to overcome them. For example:

> *Manufacturers have previously made titanium dioxide pigment by treatment of ilmenite ore with sulphuric acid. The process is effective but its liquid effluent is deep red, from the iron content of the ore, and highly acidic. Disposal of this effluent creates huge environmental problems. The present invention relates to a method for treating rutile ore with chlorine and then oxidising the so-formed titanium tetrachloride to produce the pigment. Not only does rutile have no iron content but with good process control there is no harmful effluent whatsoever.*

You may feel hesitant about telling the examiners of the 'prior art', especially if it's quite close to your improved version. But remember that examiners are pretty effective searchers and almost certain to find the close prior documents anyway. You're more likely to persuade an examiner to grant you a patent if you clearly acknowledge the prior documents and explain from the outset what's better about your version.

Some examiners get really crabby if you don't tell them about prior art you clearly knew about. This is especially marked in the US, where failure to reveal all is regarded as fraud and is a ground for revoking the patent (understandably so if in effect you have obtained your patent on false pretences). Historians and politicians among you may recognise the principle, known under such names as the Watergate or Chappaquiddick principle of: 'The sooner and in the more detail you reveal the bad news the better.'

Summary of the invention

You can now begin to go into a bit more detail on your invention and its advantages. Here's also a good place for a statement of invention with wording substantially the same as the main claim you're including or intending to include. You may wish to go further and include other statements of invention corresponding to some of your subsidiary claims, such as, 'In one preferred embodiment the invention provides a vehicle door lock comprising . . .'. Some attorneys consider that including such equivalent statements is unnecessary repetition of the wording in the claims. But it isn't if you're filing an initial application without claims. Claims can be added to the specification within the initial 12 months from the filing date, when you may have a better idea about the scope of the invention. If you haven't yet used a patent attorney to help draft the specification for the working of the claims, you may want to enlist their help now. After all, the specification is where your invention is defined. And it makes it difficult for an examiner to object that the claims don't have proper basis in the description. And it makes it easier for the competitors who want to read all about your invention – and what they must avoid – to find the details without jumping to and fro between the description and the claims.

Description of the preferred embodiment

Including a fully detailed description of at least one preferred embodiment of the invention is a legal requirement, and the heart of the disclosure. It's not good enough to say 'The invention relates to a motor-vehicle device that warns a reversing driver of the presence of another vehicle or lamppost to the rear'. You must also provide at least one way of achieving the desired objective, the working elements and the necessary functions such as a particular construction of radar gun; an electrical circuit involving a broken light beam; or simply an angled mirror hanging on the tailgate. In the words of one wise judge some years ago, 'You must not give people problems and call them specifications'. So here's where you begin to get into the real detail. The length of your detailed description depends on the nature and complexity of the invention but it must give enough by way of instructions for a reader to put the invention into practice after the patent has expired.

Drawings

Not all inventions need drawings. Most chemical and biological and information technology inventions don't. But if drawings are necessary to understand the subject matter of your invention, you must include them with your application. They're not as such part of the description so their position in the detailed description sections is not the place they occupy in the published specification. Most patent offices put them at the end of the specification, though the US Patent Office puts them at the front. However, they need a mention before moving to the description relating to them in the next section.

The drawings to be published should be of a quality that permits photocopying, as they form part of the published specification. Try to ensure that they look good. You can get away with informal versions initially as the patent examiners let you replace these by good formal versions before publication. Many third parties, notably competitors and potential infringers, make their first decisions on the strength of your case by looking at the drawings. If they look scruffy and carelessly drawn the third party may see you as an easy touch and decide to infringe anyway. Several excellent firms can prepare patent drawings. Such firms offer great value for money and their drawings impress inventors and everybody else.

Resist the temptation to include printed matter on the drawings. Sometimes inventors get away with including printed matter on drawings, but the proper course is to label the drawing with just the number of the Figure, such as Figure 1 of 4, and reference numerals and lead lines. As discussed in the next section the invention can then be fully covered within the description by reference to the individual numerals.

Brief description of the drawings

For those inventions that require drawings here's a good place to introduce their description. Devote some thought to the views they should display to show the invention to good effect. A typical collection and introduction may say:

> 'The invention is further described with reference to the accompanying drawings, in which: Figure 1 is a three dimensional view of one version of the device; Figure 2 is a side view of the device of Figure 1; Figure 3 is an end view of the device of Figures 1 and 2; and Figure 4 is a cross section through the device of Figures 1–3, taken along the line A-A of Figure 3.'

Follow your introduction with a description of the device in question, referring to the constituent elements in turn and giving them individual reference numerals, which should be repeated with each mention of the element. Work first through the structure of the device and then start again, this time describing how it works, still with mentions of each element and its reference numerals.

Examples

The examples section works almost the reverse of the drawings description. Many device inventions don't need worked examples. But most chemical and biological inventions do. For example, chemical inventions may need to specify the reactants (and not just by their brand names), their proportions, when they should be added, how they should be mixed and for how long, the temperature and pressure conditions for the reaction, and any preparative or clean-up steps. And ideally include several examples, not just one. Multiple results can conveniently be shown in tables.

Claims

The claims section should begin on a separate page with the word 'Claims' as the heading. Claims form the foundation and nucleus of your patent and define the scope of your patent protection. They're absolutely one of the most important features of your application, because they're the primary features fought over in infringement cases. Whether a patent is granted is determined primarily by the patent claims section.

Think of the claims as a fence around your back garden – they define your property ensuring that other people need your permission to enter. You want your fence to be as broad, big, and sturdy as possible. Patent attorneys try to make the first claim as broad as they can while still distinguishing it from what has gone before. But in many instances you and your patent attorney have an incomplete knowledge of what has gone before. You file a broad main claim in good faith but the examiner finds a prior publication you hadn't spotted that falls within it. To guard against this possibility the attorney includes a second claim, narrower than the first, in the hope that the unexpected prior document falls outside it. But because you don't know what an unexpected document may disclose, the attorney also includes third and fourth and probably several other claims, each narrower in a different respect from the broad main claim, building up a set of claims providing all manner of lines of defence. The hope is that at least one of these defensive lines resists the unexpected attack and leaves you with a strong defensible core of your invention. It usually works.

When preparing the claims, watch out for the elephant trap that catches many first-time inventors. They present as claims statements about the great advantages that their invention offers: 'My novel bicycle goes twice as fast as any other; it's much easier to pedal uphill; its gear train will last 100 years.' Conceivably all these wondrous features may be true. But they don't make a patent claim! They form a good basis for any marketing campaign later on, but the claims must list the technical features or elements of your invention. You aren't doing a sales pitch!

Getting in first

Most countries adopt the principle of 'first to file', meaning that if you get your application on file before someone else for substantially the same invention then you're the person with the prior rights. In the US however, if you can show that you thought of the invention first but for some good reason filed your application after someone else, then it may be held that you have the prior rights. You can appreciate that the evidence and hearings to decide prior rights gets mighty complicated. US researchers keep detailed, dated, and witnessed notebooks to provide evidence of the occasion of the Eureka moment – the occasion when they conceived the inventive idea – and the diligence they then applied to reduce the invention to practice in the form of a working prototype or effective process. The US approach has the intention of being fairer to the person whose Eureka moment came first, but for most observers the rough justice of 'first to file' is the better option. It certainly makes the early stages a lot easier to manage.

Many examiners, especially at the European Patent Office, insist upon the claims being put in the 'two-part' form, in which the first part of the claim (the *preamble*) set outs out what's already known and the second part (the *characterising part*) tells what's new about your invention. The two parts are separated by the words 'characterised in that'. For example:

> *A bicycle comprising a frame and having front forks to support the axle of a front wheel, wherein the front forks are the lower part of a member of which the upper part is tubular and is rotatable within a tubular forward portion of the frame, characterised in that the front forks incorporate spring-loaded shock absorbers.*

The two-part claim is not always the best way of defining the invention. Some good inventions are a new combination of several features that are themselves well-known but the invention puts them together in a way that produces surprising advantages. This kind of application is another instance where you may need professional help to get the best protection.

Do try to make the first claims as broad as possible. If the prototype is made of stainless steel – because that's the best material to withstand the required duty – don't limit the claims to stainless steel. If you do, you make it easy for a competitor to use a different material, maybe aluminium or an engineering plastic. Spike the competitor's guns by using wording to include all sufficiently suitable materials, and mention the others in the description. But keep a subsidiary claim specifically for stainless steel.

Abstract

The abstract should be on a separate sheet of paper with the heading 'Abstract' and carrying the same title as in the application form and the front page of the description. It will in due course be included on the first page of the published specification. It should be a concise summary of your invention as brief, complete, clear, and to the point as possible. The abstract is generally the part of the application that's read first. You may want to view abstracts from other patents to give you an idea of what's needed.

If your specification includes drawings you need to nominate which one of them is to appear alongside the abstract in the published specification. And the abstract should include after each mentioned component the equivalent reference numeral from the drawing.

Completing the application

An application for a patent should include the patent specification (which we discuss in the previous section 'Defining the patent specification'), with its full description of your invention, any necessary drawings, a set of claims defining your invention, a short abstract, a completed application form, a fee sheet, and the necessary fees. You can obtain all the forms through the UK-IPO Web site (www.ipo.gov.uk).

Some of the elements to be included with the application need not be filed with the original papers, as long as they follow within defined periods. The essential elements at day one are the application form and the full description (and any drawings). Not even the application fee is essential at day one, though oddly it is advisable to file a fee sheet (Form FS2) for zero pounds as doing so helps the UK-IPO formalities. You may be anxious to secure your filing date for the invention, and look to pay the necessary fees later.

Similarly some other elements of the application can be included with the original papers or filed later. These include the request for a preliminary search (UK Patents Form No. 9A) and a request for substantive examination (UK Patents Form No. 10). A statement of inventorship (UK Patents Form No.7) is also required if the person filing the application is not the inventor or if the application is being made in the name of a company.

The UK-IPO adopts a very user-friendly approach to lone inventors and guides you, usually by letter, on any missing elements of the applications and the date by which they're required. For example if the original application includes no search request they inform you of the date by which you must send it to ensure that your application continues – no later than 12 months from your filing date.

The patent specification should be typewritten in black ink on white paper (standard A4 letter size, shorter sides top and bottom). Rules govern the size of margins at the paper's top, bottom and sides – some insist on 2.0 centimetres, others 2.5 centimetres. A good rule of thumb is to leave a 2.5 centimetres (1 inch) all round.

The originally-filed drawings can be informal (not meeting the strict requirements on such aspects as page margins and line thickness, for example) to
be replaced by formal versions later if requested. Sometimes if the informal
versions are good enough to be photocopied for publication the strict
requirements may be waived.

The set of claims can also wait – in principle – but until they're filed the official examiners can't conduct their searching, because you haven't defined for
them what it is you consider to be your invention. See below for much more
on what the claims should and should not include.

The application can be filed by mail or by hand to the UK-IPO. You get an
official filing receipt, usually within a few days of filing, showing the allocated
application number and confirming the date of filing.

You can also submit your application online. You receive confirmation by
return email. You can submit your application in three ways:

✔ The UK IPO Web site has an online form which must be completed in
  one go. You would then need to attach to the form to your specification
  in PDF format. You pay by credit or debit card using this online process.

✔ The European Patent Office (EPO) offers an online service known as
  epoline. The service uses smart cards to ensure security and allows you
  to create and apply for United Kingdom (UK) national, European, and
  Patent Co-operation Treaty (PCT) patents online. More details about
  applying in other countries can be found in Chapter 8.

✔ The third way to file online is through the World Intellectual Property
  Organisation (WIPO) using their PAT-SAFE system that uses a personal
  password to ensure security.

Applying online means that you don't need to worry about security, postal
delivery delays, and filing date hassles. The filing receipts are also immedi-
ate. Epoline and PAT-SAFE also incorporate easy-to-use software for building
your applications, and inbuilt validation software to help you get the application right first time. More information about all these systems can be found
on the UK-IPO Web site www.ipo.gov.uk.

You're now in a position to talk to third parties about your invention because
your priority date has been formally recorded. You may need to show the
invention to a possible manufacturer or talk to other business advisers
about the idea. We always advise that you request that they sign a confidentiality or non-disclosure agreement before you show them anything. You may
wish to withdraw your application, and then re-file at a later date, in which
case the invention can't have been disclosed or placed in the public domain.
Effectively, you're buying time in which your invention's kept secret, to

Going international from the start

Under the Patent Cooperation Treaty (PCT), you can also opt to file an international application first or within the initial twelve months from filing your UK application, designating the countries you want patent protection in. Filing internationally first may work for you if:

✔ **You're in a big hurry to obtain patents abroad.** Most inventors like to wait until the last minute to file patent applications in foreign lands, which is 12 months after the filing of their application. They want to wait

and see if the invention is going to be commercially successful in their own country before applying abroad. However, because it takes three or four years to obtain a foreign patent, you can chop off 12 months by filing an international application first.

✔ **You've got plenty of money to spare.** Foreign filings cost more than a domestic one, but if you've got enough money the quicker coverage may be worth it to you.

choose which territories you'll need protection in, and to incur all the large fees associated with this part of the process. You just need to write to the UK-IPO within the initial 12-month period to advise that you want to allow the application to lapse. We cover deferring applications in more detail in Chapter 9.

If you've paid the Application Fee (currently £30), the UK-IPO makes a formality check to ensure the presence of all essential parts of the application , that the necessary fees have been paid, and writes to draw your attention to any missing elements.

It takes a well-rounded patent attorney to draft a good patent application. The strength of the eventual patent depends upon the completeness of the specification and the claims. If you have some technical savvy and basic writing abilities, you can write an acceptable description of your invention. However, the specification isn't the most important part of a patent application. What legally defines the rights of the patent owner and the area of technology covered by the patent are the claims – and you really need a patent attorney to write the claims.

IP attorneys spend years honing their claim-writing skills. In spite of all those 'how to' books about patent applications, we recommend that you enlist the assistance of a patent attorney to draft the claims. After all, you want to achieve the broadest protection possible, and ensure that the meaning of each word is construed correctly.

Disclosing Your Invention in the Specification

Writing a good patent specification requires your active participation and candid communication with your attorney. You're the only one who knows all the ins and outs of your invention and can point your attorney in the right direction when its various embodiments, applications, functions, and great advantages have to be explained. The specification must meet two basic requirements:

- ✔ **The enabling factor:** The specification must clearly and concisely disclose enough for a person skilled in the field of the invention to practise the invention without a lot of experimentation.

- ✔ **The best mode factor:** The disclosure must state what you consider to be the best manner of carrying out the invention.

Complying with one rule but missing the other can make your patent invalid. For example, you may clearly explain how to practise your invention, but this may not be your best mode. On the other hand, your description of the best way to apply your invention may be too sketchy to meet the enabling requirement. The following guidelines should keep you on the straight and narrow path to compliance:

- ✔ **Select the best mode:** In the 'Description of the Preferred Embodiment of the Invention' section of the specification, you must reveal what you believe is the most efficient way to practise your invention, which may not necessarily be the manner you use to build your own prototype. If you've thought of other ways to exploit the invention, you can add them as alternate embodiments. Don't be shy about mentioning various ways to construct a particular structure or perform a specific process step.

- ✔ **Explain enough but no more than required:** When you try to meet the enabling requirement, you're writing for a person skilled in your field so you can use technical jargon and skip obvious details. Don't waste time explaining how to use every little component or tool. Your skilled readers can figure out which tasks are necessary on their own. Just make sure that they don't need to do a great deal of experimentation before they can use your invention. You can require time of them, but no head scratching.

Remember that after your patent expires, others can use the disclosure of your invention to compete against you. Also, revealing too much may help someone figure out how to avoid your claims by designing around the patent – something that's perfectly legal.

Don't treat the specification like a promotional device or a marketing tool for your new business. It's not the place for sales pitches about your product or for disparaging comments about your competitors. Allow your attorney to stick to the legal requirements. Don't insist on adding material that's not necessary to support the claims. In infringement litigation, the defendants' attorneys can use unnecessary extra material to attack the validity of your patent.

Arguing Your Case for Patentability

According to the law, your patent application only has to include a description of the preferred embodiment of the invention and one claim. But, you need a lot more to make a case for the patentability of your invention. Convincing the examiner or the appeal judges (if you have to appeal a rejection by the examiner) that you deserve a patent usually requires a little extra. You need to provide your IP attorney with as much information as possible to establish the novelty, and non-obviousness of your invention (for the basic conditions of patentability, see Chapter 4).

How do you convince a patent examiner that your invention is the greatest thing since the corkscrew? You must persuasively demonstrate that:

- ✔ Your invention solves a technological problem that has existed for some time.

- ✔ Others have tried to resolve this problem with questionable success.

- ✔ You have taken a fresh and different approach.

- ✔ Your invention provides a marvellous solution to the problem.

And the places to demonstrate these things are the *background of the invention* and *summary of the invention* sections of the patent application.

Here's a simple approach to the background section:

1. **Define the general application of the invention.**

   'Strap-tightening ratchet mechanisms, commonly called strap ratchets, are used in connection with cargo-securing harnesses . . .'

2. **Note the shortcomings of the current devices.**

   'The ratchet mechanisms are usually provided with short tightening levers that yield very little torque force. Accordingly, the harness cannot be tightened to the full extent possible . . .'

3. **Describe the prior approaches for resolving the problem, including their shortcomings.** You can refer to prior patents, publications, or well-known devices already on the market.

   'Some mechanisms of the prior arts have been provided with extended levers as disclosed in Patent No . . .' 'The length and bulk of these extended levers often interfere with the placement of the ratcheting device near a corner of the cargo . . .'

4. **Close the section by stating that your invention is an attempt to resolve the outlined deficiencies in the prior mechanism.**

Staking Your Claim

Your patent claims define the area of technology covered by the patent, and in the end, are the only part of the patent that really count because they legally define your rights to the invention. The specification has only one purpose – to support the wording of the claims.

Notice that the claims don't define your new device or process, which is a tangible or concrete thing, but they do define the area of technology represented by that device or process. Your actual invention is an abstract construct that can't be easily or precisely defined; the specific device or process is only one of many possible applications of the invention. Your patent attorney needs to take care of the claims, but here's a crash course on what he or she does.

Less is more: Mastering the mechanics of claims

The wording of a claim has a lot in common with the description of a piece of property in a deed. Just as a deed description defines only the limits of the lot and not anything that may be on it, a claim recites only the minimum elements that must be present for a device or process to be covered by the patent. Of course, anything that falls within these limits belongs to the title owner – the landlord or the patent owner.

A claim usually covers a lot more than the limits it spells out. And the shorter the claim, the broader its coverage.

For an example of the less-is-more rule, take a look at Figure 7-1, which shows the first horseless carriage, invented by Nicolas Cugnot around 1769. If Cugnot had asked an attorney to draft a patent application for his invention, the first claim might look like this:

A vehicle comprising:

a cargo-carrying member

at least two wheels supporting said member, and

an engine driving at least one of said wheels.

Figure 7-1:
Nicolas
Cugnot's
horseless
wagon.

Cugnot's carriage had a back axle supporting a pair of wheels. The steam engine was coupled to a front wheel. But being very astute the patent attorney was also able to imagine motored vehicles riding with only two wheels because 80 years earlier, another Frenchman, Mede de Sivrac, had developed a crude bicycle. The attorney therefore listed the minimum components necessary for a workable device. And it's a good thing he did. If the patent were still in effect today, it'd cover locomotives, cars, trucks, and motorcycles.

But someone can get around the attorney's claim by using only one wheel (possibly a long roller) or by detaching the engine from the wheels (by using a jet engine). You can plug these loopholes by rewriting the claim as follows:

A vehicle comprising:

a cargo-carrying member

at least one wheel supporting said member; and

an engine positioned to propel said vehicle.

Because the second claim lists only three elements instead of four like the first, more devices out there can very likely fall within its limits. So the more concise second claim has a broader scope than the first and can catch more infringers.

Just for fun, try to redraft our example claim to cover a boat or an aircraft. It's not as easy as it may first seem and demonstrates why we must reiterate the benefits of having a patent attorney on board.

Checking the various types of claims

Not all inventions can be described by a concise list of components, also called *limitations,* as in the Cugnot example in the previous section. That's why the law provides more than one way to achieve the same result.

Listing elements in a claim

The kind of component-listing claims illustrated in the Cugnot example are commonly used with machine, device, and composition of matter inventions. A few variations on the same theme that lend themselves to other types of inventions include:

- ✔ **Using functional limitations:** If you have to list a component that has many equivalents capable of performing the same job, you can describe that component in a *means-plus-function* form. For instance, a wheel can be attached to a vehicle frame by means of an axle or a pin or with a complex articulated structure, like the one used on the front wheel of a car. You can effectively describe the component or limitation as

  '*. . . means for rotatively securing the wheel to the vehicle frame . . .*'

  Can't find *rotatively* in your dictionary? It doesn't matter. When you write claims, you can create your own vocabulary, as long as you clearly define the new term in the specification section of the application.

  In an infringement action, the judge interprets the scope of claim to cover the component described in the specification, plus any equivalent structure. An *equivalent structure* is one that achieves the same results (with insubstantial differences) as the one described in the specification, if the equivalent structure is available when the patent is granted. Therefore, enhance your patent by describing as many equivalent structures as possible in the specification. For example, in the wheel attachment component described above, the axle, pin, and complex car front wheel mounting structure should be described in the specification.

- ✔ **Grouping similarly effective components:** Another way to cover a large gamut of similar components in a single claim is to list a group of applicable elements. This US style of claim, called the *Markush claim,* is often used to define chemical inventions. The only requirement is that the group of alternate components must be introduced by the all-inclusive phrase 'to consist essentially of'. Elements not listed as part of the group are excluded from coverage. For example:

  '*. . . a dry lubricant taken from a group to consist essentially of graphite, molybdenum sulphide, and boron nitride . . .*'

The specification must mention the utility and effectiveness of all the listed components. For example, you may explain that tests have been conducted with each type of lubricant with the same effective results.

Claiming a method or process

An invention component can also be defined in a claim by its unique manufacturing method:

> '. . . a spacer made by bending a length of steel wire into a closed loop . . .'

Combining structures

A claim can recite a combination of two or more objects. It's a particularly handy method to use when the inventive gadget's utility and novelty are only evident when applied to an existing device. However, to patent combined structures, the patents must have some interaction between them. For example, a phone mounted on a washing machine for the convenience of the housekeeper isn't a patentable combination because the two devices don't work together, but are only located in the same place. However, the combination of a cylindrical eraser mounted at the end of a pencil may be patentable because the pencil acts as a handle for the eraser.

Following grammatical rules

Claim drafting is more than a science – it's an art at which any patent attorney worth his or her 'whereas' should excel and which requires every semantic and legal trick possible. Don't feel bad if you can't comprehend the full scope of each claim in your application.

Claims must comply with very peculiar grammatical rules. With apologies to your English teachers, get used to the following oddities, which demonstrate just a few of the crazy grammatical twists and turns you'll run into:

✔ A claim must be written in a single sentence, even if that sentence extends over three or more pages. So run-on sentences are okay.

✔ A claim must begin with a preamble that briefly states the framework of the invention, followed by a linking phrase such as 'which comprise(s), including', or 'which essentially consist(s) of', followed by the limitations (elements) of the invention. If necessary, you can tack on a 'whereby' clause after a limitation in order to clear up any potential confusion as to the nature, application, or function of the invention. The whereby clause doesn't define a necessary limitation of the invention and is often discarded by the judge interpreting the claim.

✔ You can't use a definite article (the word 'the') in front of an element unless you've already introduced that element in the body of the current claim or in a parent claim. For example, you can't start a claim like this:

> *'A video camera that comprises a shutter behind the lens . . .'*

The word lens hasn't been defined yet, so you have to write:

> *'A video camera that comprises a lens and a shutter behind the lens . . .'*

✔ You can use the terms 'which comprise(s)', 'comprising', 'including', 'having', and so on, without excluding other elements in the claimed invention. However, the phrase 'essentially consisting of' or 'which essentially consists of' excludes any other element. So a claim that recites 'a table which comprises a flat top and three legs' also covers tables with four or five legs. However, a claim stating 'a table consisting essentially of a flat top and three legs' wouldn't cover a four-legged table.

✔ You can reference previously introduced elements with the term 'said' without repeating the qualifying terms, for example:

> *'A camera comprising a zoom lens; a shutter positioned behind said lens.'*

✔ Don't use the conjunctions *'or'* and *'nor'* or the phrase 'such as' if they make the definition vague or ambiguous. For example, the statement 'a camera having a lens made of a material such as glass or plastic . . .' won't cut the mustard. Instead, use multiple claims, each reciting one type of lens: 'A camera having a lens made of a material taken from a group consisting essentially of glass, plastic, and silicone.'

✔ Words have the meanings that you give them in the specification, even if these meanings differ from the ones commonly found in dictionaries. Of course, you can't go so far as calling a cat a dog.

✔ Any descriptive words you use in a claim must first be defined in the specification.

As an example of using these rules, check out Figure 7-2. Now read the following claim for the structure, with all the language rules applied. Can you pick out the rules?

> *'The combination of a ratcheted, strap-tightening mechanism having a hand-operable cranking lever and a resiliently biased ratchet-locking member, and*
>
> *a manipulating tool, said tool comprising:*
>
> *a rod;*

a socket having a proximal end attached at a first end of said rod and a distal end opposite said proximal end, said socket comprising four flat joined sides defining a channel shaped and dimensioned to axially engage over said lever; and

a tongue projecting from a second end of said rod opposite said first end, said tongue being shaped and dimensioned to leveredly bear against said resiliently biased member and pry it away from a locking position to release said mechanism;

wherein at least two opposing ones of said sides taper inwardly down axially from an opening at said distal end toward said first end of the rod,

whereby said socket can be securely engaged over a plurality of levers of different sizes.'

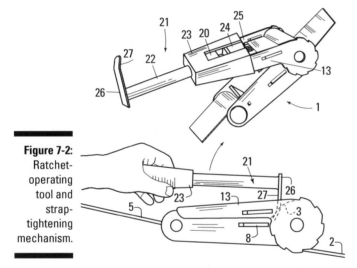

Figure 7-2:
Ratchet-
operating
tool and
strap-
tightening
mechanism.

Actively Participating in Application Preparation

The best thing you can do to ensure that you get your patent is to give your attorney as much information as possible. Your attorney may be the best on the planet, but he or she can't do the best job without having all the data.

Compiling the record

Your legal eagle needs various bits of information to help draft your patent application. If you kept a good notebook as you developed your invention (as we suggest in Chapter 5), dig out the notebook now – it contains a lot of what your IP attorney needs. Otherwise, here's a helpful list of the bits and pieces your attorney may probably ask for:

- ✔ Short definition of the general fields of technology to which the invention relates. Include any device or process to which your invention applies.

- ✔ Reasons that led you to develop the invention.

- ✔ Explanation of how the invention came about (unexpected discovery, trial-and-error approach, a flash of genius, in a dream . . .).

- ✔ Where you developed the invention (for example, as part of your employment, within the scope of a contracted job, or using someone else's resources or facilities).

- ✔ Outline of the existing problems the invention resolves.

- ✔ Account of how these problems were handled in the past.

- ✔ Your opinion about what the invention does that couldn't be done before, or why it's an improvement over past devices or methods.

- ✔ Depiction of the closest thing to your invention.

- ✔ Documents or references that best describe the most recent advances in the field of the invention.

- ✔ Lists and copies of all patents, publications, treatises, articles, and other written material at your disposal that may be relevant to your invention. You're not required to conduct any particular research. If you've done a search (described in Chapter 6), you'll have all this information at your fingertips.

- ✔ Copies of novelty search results and any professional patentability opinion.

- ✔ All records of your development efforts.

- ✔ Identification of all persons (including children) who may have contributed to the conception and a brief description of each party's contribution. Include the full names, mailing addresses, residences, and citizenships of all inventors.

- ✔ Copies of any prior filings, or prior patent applications, whether still active or abandoned.

- ✔ Copies of any assignment, licence, or business agreement related to the invention. Chapter 19 talks about assignments and licences.

- ✔ Copies of identifying documents, such as Articles of Incorporation, Partnership Certificates, and fictitious name registrations, for any business that is (or may become) owner of the patent or the invention.

- ✔ Complete description of the invention, including drawings, photographs, prototypes, test results, testimonials, and anything else that helps your IP professional understand and appreciate the invention. Don't forget the disclosure issue. It is vital, and a requirement of the UK-IPO, that your invention has not been disclosed to anyone without a confidentiality agreement in place, before you file a patent application.

- ✔ Concise description of the basic structure of your invention that can serve as a model for the *abstract* portion of the application. You don't need to get into the invention's advantages here. (See ' Understanding the Patent Application' section, earlier in the chapter.)

- ✔ Brief account of how you plan to exploit your invention through your own manufacturing, by licensing others, or by outright sale.

Looking over the pro's shoulder

You've just received the first draft of your patent application from your patent attorney and are about to review it alone or in a tête-à-tête with your attorney. We now point out the main things to look for.

Your patent attorney works for you, so don't be afraid to ask for advice to clarify anything you don't understand or to change anything that doesn't describe your invention adequately.

Scrutinising the claims

Because the claims constitute the most important part of the application, you should go over them with a fine-tooth comb. Be sure that you and the claim-drafter are on the same wavelength. Verify that the part of the technology that's recited is exactly the one that needs to be protected.

You may discover that the most critical aspect of your invention is recited in a dependant claim. Because you can claim only one invention in a patent, ask your attorney to reverse the organisation of the claims to recite the most important portion of the invention in an independent claim.

If a claim lists every detail of the structure, down to the kitchen sink, stove, and oven, talk with your attorney about eliminating or rewriting it. A narrow claim doesn't provide much of a net to catch an infringer.

Do make sure that every inventive feature is listed in one or more claims. Don't worry too much yet about whether you're claiming more than one invention in a single application. Later, you can answer the patent examiner's objection by reshuffling the claim pyramid or by withdrawing some claims to be resubmitted in a divisional application (see Chapter 8).

Focusing the abstract

Verify that the abstract describes the gist of your invention. It should be a single paragraph and written in plain language, without using legalistic terms such as *means for* and *whereas*. Typically, the abstract reflects the principal claim (usually Claim 1).

Checking the drawings

The drawings must be done in accordance with UK-IPO guidelines. Patent attorneys use professional patent draftspersons, who work from sketches prepared by the professional based on your description. The drawing must illustrate every item that's recited in the claims. It can be as simple as a block diagram or a flowchart. Don't include more figures than are absolutely necessary to describe the preferred embodiment of the invention. You don't need to draw every nut and bolt. A patent drawing is only an illustration, not a manufacturing blueprint.

Reviewing the disclosure

When you look at some patents, you may think that the drafter was paid by the page. There's too much information, including verbiage that's not legally required and doesn't advance the case for patentability.

Brevity gives you a practical advantage. When you file abroad, you'll be charged by the word or page for the translation and filing. Therefore, you can save hundreds of pounds with a little literary restraint. For example, the *background of the invention* section is no place for a lengthy listing and discussion of prior patents and publications, which come later (see Chapter 8 for more).

To make your application short and effective, cross out anything that doesn't support the language of the claims or demonstrate that your invention is useful, new, and above the skill of other people in the field.

Chapter 8

Filing Your Patent Application

· ·

In This Chapter

▶ Getting your application out the door

▶ Watching for deadlines

▶ Seeking protection in other countries

▶ Profiting from your invention in the meantime

· ·

*N*ecessity may be the mother of invention, but patents are the guardians.

In this chapter we show you how to prepare a patent that impresses everybody who sees it, including the patent examiners who decide the scope of protection they're prepared to grant you, the investors who you may wish to back your inventive project, the manufacturers who may want to license it, the potential infringers who will (we hope) back off when they see the patent's quality, and – if we ever get there – the judge(s) in court who decide whether your patent's valid and whether it covers the infringing activities.

Throughout this chapter we alert you to the traps that can destroy your patent rights, even if the invention is way better than sliced bread: things like paying the official fees a day too late, paying the wrong fees by using an outdated fee schedule, getting your co-inventor's name wrong. Some of these can be remedied – if you spot them in time – but others can't, especially in matters of fee payments. Given the difficulties of putting together a strong description that clearly defines your invention and shows its differences and improvements over anything known before, it would be a tragedy if you lost your rights because of a technical oversight.

This chapter also covers the costs of getting a patent at home and abroad, indicating how much you pay for filing the patent application and getting it to the stage of being granted.

You probably think that the hardest part is over after you prepare the patent application. True – a lot of the detail work is done. But you still have a lot of things to keep in mind when getting ready to file your application, and even more things to keep track of after your application hits the UK Intellectual Property Office (UK-IPO). Your patent attorney takes care of most of these details, but you should have a clear view of the filing process, so we've described it here in as much detail as you need. We refer you to more extensive source material in case you want to find out more on the subject.

Packaging the Application

 Whether you're using a patent attorney or agent or going it alone, the UK Intellectual Property Office Web site www.ipo.gov.uk has a wealth of information. In the section under patents, downloadable booklets and factsheets detail the different parts of the process. You can also phone the office and ask them to post the documents to you.

We suggest that in the first instance you request or download copies of the following guides at www.ipo.gov.uk/patent/p-applying/p-should.htm:

- ✔ PATENTS: Application Guide
- ✔ PATENTS: Essential Reading
- ✔ INNOVATION IN YOUR BUSINESS: Is it a business?
- ✔ PATENTS: Basic Facts

In this section, we supplement the information in these guides with a handy checklist of all the documents that accompany your application. We discuss additional material you may want to submit and run through an outline of the fees, forms, and timescales for each part of the process.

Ticking off the application checklist

In addition to the patent application specification and claims (in Chapter 7 we talk about preparing the application itself), you must fill out and send the following forms. You can download the forms from the UK-IPO Web site, www.ipo.gov.uk, by clicking on 'Patents' and then on 'How to Apply'.

The UK-IPO is forever adding, amending, and cancelling forms, however. If you're unsure which form applies at a particular stage, we suggest you phone the office.

- ✔ **To apply for a patent:** Patents Form 1; accompanying factsheet: filling in Form 1; and Fee Sheet FS2.
- ✔ **To apply for a Novelty Search:** Patents Form 9A
- ✔ **To request Substantive Examination:** Patents Form 10
- ✔ **If you're not the inventor, are applying on behalf of a company, or if there's more than one inventor, you need to complete a Statement of Inventorship:** Patents Form 7

To begin the application process you need to fill in Form 1 and send it to the UK-IPO along with a copy of your specification. You can consult a very useful factsheet about filling in Form 1 if you come unstuck with any of the questions, or are unsure of what to write in each box (see www.ipo.gov.uk/fact0177.pdf).

If of course you have an attorney on board, she completes Form 1 on your behalf. If you're not the inventor you need to fill in Form 7 the 'Statement of Inventorship'.

Post your patent application and any forms to the UK Intellectual Property Office. The UK-IPO has two offices, one in London and one in South Wales. You should check with the Web site or the Central Enquiry Unit that the following addresses are still accurate before popping it in the post:

The Comptroller, Cardiff Road, Newport, South Wales NP10 8QQ

The Comptroller, Harmsworth House, 13-15 Bouverie Street, London EC4Y 8DP

Keep copies of everything that you send to the UK-IPO. You receive a filing receipt back from them that includes an application number and confirms the filing date of your application – keep this safe too!

To continue with your application, and within the initial 12-month period from the filing date, you need to request a search. This search is to test whether your invention is novel, and whether it includes an inventive step, as we explain in Chapter 4. To request a search you need to fill in form 9A/77 and send it to the UK-IPO with the appropriate fees. If you fail to pay the fees by the date on your filing receipt your application is withdrawn, so keeping track of these dates is extremely important.

Just to complicate matters, if your application claims priority from an earlier application, the deadline for filing Form 9A is the later of two months from your filing date or 12 months from your priority date. Again, if you're unsure at all, the Central Enquiry Unit at the UK-IPO willingly provides clarification.

No later than 6 months after publication, to avoid your application being terminated, you need to file a Request for Substantive Examination. In the meantime you, or your patent attorney, have responded to the Novelty Search findings and have confidence that the application can proceed to grant. To request Substantive Examination, you need to fill in and file Form 10/77.

Accelerating the search

The novelty search is typically processed within four months of your request, but may be longer. You effectively join the back of a queue. However, if you have a strong reason for asking for a search to be completed by a particular date, the UK-IPO endeavours to meet your needs. You must however have included at least one claim with your patent specification. The search is based on the claims. You should also look to file your request for a search at the same time as filing the application.

Before asking for an accelerated publication, we strongly advise you to get advice from a patent attorney. Accelerated publication can be advantageous if you're aware of a possible infringement, as your application being published can be seen as a warning of future legal action. However, you have no guarantee that your application is going to lead to a valid patent and no guarantee that an infringement action would succeed. The disadvantage of early publication is that it can cut short your investigation into the potential market and may alert other people to your activities, as once the application is published, all the information within it is open to public inspection.

Meeting Your Filing Deadlines

Dates are everything, and we're not talking about what you're doing this weekend. In the UK, a patent application, must meet all the time frames shown in Figure 8-1:

Most countries, including the UK, require that you file your first domestic patent application before any public disclosure of the invention and that you file your application abroad within one year of the first filing (six months for a design application).

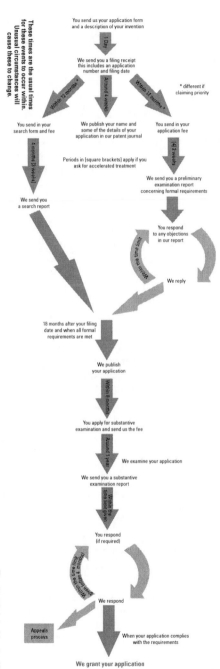

These times are the usual times for these events to occur within. Unusual circumstances will cause these to change.

You send us your application form and a description of your invention

1 Day

We send you a filing receipt this includes an application number and filing date

Within 12 months *

Around 4 weeks

Within 12 months *

* different if claiming priority

You send in your search form and fee

We publish your name and some of the details of your application in our patent journal

You send in your application fee

4 months [3 weeks]

Expires [6]

Periods in [square brackets] apply if you ask for accelerated treatment

We send you a search report

We send you a preliminary examination report concerning formal requirements

You respond to any objections in our report

Within the time given

We reply

18 months after your filing date and when all formal requirements are met

We publish your application

Within 6 months

You apply for substantive examination and send us the fee

Around 1 year

We examine your application

We send you a substantive examination report

Within the time given

You respond (if required)

Within the time given within [?] month

We respond

Appeals process

When your application complies with the requirements

We grant your application

Figure 8-1:
The timeline for a UK patent application.

Courtesy of the UK-IPO.

Keeping Your Application Under Wraps

Some 18 months after the filing date of the application or the priority date the specification is published in the weekly Patents and Designs Journal, which you can download for free from the Patents section of the UK IPO website (www.ipo.gov.uk/patent/p-journal/p-pdj.htm). Anyone can now read every word of it, buy a copy, or inspect the specification on line. What may sound like bad news can in fact be very good news. Anyone who chooses to infringe your IP risks having to pay you damages from the date of publication, although you can't institute action to try for damages until the patent is granted. We discuss the merits of the published specification in more detail in Chapter 9.

If you're aware that someone is infringing, or thinking of infringing, your IP, or indeed for any other reason, you can request early publication, bringing forward the date from which damages can run. You may want to delay costs or to keep your invention under wraps for as long as possible. However, if you want to accelerate examination at the UK-IPO you need to contact the examiner who's handling your case, with your reasons for wanting to speed things up.

Whatever you do, make an active decision. Don't let your application be published by default, especially if you're concerned about loss of your trade secret. After you're through the initial search phase, if you simply do nothing, your application automatically publishes 18 months after the filing date as long as you've completed all the formal requirements. If you're confused, talk to your patent attorney or the UK-IPO and let them help you make the right decision.

Before you decide to have your application published, consider the advantages and disadvantages. Don't forget that prior to publication you can withdraw the application and your invention then remains a secret until you're ready to go through the patent protection process again. In our opinion, the advantages of publishing are:

✔ Anyone who infringes on any published claim of your patent application is liable from the publication date, providing that the claim is part of the patent when it's granted. You can't sue the infringer until you get the patent. But, after you do, you can request compensation for all losses resulting from the infringer's activities since the date of publication. Your patent may not be granted for more than a year after publication, so these losses may translate into a lot of dosh in damages.

✔ The publication of your application acts as a public notice of your impending patent, which is particularly important if you've practised your invention publicly or sold items manufactured according to your invention before you get your patent.

The presence of the patent number (see Chapter 10 for the appropriate notice) on all items ever sold constitutes proper notice to the entire world. The legend 'Patent Pending' on a product has no legal value.

✔ You can file an application abroad claiming the priority date, based on the filing date of the UK application, providing you do so within one year of that filing date. See the next section 'Exploring Equivalent Applications Abroad' for filing applications outside the UK.

But the disadvantages of publishing are:

✔ Publication may punch a big hole in your trade-secret protection strategy. You may want to keep your invention confidential for as long as you can (see Chapters 1, 2, and 5 for more info). If you intend to rely on your trade-secret strategy to protect your invention and file a patent application simply as back-up protection, then publication may be a risk (we talk about trade-secret strategy in Chapter 5).

✔ If your invention isn't quite ready for the market, the publication gives an early opportunity to some sharks to start working around your patent claims, and beating you in the race to the market place.

Exploring Equivalent Applications Abroad

In today's global market, you may consider protecting your invention in other countries as well as the UK. For the purposes of this section we assume you've already filed an application at the UK-IPO. Filing outside the UK in the first instance is possible but, primarily for security reasons, requires prior consent from the UK-IPO. If you're resident in the UK and your application contains information related to military technology or may be prejudicial to national security or public safety, you need to obtain clearance to file abroad. For guidance on filing abroad see www.ipo.gov.uk/factpats abroad.pdf.

National applications

Provided you file an equivalent national application in another country within 12 months of the priority date of your UK application, that further application retains the UK priority date (a useful aspect of the Paris Convention – see Chapter 3). Each such national application requires local application forms and fees on filing and progresses through similar stages of publication, search and examination through – if successful – to grant in that country. You've little prospect of filing and prosecuting the application yourself in the other countries; local attorneys are almost invariably required. To ensure the use of local attorneys who can offer the expertise required for your invention, the safest route is to instruct UK patent attorneys and let them prepare and send documents in a format they know meets the local requirements, to associate attorneys they know to be capable and trustworthy. The whole process can be handled remotely. Your best bet is to find a UK-based attorney that you can trust.

A huge drawback of filing individual national applications is that, with notable exceptions such as the US and many Commonwealth countries, you're faced with substantial translation costs at a fairly early stage in your invention's life. Good quality translations don't come cheap. Arranging translations is normally best left to your patent attorney and her overseas associates who are aware of local translators with the technical skills to make a quality translation. If you wish to retain the UK priority date you should also ensure that the specification reaches the associates in good time before the due date – ideally several week s ahead – to give the translator ample time to prepare the translation and therefore avoid expedition fees for sending the documents near to the due date.

International applications

If your overseas interests extend to two or more countries, the most cost-effective way of applying is almost certainly through one of the international application systems under which at least some of the procedural steps towards a granted patent are conducted just once. For International PCT and European EPC applications (for which, see the next two sections and Chapter 3) the initial filings can then be made, in English, at the UK-IPO who forward the papers to the appropriate organisation for further processing, again in English. Translation of the specification is eventually needed in non-English-speaking countries that grant or validate patents , but these costs are put off for several years.

The Patent Co-operation Treaty (PCT)

If your countries of interest extend beyond continental Europe the easiest and cheapest route is likely to be an international application via the Patent Co-operation Treaty (PCT). Your application should be filed within the 12-month international convention period to retain the UK priority date. You can designate any, or all, of the 137 member states. Because the UK is a PCT member you can choose to pursue UK cover via the PCT and abandon the UK application for all purposes except for proving the priority right. Some applicants however choose to continue with both the PCT and UK applications, giving them maximum flexibility in choice of route as the applications proceed. For more on PCT applications see Chapter 9.

The most notable PCT absentee is Taiwan: if you want to file there you need a national application (and send the papers in good time for the translation to be ready within the 12-month convention period).

The UK-IPO forwards the application papers to the World Intellectual Property Office (WIPO) in Geneva but for UK-based applicants most of the steps are then taken for WIPO by the European Patent Office.

The PCT application should include the request form (PCT/RO/101), the official fees, and the PCT specification with contents as in the priority specification – with, at this stage, possible additions, although these additions won't have the UK priority date. Online filing is also an option (see the WIPO Web site www.wipo.int/pct/en). You need to designate the PCT members of interest, which can be by individual countries or by regions. Regional designations are possible for four systems:

- The European Patent Convention (EPC, covering 32 countries in Europe).

- The Eurasian Patent Organisation (nine former Soviet countries).

- The African Regional Intellectual Property Office (ARIPO – 16 countries, mostly in East Africa).

- OAPI (Organisation Africaine de la Propriété Industrielle – 16 countries, mostly in French-speaking Africa).

The PCT steps are substantially the same as the equivalent steps in a UK national application: filing receipt with official number and filing date; publication at 18 months from priority date (or faster by negotiation) and a prior art search and report. Optionally (and with a further fee) you can request preliminary examination, which leads to an official international preliminary opinion on the patentability of the application. This opinion is sent on by the EPO to all designated regions and countries. The preliminary examination system is very user-friendly. The examiner first sends a written opinion to the applicant indicating aspects that require attention. Effectively the preliminary opinion tells the applicant the amendments necessary to put the application into an allowable form. The applicant submits the amendments to remedy the deficiencies, making the issuance of a positive international preliminary opinion very likely.

The PCT system does not however directly grant the patent. After 31 months from the priority date (for UK applicants) the application must enter the regional or national phase.

Although using any of the regional systems is not essential, as with the PCT itself, they do offer significant cost savings compared with separate national applications. Beyond the regional countries, for example for US, Japan and South Korea, the application must proceed as an individual national application.

The European Patent Convention (EPC)

The most commonly used regional system for UK-originating applications is the EPC. Since the UK is a member, you don't need to file or to continue a UK national application (although it can be continued if you wish, see Chapter 9). The EPC application can be filed, in English (or in French or German), at your home IP office (in the UK at the UK Intellectual Property Office) designating any or all of the member countries. If you've taken the PCT route you can enter into the EPC phase from there. The EPC members include all the members of the EU, plus Iceland, Monaco, Switzerland, Liechtenstein, and Turkey (but not Norway, although it's a member of the PCT).

If you do continue with both UK national and EPC applications for the same invention you eventually have to choose between being granted a UK patent or an EPC patent, validated and effective in UK. You can't patent the same invention twice for the same territory.

The EPC application is processed by the European Patent Office (EPO) as a single application. The processing goes further than that of the PCT. After publication and a search stage (which may have been conducted at the PCT stage) the application undergoes a full examination. If accepted it becomes a granted European patent which can be validated as separate patents in your designated countries. Should enforcement of the patents ever become necessary the work is undertaken by proceedings in the respective country's courts.

Progress of an application through the EPO can be slow, especially if examiner interviews or appeals against rejection become necessary. A delay doesn't always mean bad news.

Counting the Costs of Filing

Put plainly, applying for and getting a patent ain't cheap. Not only do you have official fees to pay at many stages, some of them substantial, but if you use attorneys they add a handling charge for dealing with the action the fee involves – and that handling charge is often at least as much as the fee itself. When it comes to the professional services of attorneys in preparing patent specifications, and dealing with examiners' objections, their charge rate reflects their high levels of skills and the substantial administrative costs their office has to bear in reliable diary and reminder systems, professional insurance, and experienced support staff. And for overseas applications in non-English speaking countries you're likely to be faced with the costs of translators with the technical expertise to handle patent language. They don't come cheap either.

As you reflect on the high costs of getting patent protection, don't overlook the returns they can generate. In June 2007 New Zealander Juliette Harrington sold to Yahoo! her US patent on one-stop Internet shopping for NZ$6.55 million (£2.25 million).

The costs we mention in this section are merely indicative. A review of official fees takes place from time to time, usually on an upward-only basis, and professional advisers' fees have a way of creeping up too. Remember, too, that the amount of professional work involved varies greatly from case to case. You can check the current official fees on the UK-IPO Web site but we strongly suggest that you check in advance with your professional advisers on how much their services for a particular activity are likely to be.

In all cases official fee savings can very likely be made by filing online. The figures that follow assume communications by surface and air mail.

✔ **National applications in English:** The charges for preparing and filing a patent application in UK or other English-speaking country, using professional services, and including attorneys' and official fees, are likely to be at least £2,000.

Taking such a national application through search and examination to grant is likely to incur a similar sum of at least £2,000 in total. However there's no obligation to continue with the application if it runs into undue examination problems or if the market no longer justifies it. For complex disclosures however, costs can increase considerably, and therefore this figure should only be taken as a guide.

✔ **National applications not in English:** Translation charges add dramatically to the costs in applications using languages other than English. For European languages, such as French, German, and Spanish, the application charges may increase to at least £3,000. For applications in Asiatic languages, such as Japanese, Mandarin, or Korean, expect application charges of at least £4,000. Provided the local agent communicates with you in English (which is usually the case) the further charges through to grant may be similar to those for UK applications – which means at least £2,000. Again you have the choice of whether or not to continue with the application and associated expense.

✔ **PCT applications:** PCT applications carry substantial official fees of about £1,800. The attorneys' charges are likely to be at least as much again. The fee for the optional subsequent preliminary examination is about £1,100, plus the attorneys' handling charge. The attorneys' reporting on the search and preliminary examination and submitting observations on the preliminary examination usually add at least a further £1,000.

✔ **EPC applications:** EPC official application fees, assuming all member states are designated, come to about £1,200. The attorneys' charges may be in the region of at least £1,800. The official fee for the subsequent examination is about £1,000, plus the attorneys' handling charge. Attorneys' reporting on the search and examination and dealing with the examiners' objections can probably add at least a further £2,000.

✔ **Validating an EPC patent in individual member states:** Validating an EPC patent in UK is a simple formality. However validation in other member countries is the stage at which translation of the granted patent is needed, adding some £1,000 plus handling charges.

✔ **Renewal fees:** Renewal fees have to be paid in each country in which you wish to keep the granted patents in force. We cover their requirements and fees in Chapter 10.

Making Money and Taking Precautions While You Wait for Your Patent

You don't need to wait for your patent to be granted before you do something with your invention. Years may pass before a patent is issued and that's never a certainty. The average pending time is about 32 months, but don't count on that estimate for any serious business planning.

While you're waiting, you can exploit your invention by the same methods you'll use to make some cash after you get your patent. We discuss these avenues in detail in Chapter 19. Activities can include:

✔ Manufacturing and selling products embodying the invention.

✔ Licensing your invention and eventual patent to others for royalties.

✔ Selling the invention and patent rights.

The one thing you mustn't do is disclose your invention to anyone, except under strict conditions of confidentiality. Even once you've filed the application, within the initial 12-month period, your invention remains top secret. You may decide after 12 months to withdraw your application before it incurs a far larger strain on the bank balance, once you seek protection in other territories. If you've disclosed the application without confidentiality in place, you can't allow the application to lapse and re-file at a later date.

Of course, after your application has been published, you don't need to keep it confidential because the UK-IPO has taken care of making it public. Bear in mind however that although you may enjoy looking at your name in lights on the UK-IPO Web site, everyone all over the world now knows what you've created, and exactly how you've made it. Your next-best-thing is no longer under wraps.

You may also receive a batch of letters from various companies that track new patent filings, claiming that they have an interest in exploiting your invention, and promising you the earth in the process. Although they may dangle carrots such as fame and fortune, we advise that you do your home-work and read up on the companies before you take them up on their offer. Some of these companies barely read the patent specification, and fire letters of this sort out to all filings and new publications.

If in doubt, seek advice! The UK-IPO, an IP attorney, or even a lawyer is a great first point of call in this instance. These professionals can offer an opinion on whether the correspondence appears legitimate, and can look over any contractual issues that may arise.

You can mark your products with a *Patent Pending* notice and make your licensees do the same. The notice acts as a good deterrent to potential copy-cats. They'll hesitate to invest in manufacturing your product, for fear they may be shut down within a few months. But if you let it be known that you've just filed your patent application, a copycat may speculate that he has two or three years to compete with you without consequences.

Chapter 9

Prosecuting Your Patent Application

*A*fter you identify your invention and file your patent application to the UK Intellectual Property Office (UK-IPO), you need some patience as you push your application through the UK-IPO, – a process called *the prosecution*. Like the wheels of justice, the gears and cogs of the UK-IPO turn slowly – and all at your expense because the 20-year life of your patent is computed from the date you file the application. Expect to wait 30–54 months before you receive the patent.

In this chapter, we take you through the maze of the various objections that may arise during the prosecution of your patent application. We also advise on the best way to amend your specification and claims to the satisfaction of the examiner in order to secure the grant of your patent.

Some inventors manage to speed up the prosecution of their patent applications by filing a special request to the UK-IPO. We've known cases where the prosecution to grant of an application has only been nine months. The main reason why applicants sometimes file a request for their application to be speeded up is the imminent commercial launch of your invention or the very real threat of infringement of the IPRs by one or more third parties.

You don't need to pay extra fees for the UK-IPO to speed up your patent application, but, if your application is filed by a patent attorney, you may face added costs for his input.

No matter how ambitious you are, you probably won't be able to single-handedly answer the examiner's requests, objections, and rejections after reading this chapter. You may have to rely on your patent attorney and trust his or her judgement. All communications from the patent examiner are written in a formal style and are often accompanied by citations of statutes, rules, and controlling court decisions. They should be answered in the same way, point-by-point, with contrary citations supporting your position when appropriate.

In the narrow confines of this chapter, we can give only a basic outline of the rules and regulations that govern the prosecution of patent applications. The nuances, exceptions, and special provisions are too numerous to address.

Touring the UK-IPO

Before you tackle the substantive issues that the patent examiner may raise after looking at your application, we suggest you get more intimately acquainted with the UK-IPO. The UK-IPO is an administrative agency of the UK government that manages the following patent-related tasks:

- ✔ Accepting and examining patent applications
- ✔ Granting patents
- ✔ Maintaining a library of granted patents
- ✔ Correcting defective patents
- ✔ Registering and keeping copies of documents related to patents and patent applications
- ✔ Collecting fees from applicants and patent owners

Notably absent from the list above is helping applicants obtain their patents. In fact, whereas the IPO overall is a fairly user-friendly agency, the examination process – by design – may seem a bit contrary. That's because one of the duties of UK-IPO examines is to prevent you from getting a patent that goes beyond the merits of your invention.

For applicants, who choose to file their own application, rather than use a patent attorney, the UK-IPO has a Private Applicants Section. We've found, by talking both with members of the Private Applicants Section and with inventors, that the advice and guidance from the Private Applicants Section is first class.

The UK-IPO has absolutely nothing to do with patent infringement matters, which remain the exclusive domain of the courts, principally the Chancery Division of the High court and the Patents County Court.

Consulting the golden book

The *Work Manuals* and *Tribunal Practice Notices* govern all the UK-IPO's activities related to patents and patent applications . The *Work Manuals* list the patent laws, the regulations applicable to patents, patent applications, and all related administrative procedures, and give very detailed instructions and guidelines for use by patent examiners and UK-IPO personnel. The *Tribunal Practice Notices* contain changes to the *Work Manuals* usually as a result of a legal decision. We explain how to get hold of copies of the *Work Manuals* in Chapter 24.

Dissecting the UK-IPO

The patent examining section of the UK-IPO is divided into units. Each *unit* specialises in a specific field of technology identified by reference to one or more groups. A *group* is a subdivision of the patent classification system that includes several technological classes and subclasses (which we talk about in Chapter 6).

Within each unit, patent examiners work their legal voodoo on your application. *Patent examiners* perform the down-in-the-trenches work of reviewing hundreds of patent applications a week, conducting novelty searches, and drafting examination reports. Over many years of personal dealings with the UK-IPO, we've found the examiners to be well-trained, dedicated professionals.

Whenever you communicate with the UK-IPO about a pending application, include the application number and any other references that readily identify your application. You can find that number on the original filing receipt and on all papers from the examiner. If you know the name of the examiner assigned to the case, including his or her name may be useful.

Clearing Initial Administrative Hurdles

In your patent application you have to include an Address for Service on Patents Form 1. The UK-IPO forwards all communications (filing receipts, search results, and so on) to the Address for Service. If you filed the application yourself, all communications go to your address. However, if you take our advice – and can afford to do so – use the services of a patent attorney, in which case all the communications from the UK-IPO go direct to your patent attorney.

This section gives you insight into your step-by-step interaction with the UK-IPO and the way in which to deal with any communication you receive from an officer or an examiner.

Meeting the minimum requirements

After you send your patent application to the UK-IPO (see Chapter 8 for filing info), the Formalities Section issues a filing receipt, usually within three or four days. The filing receipt includes an application number and confirms the date on which the Formalities Section received your application.

 If you don't get a filing receipt within a week of mailing your application, assume that something went awry in the post. We suggest you telephone the UK-IPO and ask for the mailroom to determine whether your application has been received. In order to avoid such hold-ups, you can file your application by email or fax – you then get an acknowledgement of receipt (a Filing Receipt), by return.

The Formalities Section then checks your application to see whether your application meets the minimum filing requirements – a specification and drawings, if necessary. Meeting these minimum requirements puts your application in the UK-IPO's system but doesn't guarantee you a patent. Your application needs a lot more work yet (check out Chapters 7 and 8 to see what is involved) to comply with the formalities and to overcome any objections raised by the examiner following a novelty search and a subsequent request for substantive examination.

The Formalities Section writes to you, or your patent attorney, advising when you need to file other documents.

Publishing notice of your application

After filing, the UK-IPO makes public the following details of your application:

- ✔ The title of the application, for example, 'a hedge trimmer'.
- ✔ The date on which the application was filed.
- ✔ The applicant's name (the applicant can be the lone inventor; an assignee of a lone inventor where there's an assignment of the IPRs; or a patent attorney empowered to file an application).
- ✔ The official application number.

These details are published on-line in the free, weekly *Patents and Designs Journal* some six weeks after the filing of the application (see www.ipo.gov.uk/patent/p-journal/p-pdj.htm).

The UK-IPO makes no other details public at this time. If you decide not to proceed with your application, the details of your invention remain secret forever.

Fathoming foreign filing and secrecy order

Six weeks after filing your application, you're usually clear to file an overseas application corresponding to your UK application without any protest from the UK-IPO. However, we suggest you seek clearance from the UK-IPO first, to ensure that no objection to filing overseas exists.

The main purpose of controlling what may be filed overseas is to prevent UK residents from disclosing to other countries critical inventions with military applications. All patent applications with military applications are subject to review. Depending on the sensitivity of the technology, foreign filing may be denied and your application placed under a secrecy order. A *secrecy order* forbids you, and anybody else, from disclosing your invention to anyone and prevents the UK-IPO from publishing your application or allowing it to mature into a patent within the normal time period of four years and six months from the filing date of the patent application.

If your invention becomes the subject of a secrecy order, you may still prosper if a Government department (such as the Ministry for Defence) makes use of it. With the passage of time, your invention may become less sensitive as it's overtaken by other developments, in which case your patent application may proceed to grant. We're aware of patents that have been granted some twenty years or so after the original application because they were the subject of secrecy orders.

If you still want to file overseas, and the UK-IPO doesn't object to you doing so, head to Chapter 19, where we focus on foreign filing.

Filing for More than One Invention

If you file a request for preliminary search when you file your patent application, which includes a series of claims that may be for more than one invention, the search report issued by the UK-IPO may notify you that only certain claims have been subjected to the search exercise and that a search of the remaining claims can be undertaken only upon the filing of a further request and payment of the search fee.

Say you invented an electric toothbrush with bristles that have different directions and ranges of motion. You claim several species of the brush – one with a straight handle, one with a curved handle, one with a metal handle, and one with a plastic handle. The metal and plastic handle species aren't patentably distinguishable from each other because substituting a plastic handle for a metal one would be obvious and not deserve a separate patent. But using a curved handle instead of a straight one may provide some significant and not necessarily non-obvious advantages (making it easier to reach some back teeth), which would make it the object of a separate patent. You'd have to restrict your application to one of these last two species of brushes.

If a claim applies to all species of the invention, that claim is said to be *generic*. A generic claim defines the *genus* that has the basic characteristic of all claimed inventions. In the toothbrush example, a claim that recites the bristle arrangement and simply 'a handle' would be generic because it covers all the various handle species.

The best choice in maintaining a patent application for one invention, or dividing out so that you may eventually end up with two patents, is the aspect of the invention that gives you the most legal rights against your eventual competitors, not necessarily the one that you think is the most clever or innovative. When in doubt, let your patent attorney help you make the most sensible decision, especially if your patent attorney is well aware of your business interests and has an intimate knowledge of the market place for your invention(s).

Getting in on the Action: The Official Letter

After the UK-IPO publishes your application, and you've filed a Request for Substantive Examination, the examiner reviews the Novelty Search results against the invention, which forms the basis of the claims you've placed on file with your application (which we explain in Chapter 6). The examiner then issues an Official Letter (OL). The OL is the first report on the merits of your claims. If you're the exception to the rule, all is well: You receive a *notice of allowance* of all your claims and you're in the home-straight – you can now head to Chapter 10, where we show you what happens next. However, if the OL contains an adverse ruling, you have to attempt to refute that ruling, usually by amending the claims to make them more acceptable.

The examiner then fires back with another OL, giving you a further opportunity to argue or amend. Additional procedures allow the exchanges to continue until you and the examiner reach a meeting of the minds as we explain later, see Chapter 10.

The OL may contain various objections, often due to a lack of clarity in your specifications or claims. We cover the various objections in the following sections.

Overcoming an objection for lack of clarity

An objection for lack of clarity may state that your wording is incomprehensible, vague, or long-winded or contains typographic or grammatical errors (including the peculiar grammatical rules of claim drafting that we cover in Chapter 7). Lack of clarity also includes discrepancies between the written description and the drawing, and defective drawings.

As we mention in Chapter 7, it's to your advantage to have your claims as broad as possible, and broadness can be achieved by not being too precise. Here lies a tug of war between you and the examiner: You want a claim that covers as many machines and processes as possible, even at the risk of being ambiguous. But the examiner wants to make sure that one can readily assess the coverage of the claim from its wording.

You can overcome the objection of a claim for lack of clarity by tightening its wording – but be very careful not to unduly narrow your coverage.

Fighting a lack-of-utility rejection

Being rejected because of a lack of utility basically means the invention has no demonstrable practical use. (Utility, along with novelty and obviousness, is one of the tests of patentability, as we discuss in Chapter 4).

The courts have interpreted the utility requirement to mean that a person with some skill in the area can immediately appreciate that the invention is useful, and that its utility is specific, substantial, and credible. The following 'inventions' contain questionable claims content and demonstrate the kind of statements you'd see in the first OL:

- ✔ **Method for growing hair by exposure to a magnetic field:** The claimed invention has no demonstrable utility. The effect of a magnetic field on the physiology of hair growth is neither demonstrated in the specification nor credible in view of current knowledge in the medical arts.

- ✔ **Perpetual motion machine:** The claimed invention is inoperative and therefore lacks utility. The invention is a perpetual motion machine that defies the laws of physics and cannot be credible.

If you get an objection for lack of utility because the invention is absolutely nutty, you can't do much about it, so we won't waste time trying to show you how to salvage a claim to an absurd invention. But an invention with merit can be rejected if you don't do your homework when preparing the application. Your application should mention any actual, or potential, utility of your invention in the specification. But you can easily counter a lack-of-utility objection with a reasonable answer that demonstrates whichever one of the following attributes the examiner says your invention lacks:

✔ **Credible utility:** An invention, such as a perpetual motion machine, that's deemed totally incapable of achieving a useful result will be objected to for lack of credible utility. However, even a minimum of utility can salvage the invention. Just because an invention lacks sophistication, performs poorly, or operates only under very specific conditions doesn't mean it should be objected to. Demonstrating partial success in achieving a useful result is enough to avoid the objection.

✔ **Specific utility:** You must indicate at least one plausible, specific application for the invention. Claims rejected for lack of specific utility usually relate to those for chemical products and therapeutic preparations or treatments because the specification doesn't include examples and test results that sufficiently support the invention. For example, indicating that a compound may be useful in the treatment of unspecified disorders isn't specific enough to overcome an objection, without also submitting clinical test results that prove that the compound works as claimed.

✔ **Substantial utility:** You must demonstrate a use or application of the invention that's reasonably related to the invention itself and isn't insubstantial or frivolous. For instance, you can't argue that a fingernail-softening solution can also be used to fill the capsule of a bubble level, because any liquid can do that. However, arguing that fingernails softened with your solution can be reshaped for a more aesthetic appearance would be sufficient to overcome the objection.

Contesting a lack-of-novelty rejection

Lack-of-novelty objections happen when the invention is already known or is disclosed in a prior document. For a plain-English explanation of these circumstances, see the patentability checklist in Chapter 4.

Like any other legal concept, lack of novelty isn't easy to describe. A piece of prior art cited against one of your claims may look black or white, but there's always a large grey area that leaves room for argument and interpretation that can only be assessed and advised upon by your patent attorney who's the one with the necessary skill and experience in such matters. But you're here for some answers. In the sections that follow, we outline the two most common paths for rebutting lack-of-novelty objections.

Using the different invention defence

A claimed invention can be objected to for lack of novelty if the examiner believes that it's *anticipated* by the prior art because every element in the claim is explicitly or implicitly described in an alleged prior art reference. In other words, the earlier device or process must be *exactly* identical in *all* details. You then have two options:

✔ Demonstrate that your claimed invention is different from the disclosures in the prior art reference.

✔ Amend your claim to show a difference between your invention and the cited prior art. (See 'Presenting a timely and professional answer', later in this chapter, about how to amend a claim and present an argument.)

In most cases, differentiating your invention from prior art is relatively easy, although examiners have a few tricks up their sleeves to counter your defence. Be on the lookout for these common examiner comebacks:

✔ If you argue that the prior art reference, although it may be similar to your invention, doesn't disclose a characteristic listed in your claim, the examiner may cite another earlier or contemporary patent or reference. Inevitably, that citation mentions that the characteristic in question was well known, and thus inherently disclosed in the first cited prior art reference.

✔ If you claim a generic compound, the examiner can use a reference disclosing a single species of that generic compound, even if the earlier species is only a partial example of the broad generic compound (see the section 'Filing for More than One Invention' earlier in this chapter for the difference between generic and species).

✔ If you claim a species, the examiner can use a previously known genus as well as other evidence to show that a person with ordinary skill in the art would envision your species.

✔ If your claim specifies a range or a list of equivalent elements, the examiner needs only to find a prior reference partially within that range or list to make a case of anticipation.

You can't get a patent if the invention was known or used anywhere in the world before you came up with it. You also face objection from the examiner if your invention was patented or described in a printed publication anywhere (yes, even the writings of Confucius, printed on woodblocks circa AD 750 in China, are printed publications).

You're out of the game even if your invention was described (it doesn't have to be claimed) in a published patent application or in a patent before you filed your patent application.

Applying the defences

We'll try to bring all these defence tactics into focus with a hypothetical example that describes the sequence of inventing something, filing a patent application, receiving an objection, and forming your responses.

You notice that the circular pads on your rotating polishing machine wear out more quickly around the edge than in the centre. This happens because, with each rotation, the bristles on the outer edges of the pad travel a longer distance in contact with the work surface than the bristles in the centre.

You develop a new buffing pad with a graduated thickness of pile. The tufting gets tighter as it moves away from the centre, even though the length or height of the pile is the same on the entire pad. You've filed a patent application including the following claim:

> *Claim 1. A rotary polishing pad that comprises an arrangement of strands of equal length and thickness, tufted in a gradually increasing number of strands per square centimetre from a central region to a peripheral region of said pad.*

You can't believe your eyes when you read the following statement in the first OL:

> *Claim 1 is objected to as being anticipated by Abbott Publication of Application No. GB 0,000.*

> *Abbott discloses a rotary polishing pad comprising strands of equal length but gradually increasing thickness from a central region to a peripheral region of said pad.*

> *It is well known in the art and therefore inherent in the disclosure of Abbott that increase in density of a pile can be achieved by increasing the thickness of the strands or tufting the strands in a tighter pattern.*

Looking at Abbott, you notice that the application was filed just six months before yours and has just been published. You can try the 'different invention defence', but you then have to overcome the examiner's opinion that thicker strands are inherently equivalent to more strands and are therefore a substitutable method for increasing pile density.

Challenging an obviousness objection

An obviousness objection states that the invention doesn't rise beyond ordinary skill in the field. But if you thought that objections for lack of utility or novelty were tough nuts to crack, you ain't seen nothing until you wrestle with an objection of a claim for obviousness. So put on your thinking cap: we require your undivided attention.

The obviousness objection has inspired shelves-full of books and thousands of court battles. If you review the patentability criteria sections in Chapter 4, you know as much technical info as you need to know about obviousness. So here we explain the strategy you and your patent attorney must follow to challenge an objection of a claim for obviousness.

The examiner may cite one or more prior art references in raising an objection. A reference may be a patent, a published patent application, or a document published anywhere in the world – how's that for all-encompassing?

The examiner may also refer to 'well-known' facts, practices, or information without providing any documentary evidence. Each reference must have already existed at the time of the invention.

You can overcome an objection for obviousness with a gamut of defensive approaches, including:

✔ Contesting the applicability of the references on the grounds that they're disqualified as prior art or they don't meet the conditions necessary to support a lack of novelty objection.

✔ Arguing that the references belong to a *non-analogous* (unrelated) *art* into which an inventor would never look to resolve the problem addressed by your patent, and that the references don't teach anything relevant to your invention.

✔ Challenging the examiner's combining two or more references to support the objection, on the grounds that there's no basis for the combination, either in the references themselves or in the common knowledge.

✔ Specifying that the differences between the claimed invention and the prior art exceed the capability of a person with ordinary skill in the art.

✔ Demonstrating secondary factors of non-obviousness, such as wide or enthusiastic acceptance of the invention in the field, commercial success, or unexpected advantages.

For convenience, we use the handy-dandy buffing pad that we invented in the section 'Contesting a lack-of-novelty rejection' in which the tufting gets tighter as it moves away from the centre, even though the length or height of the pile is the same on the entire pad.

To your great disappointment, you also read the following statement in the first OL:

Claim 1 is objected to in the light of Abbott Publication of Application No. GB 0,000, and also over Abel British Patent No. GB 11,111,111, in view of Babele Italian Patent No. IT 22,222,222 or Chizu Japanese Patent No. JP 33,333,333.

Abbott discloses a rotary polishing pad comprising strands of equal length but gradually increasing thickness from a central region to a peripheral region of said pad.

Abel discloses a rotary polishing pad having strands arranged in gradually greater length from the centre to the periphery.

Babele discloses a car floor mat having a more densely tufted area in the centre where the heels of the driver rest.

It would have been obvious to a person with ordinary skill in the art to use the variable tufting of Babele in the manufacture of the Abbott pad instead of using thicker strands, or in the manufacture of the Abel pad instead of using strands of different lengths.

Chizu discloses a sanding belt having a coarser grade along the centre of the belt than along its longitudinal edges. It would have been obvious to a person with ordinary skill in the art to use a coarser (thicker) tufting on the Abbott or Abel pad in areas subject to greatest friction than in other areas as taught by Chizu.

The diagrams in Figure 9-1 illustrate the various pile configurations.

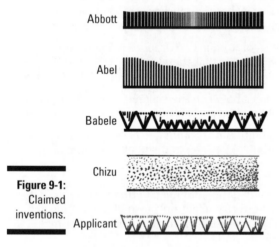

Abbott

Abel

Babele

Chizu

Figure 9-1:
Claimed
inventions.

Applicant

When you examine these references, you discover that Abbott and Abel address the same problem you noticed, but with progressively thicker or longer strands. You also observe that the different sanding grades of Chizu are intended to create contrasting finishes on polished metal surfaces for purely aesthetic reasons. Abel, Babele, and Chizu were filed several years before your application. To overcome the obviousness objection, you can try these defensive approaches, in the following order:

1. **Not part of prior art.**

   Get rid of Abbott by showing that the reference given isn't applicable. It was already disqualified as prior art because it wasn't patented or published before your application. But, the other references are too old to be polished off (pun absolutely intended) that way.

2. **Non-analogous art.**

   Try to disqualify Babele and Chizu on the grounds that they belong to non-analogous arts by arguing that your buffing pads belong in different and unrelated fields from automobile floor mats or sanding. Citing

Babele's mat is a good point. But the Chizu argument is very weak because buffing pads and sanding belts are commonly found in wood and metal shops and often used on the same work piece.

Even if you win the argument, you still have to meet the second part of the test by demonstrating that the non-analogous art reference doesn't teach anything about the invention. Babele does teach a very relevant technique of using a tighter tufting of the pile in areas of maximum wear. You can point out that Chizu suggests the use of different grades of grinding, sanding, or polishing agents on the same tool. So, non-analogous art isn't a very strong defence. Look at the other defences.

3. Improper combination of references.

You may have better luck here. To combine one reference with another, that combination must be suggested in the references themselves, or be part of the general knowledge of one with ordinary skill in the art. Moreover, the combination can't change the principle of operation of the primary reference or render the primary reference inoperable for its intended purpose. For example, if the sanding belt of Chizu was mounted on Abel's rotary machine, the combination wouldn't function as a buffer.

The remaining primary reference is Abel. The secondary references include Babele with the floor mat and Chizu with the sanding belt. Abel and Babele are designed to resolve the same problem of excessive wear in the most worked areas of the pad or mat. It'd be difficult to convince the examiner that the Babele approach can't be used practically on Abel's pad. However, the coarser sanding grade in the centre portion of Chizu's belt can't be carried over into Abel's without completely changing the operation of the buffing pad, so you can eliminate Chizu. You can win that round, and get rid of the last ground for objection.

4. Non-obvious differences.

You're left now with Abel and Babele. You can try to discredit the examiner's application of the obviousness test according to the Patents Act 1977 and established case law.

The difference between the teachings of the combined references (what you can discover from them) and the invention is extremely small. Abel recognised the problem of excessive peripheral wear in the pad and Babele demonstrates how to minimise that type of wear in a floor mat. The issue remaining is whether a person with ordinary skill in the field of buffing pads who's fully aware of the two references would be inclined to combine their teachings and develop your invention.

You can argue that Abel's use of longer strands to solve the wear problem was a poor solution because the pad now has an uneven working surface that puts more pressure on the edges than in the centre. The shorter strands in the centre of the pad won't wear out until the peripheral strands wear down to the same length as those in the centre. At which point the initial problem reappears. So Abel's invention is a nice try but is an unsuccessful way to solve the problem. We can predict the examiner answering: 'Yes, Abel didn't know about Babele, but a person with ordinary skill in the art would have.' You still have a chance to win the argument by pointing out the following observations. Buffing pad design isn't rocket science and the 'level of ordinary skill' in the field is relatively low. Abel is a good representative of the person with ordinary skill. So if Abel didn't know about Babele, neither would any other person having a 'level of ordinary skill'. That last argument might just carry enough water to win the case.

5. **Secondary factors.**

    Another opportunity to salvage the claim is to demonstrate some unexpected advantages of your invention, such as great commercial success or its important contribution to the industry, by presenting sales records, testimonials from qualified people in the field, and copies of professional magazine articles praising your achievements. An invention that is a commercial success is often referred to as a 'long-felt want'.

Proving that your invention is patentable subject matter

The Patents Act 1977 provides for the granting of a patent to 'whoever invents any new and useful process, machine, manufacture, or composition of matter or any new and useful improvement thereof.'

You may have a hard time imagining an invention that doesn't fit into one of these categories. Yet there's always someone who tries to patent (and therefore monopolise) a law of nature, a natural phenomenon, a mathematical algorithm, an abstract idea, a simple manipulation of abstract ideas, or some purely descriptive material. These subject matters are patently non-patentable. Albert Einstein wouldn't have been allowed to patent his famous formula $E = mc^2$ because it's an algorithm expressing a law of nature.

You can expect an objection of a claim on the ground that it describes non-patentable subject matter, especially if your invention is in the area of obvious perpetual motion devices or computer programmes and software inventions that involve a method of doing business.

To answer the examiner's objections you must convince the examiner that your claim describes a physical structure, composition, or process that produces a tangible result. For example, a database or compilation of information, even in an electronic form doesn't comply with these requirements and is, therefore, non-patentable subject matter.

A pure manipulation of data to obtain a final dimension or other parameter isn't an invention However, when the calculation is done by a computer coupled to an industrial process machine, such as a computer that drives a machine to regulate rubber vulcanisation, the regulation method, including the algorithm used by the computer program, may be patentable.

Showing that your disclosure is enabling

An objection for lack of enabling disclosure claims the specification doesn't demonstrate how to make and use the invention. In Chapter 7, we discuss how to meet the disclosure requirement. If you try to claim something that isn't adequately disclosed in the specification, you get an objection that's hard to overcome. If you don't spell out the enabling material somewhere in the specification, you must convince the examiner that what's missing is common knowledge to people skilled in the art, using supporting documents such as treatises, encyclopaedia excerpts, or magazine articles. If possible, also provide declarations by experts in your field to support your argument.

Accepting the one invention – one patent rule

The Patents Act 1977 'facilitates the grant of a patent to the inventor who files a patent application for protection of his or her invention' – that's one patent for each invention, not two or more. An objection can occur if you already have a patent or an application pending that claims the same invention in similar language. For example, if you have a pending UK application that's reached the allowance stage of its prosecution while you also have a pending PCT application and/or a pending EPC application, both of which may qualify for the grant of a UK patent for the same invention, the UK-IPO advises that one or other of the applications must be withdrawn thereby avoiding the situation of two UK patents for the same invention.

You can overcome the problem by slightly rewording the claims of your pending PCT and/or EPC applications so that the two claimed inventions aren't identical. The objective is to make sure that a structure or process can't infringe on both the original UK patent, if that's granted first, and the one you're applying for under the provisions of the PCT and the EPC.

Applicants have been known to maintain both of their UK national patent and their PCT/UK or EPC/UK patent by restricting the UK patent to the 'Omnibus' claim(s) usually found at the end of the claims. The scope of the 'Omnibus' claim(s) is that it's limited to the invention as fully described and shown in the drawings. Such a claim may be worthwhile in preventing 'Chinese copies (exact copies of the original) of your invention, especially if there's any doubt about the validity of the claims of a PCT/UK or EPC/UK patent.

Presenting a timely and professional answer

You usually have two months to answer an examination report on the merit of your invention. In most cases, the two months may be extended if you so request by up to two months. The Official Letter (OL) from the examiner specifies the date by which you need to file a response.. There's no need to file the request for extension before or on the deadline; just include it with your delayed answer.

In order to save time, sleepless nights, and heartache as you wait for a decision from the examiner, we suggest you respond to an OL as soon as possible with a well reasoned argument.

If you filed your patent application through a patent attorney, youl receive copies of the OL and any advice from the attorney on the response you may make. However, make sure that you agree with the proposed response before instructing your attorney to file your reply. You can instruct your attorney to file any response without delay.

Reacting to a Second Objection

You've replied to the OL with a clever amendment and what you thought was an ironclad argument proving that all your claims are allowable. Yet you get another objection of some claims or maybe an objection to the specification.

Receiving a second series of objections from an examiner isn't unusual so don't worry unduly. Simply respond as if the second lot were the first OL you've received and table your further arguments or accept any suggestion from the examiner that protects your commercial interests and keeps likely copiers at bay. Here's some more advice:

- ✔ Try to comply with the examiner's requirement in the OL.
- ✔ Make a last ditch effort to change the examiner's mind with a logical and persuasive argument.
- ✔ Amend your claims one more time.
- ✔ Answer as soon as possible to give the examiner an opportunity to review it before the answer deadline. You may get a break if the examiner reviews your application and is persuaded by your brilliant argument to pass all your pending claims.

Meeting the Examiner

At any time during the examination of your application, you can request a face-to-face interview with the examiner to try and resolve pending objections. Make the request directly to the examiner in writing or by fax, e-mail, or telephone. The request must specify the topics to be discussed.

We don't suggest that you personally engage in an interview with an examiner. Let your patent attorney act on your behalf. Examiners aren't particularly keen on dealing with a non-professional who isn't versed in patent law and doesn't speak the legal lingo. More significantly, on your own, you're more likely to agree to a concession offered by the examiner even if that concession is detrimental to your case. Your patent attorney can help you interpret and consider any written concessions.

If you're an unrepresented inventor/applicant you have to communicate direct with the UK-IPO. Doing so is not too onerous a task because your patent application has already been dealt with by the Private Applicants Section the staff of which are especially trained to provide practical guidance and advice on the steps you need to follow in order to obtain a patent for your invention.

We can't overemphasise the advantages of a heart-to-heart conversation with the examiner, especially when the outstanding patentability issue or the invention itself is very complex. Occasionally, with a few minutes of live conversation, we've been able to resolve rejection problems that would have consumed months of written communications.

If you request in advance, the UK-IPO makes audiovisual equipment available to you so that you can play a video showing your invention in action. You can even bring your computer or a small prototype to your meeting to demonstrate the workings of a piece of software. With prior notice, you may even be able to arrange a long-distance interview through the UK-IPO Video Conference at Harmsworth House in London.

Chapter 10

Entering the Home Stretch: Getting Your Patent Granted

In This Chapter

▶ Reviewing your patent strategy

▶ Taking care of clerical errors and other omissions

▶ Paying maintenance fees

▶ Slapping down your patent number

Many pitfalls and problems face you when you decide to apply for a patent (as this book clearly demonstrates). However, hopefully the day arrives when you (or your patent attorney) go to the mailbox and find a letter from the UK Intellectual Property Office (UK-IPO) telling you that your patent application is in order for allowance and is shortly to be granted.

However, you still have a few more issues to consider before you get that longed-for patent. This chapter walks you through one last reconsideration of your patent strategy and explains how to finally secure your patent. Because problems can occur and corrections may be necessary even after you get the piece of paper, we also help you tie up the loose ends after a patent is granted. Finally, we take you to the finish line with a few comments on correctly affixing your patent number to your now-patented invention.

Reviewing Your Patent Strategy One Last Time

In Chapter 5, we detail alternatives to acquiring a patent for protecting your IP assets. Now, two or three years down the line, you may be staring a possible patent in the face.

Thoroughly re-evaluating your patent strategy with the help of your patent attorney (and your marketing adviser, if you have one), even at such a late date, isn't a bad idea. Take a good look at the claims allowed by the examiner that are to be published in your granted patent, the claims being the part of the patent that spells out the extent of your protection, and with a cool head, ask yourself the following questions:

- ✔ Do the allowed claims give you the scope of protection you originally expected? If not, is the protection they do give sufficient to enhance your market position?

- ✔ Can you enhance the degree of protection under one or more alternate forms of intellectual property rights (IPRs)? Confidential information that did not need to be disclosed in the patent application may still be regarded as trade secrets and used to protect your invention. You may also enjoy copyright, unregistered design right, registered design, and some effective trade mark(s) that complement the monopoly afforded by the granted patent.

You may be having your invention manufactured and packaged abroad at a really competitive cost that allows you to establish a very lucrative market position in the countries where you've filed corresponding patent applications to that which has just been granted. These factors should be taken into consideration when evaluating the worth of your newlygranted patent.

In order to fully protect your interests, we suggest that you file a patent application in the country where you may have your products manufactured (probably China or Japan). Doing so prevents the manufacturer from infringing your IPRs by manufacturing your products for his own use and sale in that country, and in other countries where you have no patent protection. You may consider offering your foreign manufacturer a licence under your Chinese or Japanese patent upon terms that give you and the licensee(s) added security within your relationship as licensor and licensee.

Your patent attorney and marketing executive can advise you about whether you have a worthwhile patent monopoly substantiated by other IPRs, or if further action is needed by way of seeking registered design and/or registered trade mark protection.

Taking Corrective Action

Put down the champagne. Slowly back away from the bottle. Even though you've just received that long-awaited patent, don't celebrate until you've carefully gone over every line of the document. If you spot a glitch, you need to talk to your patent attorney about fixing it. Some glitches may simply be a clerical errors such as misspelling your name, address, or the name of a constituent in a chemical composition. More serious anomalies, however, need addressing without delay, especially if the full scope of the granted rights isn't clearly defined due to a discrepancy in the specification, or claims that arise between allowance by the examiner and publication of your patent.

The UK-IPO readily amends any errors or omissions that you, or your patent attorney, bring to their attention. You can easily fix typographic or grammatical errors and omissions if your intended meaning is obvious from the specification and claims despite the minor errors or omissions. You can file a letter at the UK-IPO explaining your corrections. You need to accompany your letter with a Patents Form 11 and a fee (currently £40). The UK-IPO addresses the matter and in due course, if they're satisfied, publishes an errata notice, which is attached to the granted patent with retrospective affect.

Other corrections take a bit more work, however, and we address these in the sections that follow.

Correcting the inventors' names

A patent that misstates the names of the inventor or names the wrong patentee may be declared invalid and unenforceable, which is pretty serious, especially if an infringer's attorney discovers the error when entering into an infringement action. If all parties agree that an inventor or a patentee was omitted or listed by mistake on the patent you can take the necessary action to clear up the issue.

You simply file a Statement of case in duplicate at the UK-IPO to correct the names of the inventors listed (or omitted) on the patent or to correct the names of the assignees. The Comptroller forwards details to anyone listed in the application to amend and, if no objections arise within a set period (usually three months), the amendments are allowed.

The UK-IPO publishes an errata notice, which is attached to published copies of the granted Specification.

Narrowing the claims

You may wonder why you'd ever want to narrow the scope of your patent – you just got a lucky break, right? Wrong. Your deceptively broad patent can be declared invalid by a judge if you try to sue an alleged infringer. (Incidentally, in such circumstances we strongly recommended that you seek the advice of a patent attorney, lawyer, or even Queen's Counsel (QC), especially if an infringement action is being contemplated and your lawyer recommends seeking the opinion of a QC before proceeding.

Assume that you've been granted a patent for an engine without mentioning its application to lawnmowers. You've just discovered that in the past, the same type of engine was used on small handheld power tools, such as leaf blowers and string grass trimmers. However, you were the first to draw enough power from this kind of engine to drive a lawnmower or any other device requiring more than one horsepower. Your invention uses a weighted lawnmower cutting blade as a flywheel to smooth out intermittent power gaps inherent to your five-stroke engine.

Because your current claims describe elements found in prior art machines, they shouldn't have been allowed (see patentability requirements in Chapter 4). However, because no prior patent or documentation existed for that kind of engine, you couldn't have discovered it through a comprehensive anticipation search. And, of course, you didn't hear about use of the engine on handheld power tools until recently, so the error isn't due to any deception on your part.

You need to promptly file an application for amendment of your claims to a narrower scope by describing the lawn mower or any other tool that requires more than one horsepower. You may also, for good measure, add some claims that simply mention the flywheel as long as there's fair basis for the new claim's structure in the patent specification you filed originally and no added matter is involved.

Correcting the disclosure

As explained in Chapter 7, the disclosure consists of the specification supported by a drawing of the invention. If you unintentionally misstated some facts in the specification or inaccurately drew a particular structure, you may be able to set the record straight – as long as the error didn't prevent someone from practising the invention and your proposed corrections don't introduce *new matter* (information necessary to use the invention that wasn't present in the original application).

If you didn't appreciate the regulating effect of the flywheel blade in the new lawnmower engine you've patented, you may have given some other incorrect explanation for the engine's exceptional performance. No sweat. That error didn't prevent someone with skill in the mechanical field from building your lawnmower. You may be able to correct the problem with an acceptable explanation.

Once again, you may directly, or through your patent attorney if you're so represented, file a Statement of case in duplicate. If the application to amend is successful, the UK-IPO issues an errata notice that is attached to copies of the printed specifications issued thereafter.

However, if the agreed amendments are extensive, the UK-IPO may request that you file an amended Specification, which is then re-published as a 'C' document.

Publication as a 'C' document follows the initial publication of your patent application as an 'A' document and the subsequent publication of the granted patent as a 'B' document. The notations 'A', 'B' and 'C' appear after the seven figure number of the patent specification on the front page of the specification.

Although you've no set period to file for amendments to correct an error or omission, we recommend that you immediately attend to any clerical error or omission that may affect the scope of your monopoly. It may be to your disadvantage if you don't take steps to amend any errors or omissions that modify the scope of protection you thought you had as soon as you become aware of the situation. The reason is that a third party may 'infringe' your IPRs because they were acting in good faith when they considered your patent wasn't infringed by their action, all due to the misinformation caused by errors or omissions in your granted patent.

Dealing with extensive amendments of patent specification and claims

As a result of Court decisions in an infringement action, your patent specification, claims, and drawings may require extensive amendment. Under such circumstances, the UK-IPO requires you to provide a new specification, claims, and drawings, if necessary, for publication as a 'C' document as mentioned in the previous section.

The effect of the extensive amendment is as if your patent had been granted in the form of the 'C' document.

Paying Maintenance Fees

Granted patents become subject to annual renewal fees from the fifth to the twentieth year. The first four years after the filing date of a patent application are free (no annual renewal fee is due during that period). From the end of the fourth year, you need to pay renewal fees for the fifth and subsequent years together with a Patent Form 12 to maintain your patent in force. The renewal fees cost from £50 for the fifth year increasing annually to £400 for the twentieth year (see the UK-IPO Web site at www.ipo.gov.uk for up-to-date information on fees).

You can pay renewals up to three months before the payment is due. Payment day is the last day of the month in which the anniversary of filing your application falls. So, if you filed on 12th July, you need to pay your fee by 31st July each year. You're not charged for late payment of any renewal fee up to one month after the due date. However, if the renewal fee is up to six months late, you need to pay £24 per month on top of the renewal fee that is due.

You do have provision for filing an application to restore a lapsed patent up to nineteen months after the renewal date. However, you must have acceptable reasons for restoration such as something that was out of your control such as fire, or prolonged incapacitating illness; merely stating that you forgot isn't good enough!

The UK-IPO isn't likely to restore a lapsed patent if they detect a lack of urgency between the time that you became aware of the situation and the time when you filed your application for restoration.

Failure to pay a renewal fee on time (or late with penalties) results in the lapsing of the patent. Many granted patents lapse before the patent holder intended because of various circumstances including, but not limited to, renewal fees not being paid. You can revive a lapsed patent by filing a Patents Form No.16 accompanied by an explanation of why the renewal fee was not paid or an explanation of other circumstances, which led to the lapsing of your patent.

After giving any interested party a chance to oppose the reinstatement of the lapsed patent, the Comptroller, at his or her discretion, may order that the patent be reinstated.

Provision in the patents Act 1977 relates to any third party, who, acting in good faith, has begun to avail themselves of the patented invention between the time when the patent lapsed and the date of restoration. The provision means that such a party, or parties, may continue to avail themselves of the patented invention. However, they cannot extend any such use; for example, if the third party or parties has established a facility for the manufacture of a product and has begun to use and sell that product, they may continue with such activity. But they cannot extend their business by building another facility or extending the capacity of their present facility without entering into a licence arrangement with you.

In order to safeguard against the erroneous lapsing of your patent due to renewal fees not being paid, we strongly recommend that, if you haven't retained the services of a patent attorney, you register your patent with a patents renewals service. Such a service gives you plenty of notice before any forthcoming payment and can even pay the renewal fees on your behalf, for a small charge. You can get information on one of the oldest, and most reliable, patent renewals service providers by going to www.cpaglobal.com.

Most importantly, keep the UK-IPO, and your renewal fee service provider, informed of any long-term change of address.

If you're represented by a patent attorney, all communications relating to your granted patent(s) are addressed to her. Your attorney looks after all of your interests – including the prompt payment of renewal fees if you instruct her to do so.

 When you check your patent after it's been granted don't automatically assume that it's still effective. It may have lapsed due to non-payment of a renewal fee. You can check the status of your patent by visiting the UK-IPO Web site at www.ipo.gov.uk/patent/patentmanage/patentstatus.htm. In addition to the status of your patent you can also see details of your address, the Address for Service, any licensees under the patent, and any changes.

Marking Your Widgets with the Patent Number

You may put your patent number on all products covered by your patent or made according to your patented process. If you've granted a licence to any third party for the commercial exploitation of your invention, the conditions of such a licence can be that any products, packaging, and trade literature must contain details of the patent number and that the products are licensed from you.

 Don't place a false patent or patent pending notice on your product. Note that a patent pending notice has no recognised legal value. It just acts as a deterrent to potential infringers by warning them that a patent may be granted at any time. It can only be used when, and only as long as, an application is pending.

Part III
Knowing Your Copyright

In this part . . .

Whether you're writing a novel, creating an architectural drawing, developing new software, or filming an instructional video on the care and feeding of pet ferrets, you own a creative work that automatically enjoys copyright protection upon creation. In this part, we categorise, dissect, and otherwise pick apart the wide variety of creative works that are protected by copyright.

But you have to make sure that you actually own the creative work, so we give you some tests, tips, and tricks to help you make sure that it belongs to you and not your employer, employee, or someone else who had a hand in the creation. And even though you enjoy automatic copyright protection (who said there's no such thing as a free lunch?), we explain how to put some teeth into your protection.

▶ Filing for UK registered design protection

▶ Looking at registered community design

▶ Qualifying for design right

• •

*I*n Part II of this book, we focus on identifying intellectual property and how to protect it by filing a patent application. However, relying on a patent strategy alone is not the only way, or possibly not even the best way, of protecting the fruits of your labour. And a patent strategy is certainly not the cheapest or quickest way to protect your invention, because your development may have design features that can be protected by a registered design in addition to those features of construction and function that may be protected by a patent.

Lone inventors, and small to medium-sized enterprises (SMEs), often overlook the world of designs and other forms of protection available in the UK and elsewhere. You may know more about patents because of the fame and glory often attached to past inventors or because of the fortunes made by a few modern inventors, such as Mandy Haberman for her baby mug and Sir James Dyson for his cyclone vacuum cleaner. Both inventors have relied heavily on their patents to ward off plagiarists who have tried to enter the marketplace with similar products.

However, the products of both Mandy Haberman and Sir James Dyson also qualify for protection by registered design. Unlike a patent, which protects the structure and functional aspects of an invention, a registered design protects the non-functional aspects, such as the shape and configuration.

Choosing to rely solely on a registered design to protect your invention is a difficult decision. If your invention is simply an object, for example a chair, table, or candlestick, a registered design may serve your best interests. Registering your design saves you a lot of money and gives you the security of obtaining defensible protection in considerably less time than that required for the grant of a patent.

If, on the other hand, your chair contains moving parts that facilitate the alteration of the chair to cater for a person resting with raised legs, inventive content may then exist in the function of the moving parts – in which case, both patent and registered design protection may be the order of the day.

If you've any doubts about which way to proceed, we suggest you phone the UK Intellectual Property Office (UK-IPO) or talk to a patent attorney.

Understanding UK Registered Design

A registered design automatically gives you a monopoly on the rights to use that design.

The design may be:

- ✔ **The shape of a product:** a new leg for a table or chair.
- ✔ **The decoration applied to a product:** a flowering rose applied to pieces of crockery.
- ✔ **Both the shape and the decoration of a product:** the shape of a teapot which may also have a specific pattern.

The specific pattern itself, such as a floral pattern, is protected, no matter what product is named in the application form. Therefore, if somebody uses your protected floral pattern on their own product(s), they're infringing your rights.

You can protect an entire product or just part of that product's features as in the following examples.

- ✔ **Lines:** the outline in plan of a roof tile.
- ✔ **Contours:** the undulating upper surface of a bold roll roof tile.
- ✔ **Colours:** the colours for a new pattern to be applied to a fabric for a range of furniture.
- ✔ **Shape:** the shape of a vacuum flask.
- ✔ **Texture or materials:** the fabrics chosen for a range of luggage.

Registering your design with the UK Intellectual Property Office (UK-IPO) gives you the exclusive right to the design in the UK and the Isle of Man for up to 25 years. This period is made up of an initial five-year term from the date of filing the application and is followed by four further terms of five years upon payment of requisite renewal fees, which we explain in the later section 'Paying to protect your design'.

As you develop your product, you may take advantage of a grace period of up to 12 months to test the market for your design, but you should not delay filing your application any longer than is necessary.

Bear in mind that if you take advantage of the 12-month grace period, you may undermine your rights in respect of filing a design application outside the European Union (EU). An application for an EU registered design for all member states of the EU is filed at the Office for Harmonization in the Internal Market (OHIM).

You also have a grace period of up to 12 months for applications filed through OHIM. The UK is one of the European territories covered by such an application. Therefore, no anomalies arise whether you file in the UK in the first instance, after making use of the grace period, or file at the OHIM office, based in Alicante, Spain.

If you plan to market your product in Europe but nowhere else, then making full use of the grace period may be to your advantage. The reason is that you may be able to determine the commercial viability of your product and to secure a positive response from a manufacturer and/or distributor, who may be interested in a licence for your product, preferably on equitable terms.

However, if you think that your product may have worldwide appeal, use of the grace period for up to 12 months prevents any valid protection being obtained in territories outside Europe in, for example the US, Australia, or China, where you may need to have your products manufactured and packaged ready for sale. All countries have requirements in respect of novelty, with most requiring absolute novelty. That means that if your product is to be protected by a valid registered design, products of the same design cannot have been available anywhere in the world before the application for the new design was filed. Therefore, if you've made use of the grace period allowed by the UK-IPO or OHIM and placed your new design in the public domain, it's fatal to the validity of any design protection you seek in those countries.

Designs are classified into some 32 Classes (from Class 1: foodstuffs, through such others as Class 8: tools and hardware; Class 21: games, toys, tents and sports goods, to Class 31: machines and appliances for preparing food or drink, and Class 99: miscellaneous). You don't have to specify the class when you file a design; this is done by the UK-IPO Designs Registry or OHIM.

Filing Your UK Registered Design Application

Now that you have most of the relevant information for securing registered design protection for your product, you can file your design application. You can file the application yourself and save yourself several hundred pounds, or you can instruct a patent attorney to prepare and file the application.

To register a design at the Designs Registry of the UK-IPO, you complete and file illustrations (which we explain below) of the design, the appropriate forms, and the relevant fees (we set out the costs you need to meet, even if you prepare and file your own application, in the section 'Paying to protect your design' later in this chapter). An application may be for one design or a set of related designs, for example one roof tile or a set of complementary roof tiles.

For most UK design applications, you complete and file Form DF2A. You can obtain the relevant forms, and notes on how to complete the forms, from the UK-IPO or from its Web site at www.ipo.gov.uk. You can obtain a booklet entitled 'How to apply to register a design', from the UK-IPO or download from the Web site.

Your application should include the completed Form DF2A and a Fee Sheet FS2, one set of the illustrations of your product, and your fee. The illustrations may be line drawings in black ink, but don't include hidden details in dotted lines unless such details form an essential part of the design. The illustrations may also be photographs or computer-generated graphics. Make sure that you provide sufficient views of your product to ensure the visibility of its novel features.

Sometimes only one or more parts of a product are novel – in such cases, it's acceptable to indicate the part or parts for which protection is being sought by applying a blue colour wash to those parts in the illustrations. Alternatively, in a line drawing, the novel part or parts may be drawn in full lines, with non-novel part or parts shown in dotted lines. Circling a novel part or parts in red ink is also permissible.

Looking at illustrations

Present the illustrations on one side only of A4 plain white paper. If your design is not two-dimensional or merely decoration, include a series of views and label what each view illustrates, for example 'Front view', 'Plan view', or 'Upper right-hand side perspective view'.

If you have more than one sheet of illustrations, number the sheets consecutively as, for example, 1/4, 2/4, and so on if you have four pages, or 1/7, 2/7, and so on if you have seven pages.

You may file informal illustrations, which must clearly show all the features of the design for which protection is being sought. Often, informal drawings are good enough for the application to proceed. The examiner asks for replacement drawings if your informal illustrations aren't satisfactory. We find that good computer-generated drawings are often satisfactory and save a great deal of time and money.

The more professional your illustrations, the better your chances of success in warding off unwelcome attention from plagiarists. If your illustrations aren't up to scratch, plagiarists may feel encouraged to take a chance. They may manufacture and sell the same products, costing you dearly. At this point you may consider seeking redress by suing the plagiarist – but if your illustrations lack definition and clarity, your action for infringement of your registered design may fail.

Several firms offer high-quality drafting services. Using a drafting service pushes up the cost of protecting your design, but we think that it's a worthwhile cost in the long run.

Paying to protect your design

We've based the figures in this section on the 2007 fee schedules. For up-to-date fees, head to the UK-IPO Web site at www.ipo.gov.uk.

The application fee for a design included in a UK application is £60 if you give consent for publication in the *Patents & Designs Journal*. The fee is reduced to £40 if you delay consent for publication.

Where a second design is included in the application, you pay a further fee of £40 if you give consent for publication given, or £20 if you delay consent for publication.

Renewal fees for a UK registered design are as follows:

- ✔ £130 for the second five-year period
- ✔ £210 for the third five-year period
- ✔ £310 for the fourth five-year period
- ✔ £450 for the fifth five-year period

Seeing what happens at the Design Registry

You're satisfied that your design is new and is different from any previous design for similar products and so you prepare and file your registered design with the appropriate documents and fee at the Design Registry of the UK-IPO.

Upon receipt of your application, the Design Registry issues a filing receipt giving the application an official number and a date of filing; this date is also the priority date for any corresponding overseas applications filed within six months of the application/priority date.

An examiner checks your application and, if satisfied, sends you a letter advising you of the outcome. The examiner's letter may inform you that your design is acceptable and that it can proceed to registration.

If the examiner is not satisfied that your design is acceptable, the examiner advises accordingly. You then have a two-month period in order to convince the examiner that the objections aren't justified.

If your arguments don't sway the examiner, you can seek a formal meeting with a hearing officer. Your chances of success at this stage may be enhanced by the presence of a patent attorney with experience in such matters. If you still fail to convince the examiner or the hearing officer, you then have no alternative but to withdraw your application.

We can't over-emphasise the importance of using the services of an IP professional if you've any doubts about your own competence in preparing and filing your own registered design application.

Protecting spare parts

The issue of design protection for spare parts is the source of ongoing dialogue both in the courts and elsewhere.

The manufacturer of an original product usually wants to be the sole supplier of spare parts for that product. The manufacturer wants the spares to be of good quality, not risking damage to other parts of the product and not harming the manufacturer's reputation. The manufacturer may also have unregistered design rights (see the section 'Uncovering UK unregistered design rights' later in this chapter) in the parts, whether the parts are protected by unregistered or registered design rights.

On the other hand, some companies' entire business is concerned with the making of good-quality replacement parts. Such companies argue that many spares have little or no design content and that the original manufacturers use their doubtful rights to overprice routine items that should be freely available from any competent source.

Principles known as 'must fit' and 'must match' have been created by the courts to decide whether spare parts should gain design protection. Broadly speaking, if the shape of a spare part is dictated by the need to fit a specific location, then the part has no design element. However, if the part contains design features that give the part a distinctive appearance, then design rights may be a possibility. In the case of an unregistered design right, the distinctive appearance must be the three-dimensional features of the spare part.

Consider motor vehicle parts, a field in which many disputes have arisen. Exhaust pipes can't be design protected, as the exhaust pipe must fit the available path between the engine and the rear of a vehicle. Body panels and doors can't be design protected, as they must match the shape of the rest of the vehicle.

Wing mirrors, however, can be protected by design. Wing mirrors come in a variety of shapes and configurations that have nothing in common with the shape of the vehicle on which they're mounted; thus, they need not fit or match that vehicle. Likewise, car wheels can be design protected, because wheels come in a wide variety of different designs.

Uncovering UK unregistered design rights

UK unregistered design right (UDR) prevents others from copying your design. UDR is an automatic right that comes into force upon the creation of a design. The ownership of the right belongs to the creator of the design unless they were commissioned to do the work – if the commissioning document is drafted properly and includes the assignment of the work, the UDR belongs to the commissioner.

UDR is not a complete right as it covers only three-dimensional aspects of a product. UDR does not protect any surface decoration applied to the product or any two-dimensional pattern such as a wallpaper or carpet design.

There's no official requirement for registration of a UDR akin to the registration of registered designs. However, several firms offer registration facilities for a fee. This service may be useful if at any time you have to prove the date of creation of the design and title to the UDR.

The duration of a UDR is 15 years from the end of the calendar year in which the design was first recorded in a design document or an article made to the design, whichever occurred first.

If articles made to the design are available for sale or hire anywhere in the world within five years from the end of the calendar year in which the design was first recorded, then the duration is ten years.

A proviso in the Copyright Designs and Patents Act 1988 is that a compulsory licence may be requested during the last five years of a UDR.

In addition, during an infringement action, a defendant may request a licence of rights on terms to be agreed as between the rights holder and the defendant.

If you become embroiled in a situation that requires remedial action for infringement of the rights you own in a UDR, seek the assistance of a patent attorney or an IP lawyer well versed in such matters.

Considering copyright in design

In addition to the registered design and unregistered design rights that may be attributed to a new design, there may also be copyright in the design. This right applies to documents detailing the design in addition to any artistic and/or literary work incorporated within the finished product.

Reviewing Registered Community Design

A registered community design (RCD) affords essentially the same rights as in a UK registered design except that the protection extends to all the signatory states of the European Union (EU), currently some 27 countries including the UK.

The RCD offers a very attractive way of registering your design or set of related designs across the whole of the EU, as you need just one application. The wide range of what you can protect extends to many signs and symbols that may also qualify for trade mark protection.

The office responsible for granting RCDs is the Office for Harmonization in the Internal Market (OHIM) based in Alicante, Spain. OHIM is also responsible for receiving applications for EU trade mark applications.

An application for an EU registered design can be filed at OHIM, with a completed official application form, by mail or online at `oami.europa.eu`.

Alternatively, you may file an application form at the UK-IPO, which then forwards the application to OHIM. You must complete the fee sheet for OHIM application (UK Form FS3) and must pay a handling fee of £15 to UK-IPO. Subsequent communications and all fees except the UK handling fee must be sent directly to OHIM.

You can obtain the application form online or as a hard copy from OHIM or the UK-IPO. The form can also be created on your own computer but it must be in the same format, and give the same information, as the official version. The application form may be completed in any of the OHIM official languages (English, French, German, Italian, or Spanish) but it must also specify a second of these languages. Therefore, if your principal markets are going to be in the UK and France, French as the second language is an obvious choice.

The application form contains pages on which the illustrations of a design need to be provided; in addition, it contains boxes in which the number of sheets and the number of designs in the application should be provided in sequential order.

The UK-IPO publishes an excellent guide called *How to Apply for a Registered Community Design*. You can obtain a copy from the Central Enquiry Unit at Concept House, Cardiff Road, Newport NP10 8QQ – telephone 08459 500505.

Exploring the examination procedure

OHIM examines the application and advises you of any problems with it. The application needs no official searches or novelty examinations but it's checked for basic formal requirements, such as including adequate drawings or photographs and using the correct forms and paying the fees due. If any documents or information is missing you're required to submit them within a two-month period.

Registration and publication of the design typically occurs about three months after filing.

Like the term of a UK registered design, an EU design registration is also for an initial five-year period, renewable for four further five-year periods up to a total of 25 years.

Counting the costs

The official fee for an EU design application is in two parts: a registration fee and a publication fee. You must pay all OHIM fees in euros – no other currency is accepted.

The registration fee is:

- ✔ €120 for one design
- ✔ € 115 for each extra design up to 10
- ✔ € 50 for each extra design above 10

The publication fee is:

- ✔ €120 for one design
- ✔ €60 for each extra design up to 10
- ✔ €20 for each extra design above 10

You can ask OHIM to defer publication by paying the following fees instead of the publication fee, but they must be paid with the application (and you still have to pay the above publication fee when you do ask OHIM to publish the application):

- ✔ €40 for one design
- ✔ €20 for each extra design up to 10
- ✔ €10 for each extra design above 10

Renewal fees for an EU registered community design are:

- ✔ €90 for the second five-year period
- ✔ €120 for the third five-year period
- ✔ €150 for the fourth five-year period
- ✔ €180 for the fifth five-year period

These fees are based on the 2007 fee schedules and may change from time to time. The fees payable at any one time may be found by visiting the OHIM Web site or enquiring at the UK-IPO.

You need to add your patent attorney's fees to the above fees. Preparing and filing the EU application may cost £500–1000 depending on the amount of work involved in preparing illustrations of the products for which you seek protection. For the various fee-paying stages, a rough guide is to assume that the attorney's charge is about the same as the fee itself. Given the wide coverage and protection achieved by the EU registration, you may see the total fee as a considerable bargain, especially where the sale or licensing of the registered design and the sales of the products realises a healthy return on your investment.

Using a representative

If you live in an EU country you don't have to use a professional representative to prosecute your design application, but applicants from outside the EU must appoint such a representative.

However, we strongly recommend that you do use a professional representative, as the laws, rules, and time limits can and do create difficulties. OHIM requires that the representative is qualified in IP matters in an EU country and is on their list of representatives. This effectively means choosing a patent attorney or a trade mark attorney as your professional representative.

Enforcing your design rights in the UK and the EU

Be vigilant about maintaining and enforcing your registered designs. They are your absolute responsibility. Keep good diary records to make sure that you do not miss paying your renewal fees.

Designs share similarities with patents in terms of dealing with suspected infringers, so check out the section on patent enforcement in Chapter 20. Where possible, we suggest resolving problems without resorting to the use of expensive lawyers and counsel – negotiating a deal that's acceptable to all the parties concerned can help you avoid court actions. You may also consider mediation as a solution to any problem areas.

Unearthing unregistered community design right

Unregistered community design offers protection from copying the design on any item. Protection last for three years after the design has been made available to the public and covers all EU countries. Like UK design right, unregistered community design is an automatic right that you don't need to apply for.

Qualifying for Design Right

To qualify for any of the registered and/or unregistered design rights, your design must be:

- **New:** This means that it must not be the same as any design that's already been made available to the public.
- **Individual:** This means that the overall impression the design gives the informed user must be different from any previous designs. In assessing individual characters, the degree of freedom of the designer should be taken into account.

Also, remember that you can't register your design if:

- ✔ More than 12 months pass between the design being disclosed and published.
- ✔ The design is dictated only by how the product works.
- ✔ The design includes parts of complicated products that can't be seen in normal use (for example, vehicle spare parts or the parts inside a computer).
- ✔ The design is offensive according to the Designs Act, the Designs Registry, and the courts.
- ✔ The design involves certain national emblems and protected flags.

As with other intellectual property rights, owning a registered design means that you can sell, lease, rent, or franchise your rights.

Chapter 12

Entering the Whimsical World of Copyright

*O*f all the types of intellectual property (IP) rights, copyright is probably the easiest to understand and certainly the easiest to acquire. However, for all its apparent simplicity, the concept of copyright resembles a fish under water: Easy to see but hard to get a good grip on. In this chapter we help you get a handle on the concept of an original work of authorship (OWA). We explain which part of an OWA is covered by copyright and show you the scope of protection copyright law provides. We also define the various kinds of work protected by copyright, analyse the rights held by a copyright owner, and cover some common copyright acquisition and ownership issues.

In this chapter we cover only the basic nature and limitations of copyright. You find full details of copyright in the Copyright, Designs & Patents Act 1988 – although we recommend you leave the interpretation of the Act to an IP professional, who specialises in the law of copyright.

If you have a patent attorney acting for you, she can advise you on lawyers who specialise in the law of copyright. If you don't have a patent attorney, you can seek advice from the Chartered Institute of Patent Attorneys or the Law Society in London.

Getting to Know Copyright

A *copyright* is primarily an exclusive right to reproduce an original work. Copyright falls to the person who created the work or to that person's employer. This is a simplified description, however. Copyright is a legal matter and consequently the full explanation is somewhat more involved and complicated.

The ownership of copyright depends on who creates the work. For example:

- ✔ If you alone create a work for your own purposes, the copyright belongs to you.

- ✔ If you're employed by a third party and the creation of the work stems from your employment, the copyright belongs to your employer.

- ✔ If you're commissioned to create a work and you're paid for doing so, the ownership of any copyright in the work depends on whether an assignment has been executed between you and the commissioner of the work. If no assignment exists, the copyright remains with you until you assign the copyright to the commissioner.

If you commission a design house to manufacture a product to your design, you must always ensure that all the IPRs, including copyright, are assigned to you upon completion of the work.

Unlike patents, which we talk about in Part II of this book, copyright is not granted by the government after a complex and expensive application process. Instead, copyright automatically attaches to an original work the minute it's created. As soon as you write your book or your song, your work is protected by copyright. You can even mark copies of your work with a legal notice including the symbol ©, as we explain in Chapter 14.

Defining an Original Work of Authorship

An *original work of authorship* (OWA) is a substantial and fixed creative work originated by its author. We break down this definition into four basic parts, which we cover in the following sections. Each section outlines one of the requirements that an OWA must meet in order to be protected by copyright.

An *author* in a OWA can be, for example:

- ✔ The writer of a book.
- ✔ The writer of music and/or lyrics.
- ✔ The designer of a piece of machinery.
- ✔ The creator of a range of furniture.
- ✔ The writer of software instructions for a computer.

A fixed creation of the mind

An OWA is the result of creativity originating in the author's mind and not merely a discovery of something that already exists. The work isn't considered 'created' until it's fixed, tangible, permanent, or stable, and reproducible or otherwise communicable. Observing something and carefully listing its characteristics is not an OWA but a mere representation of pre-existing conditions. For example, the diagnostic of a psychologist that gives only brief details of the personality profile of a patient can't be protected by copyright. However, the actual text, which may be short or quite substantial, can qualify for copyright protection for the author.

Some examples of OWAs include:

✔ Making a natural-looking plaster-cast replica of a tree trunk to serve as a pedestal doesn't require any mental creativity. But, composing a symphony that suggests wildlife sounds of a virgin forest requires many mental steps to select and arrange sounds in a pleasant composition.

✔ Giving an ad-libbed speech or improvising a musical composition doesn't result in a fixed creation and doesn't qualify as an OWA unless it's recorded simultaneously.

✔ Once upon a time, video games were denied copyright protection on the grounds that the moving images occurred only in response to a player's commands and were, therefore, not fixed and reproducible. Eventually, it was recognised that coded instructions stored on a computer chip dictate everything on the screen. For example, by manipulating a joystick, mouse, or other control device, the player selects a series of pre-recorded program sequences. Thus, the screen images are recorded and also reproducible at will.

For your own protection, you must make a record of your work as early as possible. If you develop a teaching method or an aerobic dance routine, ask somebody to record the routine as you go along. If you create an original knitting design, take pictures of your knitting. Keep track of the date you recorded and distributed your OWA – you need that information later, as we explain in Chapter 14.

Even an E.T. can create an OWA – with some help

A few years ago, a court in the US was asked to decide whether a text that had been 'authored' by celestial beings qualified as an original work of authorship – like asking whether Moses could have obtained a copyright on the Ten Commandments. In a thoughtful exercise of common sense sprinkled with a pinch of scepticism, the court declared that, so long as the text was transcribed, compiled, and collected by mortals, it was protected by copyright.

A substantive and non-trivial mental activity

To qualify as an OWA, the work must have significant complexity, scope, length, or duration. To test compliance with a requirement, you have to use different measuring sticks, according to the nature of the work.

Written, pictorial, and non-musical works must have a certain degree of complexity or length. Here are some examples:

- Titles, slogans, maxims, two-verse poems, and reproductions of common geometrical figures don't meet the test. On those grounds, the slogan, 'You got the right one, uh-huh' used to promote Pepsi-Cola was denied copyright protection. That was also the fate of the folder icon by Apple Computer, Inc., depicting a common cardboard folder together with the term 'Waste Basket' to identify a discarded folder.

- A limerick barely passes the threshold of substantiality.

- A simple line drawing of a dove in the hand of Pablo Picasso is considered complex (and original) enough to get copyright protection.

Sounds are measured with a shorter yardstick than are words. In a musical composition, a single distinctive bar may be sufficient to deserve protection. The four opening notes of Beethoven's Fifth Symphony, used as a hook throughout the symphony, are a case in point. They would have enough substance to deserve copyright protection if they were composed today. Of a more recent vintage is the one measure 'hook' of another commercial song used in connection with Pepsi products. Although it consists of only four repetitions of the phrase 'Uh-oh' in rap music rhythm, that jingle is protected by copyright.

A non-functional creation

To qualify as an OWA, the work must not be primarily functional, such as a belt buckle or other useful article. However a degree of functionality in a work isn't necessarily fatal to its protection.

An architectural drawing has a function – to guide the construction of a building. But its functionality resides in the use of the drawing and isn't inherent in the drawing itself. The drawing embodies an imaginative rendition of a non-existing structure, including a representation of its shapes, proportions, arrangements of openings, and other characteristics that reflect the architect's talented vision, and so is protected by copyright.

The mere rules of a board game aren't protected because they're purely functional steps; however, the text may be copyright protected. Moreover, the decorative graphics on a game board, or the design of a chess piece that represents a whimsical character, are non-utilitarian, protected creations. Indeed, the *ornamental design* of a useful article, as distinguished from the article itself, may be considered a visual OWA.

For example, a water jug may simply be a conventional design like many others and isn't capable of copyright protection even though you've produced sketches of your proposal. On the other hand, you may draw a water jug having a novel shape and configuration; consequently, you own the copyright in the sketches of the novel water jug.

However, copyright of an ornamental design only applies if the design can be identified separately from, and exists independently of, the article's function. For example, the shape of a belt buckle – no matter how creative – can't be separated from the buckle and isn't protected by copyright. But a medallion depicting a novel feature affixed to the face of a buckle is protected because it isn't primarily a functional element.

An original work

The originality of an OWA doesn't imply that it's new, unusual, or innovative. The work is original if it isn't copied from a pre-existing source and is independently created. It doesn't matter that the exact same work was created in another place or time by someone else, so long as the author wasn't exposed to, or influenced by, the earlier work. This state of affairs may arise when an occurrence (severe flooding for example) is reported widely in the press and on television and results in similar creative processes being experienced by you and some other person. You may both propose more or less the same preventative measures for keeping your dwellings safe from flood damage. You draw up your proposal and mark your drawings with the date and the © symbol only to find, perhaps through the publication of the other person's patent application, great similarity between the two proposals that were created in isolation one from the other.

If you create an OWA that's based on or incorporates one or more pre-existing works, the copyright attaches only to that part of the OWA that's exclusively yours. For instance, if you write a cookbook, you may select recipes from various sources, including previously published cookbooks. You then arrange those recipes in a sequence and format of your choice, describe them in your own words, and add comments and illustrations – all mental steps that together constitute an OWA protected by copyright. If you transcribe the recipes as you find them in a cookbook (with the authors' permission) you get no copyright in the copied text. The recipes themselves function merely as processes and aren't protected by copyright.

Determining What May and May Not Be Protected by Copyright

In order for a copyright to attach to your work, your work must be an OWA meeting all the basic requirements that we list in the section 'Defining an Original Work of Authorship' and a few more requirements spelled out in the Copyright, Designs & Patents Act 1988. The concept of OWAs is elastic and is occasionally extended to cover things that the law hasn't anticipated. For example, video games, inconceivable a few decades ago, are now considered OWAs. In this section we give the low-down on what is and isn't considered copyrightable.

Considering copyright categories

OWAs fall into various categories. A work may fit into one or several categories or incorporate several works falling in different categories. For example, a puppet show is a dramatic work and a choreographic work. A motion picture is an audiovisual work that may include literary, musical, dramatic, choreographic, and pictorial works.

Your OWA may fall into one of the following categories:

- **Architectural works:** Building designs that are embodied in any tangible medium of expression, including buildings and architectural plans or drawings. Each architectural work includes the overall form, as well as the arrangement and composition of spaces and elements in the design. However, it excludes individual standard features such as doors, windows, and balconies.

- **Dramatic works:** Any work that incorporates the spoken word, including accompanying music, to be performed by one or more characters.

- **Literary works:** Any written or recorded sequence of words, numbers, or symbols, including the instructions that constitute a computer program.

- **Motion pictures and other audiovisual works:** Works that consist of a series of related images together with any accompanying sounds that are designed to be shown on a machine or device such as a projector, cassette or disc player, or other electronic contraption.

- **Musical works:** All musical compositions and their accompanying lyrics, from commercial jingles to epic operas.

✔ **Original designs of useful articles:** Protection applies to the original design of a useful article that makes the article attractive or distinctive in appearance to the public. Useful articles include practical objects from safety pins to locomotives as long as the designs are novel.

✔ **Original mask works for semiconductor chip products:** Mask works look like photonegative films and are used to manufacture multilayered microchip circuits. They're used in photo-sensitive processes to form the intricate semiconductor layers and metallic connecting straps that constitute an integrated circuit.

✔ **Pantomimes and choreographic works:** Any non-vocal performance, from classical ballet, through bump-and-grind gyrations, to trapeze acts and clowns' silent routines. Even a clown routine can be written down or recorded in some tangible way that lends itself to being protected by copyright!

✔ **Pictorial, graphic, and sculptural works:** Two- and three-dimensional works of fine, graphic, and applied art, including photographs, prints, art reproductions, maps, globes, charts, diagrams, models, technical drawings, and architectural plans.

✔ **Sound-recording works:** Works that result from the fixation of a series of musical, spoken, or other sounds on phonograph records, tapes, digital memory chips, or any other embodying device. The sound-recording category doesn't include the sounds themselves, only the result of preparing, directing, recording, mixing, editing, and other steps in the recording process.

Looking at works without copyright protection

Some works don't pass the OWA test and therefore aren't copyrightable. Whether a particular work falls into one of these exceptions isn't easily resolved because you can't apply any defined rule of thumb. Lawyers and judges must rely on common sense and a continuing familiarity with legal precedents when they give opinions or rulings on these issues. Categories of works that don't benefit from copyright protection include the following:

✔ **Clothing designs:** Fashion designers must resort to registered designs to protect their creations.

✔ **Information in the public domain and containing no original presentation:** Calendars, scientific charts and displays, and statistical charts.

✔ **Transitory works:** Unrecorded improvised speeches, radio and television broadcasts, and unrecorded dramatic and choreographic performances.

✔ **Typeface designs:** However, computer programs used to generate unprotectable typeface designs can be protected by copyright. See the section 'Separating facts from expressions in computer programs' for more information

✔ **Unsubstantial works:** Titles, names, short phrases, slogans, common symbols and designs, mere listings of ingredients or contents, bumper stickers, and traffic signs.

Discovering the Scope of Copyright Protection

In this section we cover one of the most subtle and critical aspects of copyright protection, which is the source of a great deal of misunderstanding and endless litigation. The golden rule of copyright is simple to define but much harder to interpret. Copyright doesn't protect the idea behind an OWA; rather, copyright protects the *original expression* of that idea.

In no case does copyright protection for an original work of authorship extend to any idea, procedure, process, system, method of operation, concept, principle, or discovery, regardless of the form in which it's described, explained, illustrated, or embodied in such work.

Distinguishing between the fact or idea embodied in a work and the manner in which the author expresses that fact or idea isn't always easy – but in the following sections we try to illustrate how to make the distinction.

Comparing facts and expression of facts

Consider the following scenario: Maggie, a newspaper journalist, witnesses a major traffic accident involving a famous rock singer. Maggie writes her article at the scene of the accident on her notebook computer and sends it to her editor, via unsecured email. However, before Maggie's editor has a chance to read the email, a local TV station intercepts the message and broadcasts a special announcement relating to the accident using only the facts in Maggie's pilfered message.

Does Maggie's newspaper have a cause of action for copyright infringement against the local TV station? The answer, like the answer to every legal question, is: 'It depends.' The answer depends on whether the local TV station reported only the facts of the accident, which aren't protected by copyright, or whether the TV station copied Maggie's exact words and phrases – that is, the manner in which she *expressed* those facts – in which case there may be infringement. However, if Maggie used a telegraphic style to draft her report, as we show below, the message doesn't have a substantial amount of original expression and no copyright protection can attach to it.

> *Mond. – 4pm – Accident in the High Street – Rock WIGGLEBUTT's limo bumps milkman's van – Singer taken unconscious to A&E hosp. – suspected neck injury.*

That was an easy one to resolve. We raise the ante in the next section.

Unlocking the flow of ideas

The purpose of copyright is to permit the free flow of ideas, as the following example shows.

Sam writes a successful novel about John Applebrown, an American who traces his ancestry to a famous British lord and goes to England to look for remaining relatives. When John Applebrown reaches England, he locates and eventually falls in love with a distant cousin who's heir to a great fortune.

Maxine, inspired by John Applebrown's story, decides to write the saga of Suho Chizu, a Japanese-American who discovers that her great-grandfather was a powerful shogun. Suho Chizu travels to the Land of the Rising Sun and finds a cousin in a high government position who offers her marriage.

Do you think that there's a copyright infringement here? Again, it depends. The concept of someone looking into his or her ancestry, discovering an illustrious foreign lineage, and then locating and eventually marrying a rich or powerful relative in his or her country of origin may be considered a 'scène à faire' – a French phrase meaning loosely 'a story to be told'. A 'scène à faire' is a basic idea or concept excluded from copyright protection. However, if Maxine copied some of Sam's flowery sentences or used some of the same colourful characters that lend life and interest to Sam's book, Sam has a good cause of action against Maxine and her publisher.

As the details of a 'scène à faire' develop, *protected expression* begins to emerge. That's a situation in which the storyline in Maxine's book is the same or very similar to that in Sam's book. You can't copy a very complex plot with impunity, even if the imitator's writing style is quite different from the original author's. Determining when someone crosses the line isn't always obvious. In a nutshell, unless the author adds distinctive twists to the basic scenario, basic plots such as 'boy meets girl, boy loses girl, boy gets girl' won't be protected.

Separating facts from expressions in computer programs

In this section we delve into the intricacies of copyright and computer programs. In what most people call a creative and welcome expansion of copyright protection, a few years ago coverage was extended to computer programs.

A *computer program* is a set of statements or instructions used to bring about a certain result, regardless of the form in which the program is embodied. The program source code, and the object code burned as ones and zeros into a read-only memory chip, are protected by copyright. However, the process performed by the computer program isn't protected. Therefore, you can write a program to perform the same functions as someone else's program, as long as you don't copy their code. For example, of the many accounting programs out there, as long as each is written without copying the code from another program, all the programs are protected.

You can draw an analogy with the plot of a novel, like the one we discuss in the section 'Unlocking the flow of ideas', to determine how much of the original program is protected. The process run by the computer corresponds to the 'scène à faire' of the book. If the program is very simple and there's only one practical way to code the instructions, the expression of the process has no substance – it's merely an idea or concept and therefore can't be protected. However, as the program becomes more elaborate, it acquires distinctive characteristics that reflect a unique way to code the program. Because this particular approach isn't the only way to 'express' the program, the approach that the original programr selects is protected.

The issue of which components of a computer program are protected goes to the core of the idea/expression conundrum. The components issue is extremely important because copyright has, by far, become the preferred method for protecting software. In software infringement cases, the courts have refined the criteria used to separate protectable expression from unprotectable ideas and concepts. The last chapter on the subject probably hasn't been written yet, so if you're dealing with similar issues, check with a computer law specialist.

Working Out What Copyright Can Do for You

As the author of an OWA, you have some exclusive rights to control how your creation is used. Those rights extend far beyond preventing others from copying your work – we aim to clarify them in this section. Like patent rights, copyright are subject to a time limitation. Also, some exceptions in specific circumstances allow other people fair use of your work without your permission.

Reading your rights

Copyright endows you, the owner of an OWA, with a number of *exclusive rights* or powers that you alone can exercise. In this sections we discuss the nature and scope of these exclusive rights applied to the various categories of works.

Dealing with duplication

The primary and most important right held by the creator or owner of an OWA, regardless of its category, is to exclude others from duplicating the work. The mere copying is what's forbidden, even if the copy is never used. Here are some examples:

- You can't make a copy of your own portrait bought from a photographer without infringing on the photographer's copyright. The fact that you paid good money for the original and some copies of the portrait doesn't automatically transfer the copyright to you.

- The minute you duplicate a pirated copy of a song or computer program onto your hard drive, you commit an act of copyright infringement.

- You can't download or install a legitimate copy of software without a licence to do so.

- Using popular music as background for your home video production is a clear violation of the composer's or songwriter's copyright.

Prohibiting preparation of derivative works

Based on one or more pre-existing works, a *derivative work* can be a translation, musical arrangement, dramatisation, fictionalisation, motion picture, sound recording, art reproduction, abridgment, or other form in which a previous work is recast, transformed, or adapted. *Adapted* covers many activities, such as making editorial revisions, annotations, elaborations, or any other modification that by itself is original and substantive enough to qualify as an OWA. Nobody has the right to make a derivative work of your OWA without your permission. Some examples of derivative works include:

- A statue or puppet drawn from a cartoon character.

- A TV sitcom based on a novel.

- A photograph of a statue (unless the statue is in a public place).

- Modification of a computer program to make it compatible with a different hardware or software product.

In the US a young man wrote a script for a sequel to a popular motion picture. He sent it, unsolicited, to the movie's producer, asking for compensation if his script was used. When a film based on his script was released and the producer didn't respond to requests for payment, the scriptwriter sued, claiming infringement of copyright. The producer counterclaimed for copyright infringement and won the case. The young fellow had no right to write a sequel to the original film without permission of the copyright owner, and consequently he acquired no right in his own creation. Worse, the script was an unauthorised derivative work that infringed on the copyright of the original film.

The situation is considered to be the same in the UK, so beware if you intend to adapt an earlier work without first seeking the author's consent. If in doubt about your legal position, obtain the advice and opinion of a copyright lawyer.

In order to spice up the sauce, here are a couple of exceptions to the prevention of derivative works:

✔ The owner of the copyright of a sound recording can't legally prevent someone from making a recording that faithfully simulates the sounds of the original recording, so long as the new work records a different performance. However the owner of the copyright of the song or other recorded OWA can.

✔ A derivative work consisting of photographs or paintings of a building or other architectural work is permitted.

Ruling out handouts

Distributing copies or adaptations of a work, whether by public sale, free distribution, rental, lease, or loan, is an infringement, even if you didn't actually make the copies. For example, copying a clipping from a newspaper or magazine about the impact of second-hand tobacco smoke and giving copies to all your chain-smoking relatives is a no-no. So is passing a copy of a spreadsheet program, licensed only to you, to one of your associates.

Barring public performances

You can prevent the public performance of a work protected by copyright that falls under one of the following categories: literary, musical, dramatic, pantomimes and choreographic, and motion picture and other audiovisual work.

If you own a copyright on a piece of popular music, you can prevent anyone else from playing a recording of it in public, such as background to an exercise class or at a university graduation ceremony (see Chapter 20 about performing licences).

A radio or TV station can't broadcast any music or video programme without a licence from the copyright owner. In Chapter 20, We explain how public broadcasters obtain such licences.

Proscribing public display

Not only the performance, but also the mere public display of a literary, musical, dramatic, pantomime or choreographic work, pictorial, graphic, or sculptural work, or an individual image from a motion picture or other audiovisual work can be prohibited by its copyright owner. For example, an unauthorised display of a protected statue in an art gallery is a copyright infringement. In addition, public display of sheet music, textual documents, or photographs of a ballet performance are controlled by copyright.

Quashing digital audio transmissions

The digital transmission of words or music from a sound recording is forbidden without a licence from the copyright owner. The transmission restriction is key in the music industry's attempt to control the peer-to-peer music sharing practices that are so common between Internet users.

Protecting your artistic reputation – moral rights

A *work of visual art* is defined as a painting, drawing, print, still photograph, or sculpture existing in a single copy or in a series of a signed and consecutively numbered limited edition. If you create a work of visual art, during your lifetime you've certain rights designed to give you credit for your work and protect your reputation even if you transfer your copyright in the work to someone else. You can:

- Claim authorship of the work.

- Prevent your name from being used as the author of a work that you didn't create.

- Prevent any intentional distortion, mutilation, or modification of one of your works that's detrimental to your honour or reputation, as well as prevent your name from being used as the author of such a work.

- Prevent the intentional or grossly negligent destruction of any OWA of recognised stature, such as a piece of public art or the work of a renowned artist.

Knowing your limitations

If you read the section 'Reading your rights', you may feel a bit nervous about the number of times you've infringed on copyright. If all these copyright owners' rights were always enforced, we'd all be in jail. But those rights have numerous limitations, restrictions, exceptions, and exemptions, as we explain in this section.

Noting that nothing lasts for ever

The length of protection in an OWA depends upon the nature of the OWA. In the UK the terms are as follows:

- ✔ 70 years after the death of the author of a literary, dramatic, musical or artistic work including a photograph.

- ✔ For a film, 70 years after the last to survive of:

    • the principal director

    • the author(s) of the screenplay and dialogue

    • the composer of any music specially created for the film

- ✔ 50 years from the year of publication in respect of sound recordings.

- ✔ 50 years for broadcasts.

- ✔ 25 years for published edition of the whole or part of any part of one or more literary, dramatic or musical works.

Outside of the UK and the European Economic Area, the terms of copyright protection may be different.

An extension of protection after the lapsing of a period of copyright in a literary, dramatic, musical, or artistic work may be protected by 'publication right' if such works have never been made available to the public. 'Publication right' gives an automatic right to the first person who makes a relevant work or film available to the public within the European Economic Area. The period of the extension is 25 years from the time that the work is made available to the public and gives similar rights to those given by copyright.

A copyright always extends to December 31st of the year of expiration.

Losing control

After you sell or otherwise transfer a copy or recording of your copyright work (see Chapter 13 for ownership-issues info), you can't prevent the resale or transfer of that copy and you can't continue to collect a fee or royalty every time it changes hands either.

Playing fair

The concept of fair use allows others to use your copyright work (published or unpublished) without your permission. Of course, fairness is one of those subjective criteria about which you and the user of your work may disagree – so the law spells out what is fair use of copyright material. Copying is allowed for:

- ✔ Reviews or criticism of the work

- ✔ News reporting

- ✔ Teaching (including classroom use where text from a copyright work is copied onto a chalkboard or whiteboard)

- ✔ Scholarship

- ✔ Research

Four factors determine whether the use of the original work is fair:

- ✔ The purpose and character of the use, including whether the work is used for a commercial or a non-profit educational purpose. A commercial, for profit activity is unlikely to be characterised as fair use.

- ✔ The nature of the work. A work that represents a lot of talent or considerable labour is less subject to fair use than a cheap or trivial one. For instance, a cheap novel carries less weight than a public monument or sculpture, and a home-made video production less than a sophisticated ballet performance.

- ✔ The amount and substantiality of the portion used in relation to the entire work. Lifting three or four pages from a three hundred page novel is more likely to be tolerated than reproducing an entire short poem. However, don't count on it. It may transpire that the three or four pages form the core of the original plot for the novel and you then find yourself having to defend an action for infringement.

- ✔ The effect upon the market or the value of the copyrighted work. A teacher can't routinely make and distribute copies of an entire textbook in order to save the students the cost of buying the textbook.

Claiming exemptions and privileges

Some activities that would otherwise infringe on a copyright are allowed for specific non-profit, charitable, or educational purposes.

- **Computer programs:** You may make one copy of a computer program as part of your use of the program or for your archives without permission from the copyright owner. You can also adapt that copy to your hardware. It isn't an infringement to let your computer generate an extra copy of a program to use for maintenance or repair. The archival copy may be transferred with the sale of the original program, but the repair copy must be destroyed when the maintenance or repair is done. Most program licences don't allow you to transfer the program to another computer, even if the computer with the original program is destroyed.

- **Copies for visually impaired people:** Non-dramatic literary works reproduced or distributed as copies or recordings in specialised formats exclusively for use by blind or visually impaired people are copyright exempt – Braille copies of a text being an obvious example of this type of exemption.

- **Ephemeral recordings:** Radio and television studios may make temporary recordings of their broadcast programmes for internal use, under certain conditions.

- **In-house retransmissions:** Some secondary retransmissions of the performance or display of a work may be exempt under certain circumstances and settings, such as by a hotel or apartment house to individual rooms or flats.

- **Library and archive copies:** Public librarians and archivists may reproduce and distribute one copy or recording of a work for a non-commercial purpose, providing that a notice of copyright appears on the reproduced copy or recording.

- **Private transmissions:** Retransmitting the performance or display of a work for public reception on a single receiving apparatus (such as a home theatre) is exempt if the public isn't charged and you don't retransmit it publicly. For example, if you appear on a TV show, you can receive the programme on your regular TV set then rig a cable connection to communicate it to a large plasma screen on your patio for a viewing party.

- **Recordings for personal use:** Finally, an exemption familiar to everybody. You may record a radio or television programme while it's played on the air for later listening or viewing by you and the members of your household. You may not, without permission from the copyright owner, copy, sell, lend, or publicly play your recording.

- **Teaching materials:** Teachers can perform or display a copyright protected work for their students in a face-to-face teaching activity in the classroom.

Chapter 13

Untangling Ownership Issues

. . . .

In This Chapter

▶ Getting the copyright in a work made for hire

▶ Transferring your copyright

▶ Checking the copyright status of a work

. . . .

Copyright law casts a very broad net. It's hard to imagine a human endeavour that doesn't have a copyrightable component. Whether you write a book, sell ice cream from a van, coach aerobic exercises, teach a knitting course, sell property, or design a sophisticated scientific instrument, copyright issues affect you.

This book is a literary original work of authorship (OWA) and therefore copyrightable. The illustrations in this book – as well as the decoration on your ice cream van – are pictorial OWAs. As you bounce about your exercise studio, teach your knitting class, or broker house sales, you use recorded music, textbooks, audiovisual teaching aids, or multiple listing compilations, all works protected by copyright. The list of OWAs that you generate or use when you develop, manufacture, and market your scientific instrument – from advertising brochures and technical manuals to mask works and computer programs – is endless.

Each of these OWAs raises ownership and protection issues and conceals potential legal pitfalls for the unwary. As you create your masterpiece, or hire someone to do it for you, understanding who created an OWA, and consequently who holds the rights to it, is vitally important. An oversight or mistake in this area can have disastrous consequences.

In this chapter, we talk about how to decide whether you own a copyright (and if not, who does), how to give or sell your copyright to someone else, and how to track down copyright ownership. Often these issues are fairly simple and you can figure out the information yourself. But if this chapter seems incredibly confusing, ask your IP (intellectual property) attorney to help you unravel the tangle of copyright ownership.

Staking a Claim: Making Sure That You Own the Copyright

Any original creation is a potentially valuable intellectual property right. When you start throwing around the word 'valuable', you know that things won't remain simple for long. If you've been locked away in your home office writing a great novel or developing the next world-famous pantomime routine, the question of who owns the original work of authorship (OWA) is probably simple – you do. However, if you develop a script while working for a movie production studio, or write the movie's background music as a freelance composer, chances are the studio owns the copyright in your creation.

Many of the difficulties and costly litigations that you can have with copyright involve questions of ownership. The usual participants in the great ownership debate are you and your associates, your employer or employees, your collaborators, and your contractors. Anyone who contributes to an OWA may have a full or partial interest in the work. You need to be aware of how the legalities of ownership affect your role in the creative process.

Juggling joint ownership

If you work on your own (not as someone's employee) with a co-author, you and your co-author jointly own the copyright, unless you have an agreement to the contrary. Joint ownership of the copyright, just like business partnerships and marriages, can be messy and quickly turn nasty when a disagreement surfaces. Joint owners of a copyright must provide details of monies received and provide a full account to each other for any benefit realised from the licensing or sale of the work or the copyright – and share the benefit on equal terms or in accord with the terms and conditions of an agreement between them. However, a joint owner can exploit the copyright, or even transfer it to a third party, without permission from the other owner – which can lead to very awkward situations.

If you can't avoid joint ownership of a copyright, make sure that you and the other joint owner sign a written comprehensive agreement that spells out all critical and potentially contentious issues. You can obtain copies of agreements from any number of sources, particularly companies providing IP advice. Usually, such companies provide copies of agreements on their Web site and allow copies to be downloaded for a price. You can simply search for 'copyright agreements' on a search engine such as Google. Potentially contentious issues may include:

✔ **Joint or separate rights to exploit the copyright.** You must decide whether or not you and the other co-owner are equal owners, and whether you can exploit the copyright jointly or allow each other to take advantage of any opportunity separately. You must also decide whether to pool your benefits or let each party keep their own income from their share of the copyright.

✔ **Percentages of ownership.** The interest of co-owners of a copyright can be apportioned in any percentages the parties decide. If you can't agree, the law presumes that all parties have an equal, undivided interest in the copyright.

✔ **Right to prepare a derivative work.** A derivative work can become more lucrative than the original, even to a point where there's no more market for the original.

For example, John and Rob together devise an asset management computer program, tailored to Rob's tool-rental business. Both are co-authors of the program and co-owners of the copyright. Dave, Rob's friend who operates vending machines, hears about the program and asks Rob to help him write a similar program for his business.

Starting with the tool-rental management program, Rob and Dave develop a more sophisticated program to manage Dave's vending machine operation. The new program adapts easily to other businesses. Rob and Dave, finding more and more applications for the program, embark on a very lucrative licensing venture.

Rob must account to John for all proceeds collected from the exploitation of the initial program. However, knowing that the new program is far more elaborate than the original program, Rob thinks that John only deserves a very small percentage of the proceeds from the second program (if any).

If John sues Rob and Dave for a reasonable share of those proceeds, a court would most likely award half of the proceeds to Dave (the half owner of the new program) and a quarter of the proceeds to each Rob and John, the owners of equal and undivided shares of the copyright in the original program, upon which the derivative work is based.

Here's why: Although John and Rob created the original program, when the second program was developed, Dave also became a part-owner. If John didn't want any more partners, he should've specified that each party has veto power over a joint authorship of a derivative work with a third party, in the original agreement.

✔ **Succession in case of death or disability of one party.** Succession laws vary from country to country. You can bypass those laws with a well-drafted agreement that guarantees an orderly transfer of the copyright to the surviving co-owner upon paying a stipulated sum to the deceased party's estate. You can fund and guarantee that payment by each taking an insurance policy on the life of the other.

✔ **Transferring interest to a third party.** If you aren't comfortable with the idea of being in joint ownership with a stranger, you should arrange for each party to have first choice in buying the interest of the other.

All these considerations have important legal implications that deserve the attention of a competent lawyer and preferably one who practises IP, particularly the laws of copyright.

Considering commissioned works: When the creator isn't the legal owner

A commissioned work is an OWA created by an employee within the scope of his or her employment, or an OWA commissioned under a special assignment agreement – which we explain in the following sections. In both cases the legal owner of the work isn't its actual creator, but the employer, or the commissioning party, whether that's an individual or a corporation. The copyright in a commissioned work never belongs to the actual creator of the work.

Employees' creations

An *employee* is someone regularly employed by another person – the *employer* – and subject to an agreed salary for their employment. Freelance operators and independent contractors aren't considered employees in the context of creations – for more on these, see the next section.

The law considers the employer to be the author of the work based on the theory that an employee is just a robot that executes the task upon the direction of their boss: 'Bob, fix me a cup of tea. And while you're at it, write me a computer program.' It's all in a day's work.

The ownership aspect of copyright law is totally inconsistent with patent law, which requires that the genuine inventor be listed on a patent application (as we explain in Chapter 10).

Works commissioned from non-employees

A creation by a non-employee is a commissioned work if it falls within one of the nine qualifying works categories in the following list and the work is specifically commissioned under a written contract, including an assignment of copyright in the works, signed by both parties. If the written contract doesn't include an assignment of the copyright, the commissioner may have difficulties later on when suing for infringement of copyright. The reason is that the commissioner would have to show the Court that he owned the copyright before being allowed to sue anyone for infringement.

- ✔ **Answers for a test:** Usually provided at the back of a maths text book and giving the answers to the problems set out in the text book.

- ✔ **Atlases:** Any collection of territorial maps and related textual material.

- ✔ **Compilations:** A work formed by collecting and assembling pre-existing materials or data. The way that this material is selected and arranged creates a work that, as a whole, constitutes an OWA. A collective work is also a compilation, but a compilation can be authored by a single person. Reference works such as dictionaries and lexicons, directories, cookbooks, and anthologies qualify as compilations.

- ✔ **Contributions to a collective work:** A *collective work,* such as a periodical, anthology, or encyclopaedia, contains a number of separate and independent contributions assembled into a collective whole. Any contribution to such a work is a commissioned work. When two or more non-employees contribute separate portions of a single work under a requisite agreement, the commissioner of the works legally becomes the sole owner of the copyright and is presumed to have all rights in the work as long as the agreement includes the assignment of the copyright in the work.

- ✔ **Instructional text:** Any work intended for use in a systematic teaching activity, ranging from scholarly treatises to simple ABC books used by nursery schools.

- ✔ **Parts of motion pictures and other audiovisual work:** Composing background music or designing graphic stage sets for a film, writing a script for a teaching DVD, or laying out a dancing act for a movie ballroom scene are examples of qualifying works.

- ✔ **Supplementary work:** A work prepared for publication that is adjunct to a work by another author, such as an introduction, preface, foreword, epilogue, afterword, conclusion, illustration, explanation, revision, update, commentary, map, diagram, chart, table, editorial notes, musical arrangement, answer sheet, bibliography, appendix, glossary, index, or anything that may assist in the use of the principal work. (However, frequently, if an author is well-known, he retains rights to his introduction.)

✔ **Test:** Such as MENSA, any literary or graphical work that solicits a subject's written, oral, or physical answers or reactions.

✔ **Translation:** From written or aural text in one language to another language.

A contract commissioning a work from a non-employed third party must be signed by all parties and must include an assignment of the copyright in the work in order that the commissioner owns the copyright in the work!

Changing Owners: Transferring Interest in a Copyright

The copyright to an OWA can be sliced like a sponge cake into separate ownership portions – legally called *interests* – which you can then assign – *transfer* – to different people. You can also assign to different parties all the various exclusive rights of a copyright owner that we painstakingly list in Chapter 12. For example, a motion picture studio can get the right to make a TV sitcom from your story, and a magazine can serialise the same story over a number of weeks.

The law is very clear that an OWA isn't created until it's *fixed* (in a tangible or reproducible state, as we describe in Chapter 12). Furthermore, when a work is prepared over a period of time, the portion of it that is fixed at any particular point in time constitutes the work as of that time.

You can only transfer copyright ownership on what is fixed at the time of the transfer. The transfer doesn't automatically cover any part of the work that you create and fix in the future unless an assignment for the transfer of copyright in a work specifically includes future copyright in the commissioned work that results from improvements in the work.

The basic rule of transferring an entire copyright interest is to get it in writing. Any transfer, other than by court order, inheritance, or other automatic manner specified by law, is invalid unless it's in a written *conveyance* (the transfer of an interest from one person to another) signed by the owner.

Investigating the Status of a Copyright

To use copyrighted material in your own work, you need permission from the owner of the copyright. For example, imagine yourself in one of the following situations:

✔ You write a coffee-table book about Renaissance gardens. You find an encyclopaedia containing beautiful engravings of wild roses and you want to use the engravings to illustrate your own work. You need to find the owner of the copyright covering the engravings and get permission to copy them.

✔ You write a short ditty for a high school performance and want to use the music of a popular song with your own lyrics. You need permission to create your derivative work from the song's copyright owner.

✔ You own a small bronze statue of a Harry Potter character that you'd like to reproduce as part of a painting or photographic print. You can't do it without permission from the copyright owner.

✔ You want to incorporate a number of pre-existing OWAs in your own creation, but don't have the time or resources to obtain necessary licences or permissions from copyright owners.

Your course of action in any of these four situations isn't easy. In addition, the older the work, the harder identifying the current copyright owner becomes. If you identify and find the copyright owner, getting a licence or permission can be like pulling teeth, unless you're ready to offer a good amount of cash.

Before you spend time and money searching for a copyright owner, keep in mind that finding the owner is no guarantee that you'll readily get the licence or permission you need. The copyright owner may be unwilling to grant you one or may be under a legal obligation to prohibit anyone from using the work. The price you pay for the permission or licence sometimes isn't worth the additional charges that the copyright owner's attorney may charge to prepare the necessary paperwork.

If you can't secure the permission, don't even think of using the copyrighted material without it. As we show you in Chapter 20, a copyright owner can get a relatively large damage award for a single infringement act – without having to prove any loss resulting from the infringement. Not good news for you.

The general guidelines below can help you find the copyright owner and secure permission:

✔ If you're absolutely certain that a work has been available in the market place anywhere in the world for a considerable number of years, you can safely assume the work is in the public domain. However, make sure that you're not copying a more recent edition of a work that may still be under copyright.

✔ To use text from a book, first contact the publisher. You may get lucky and talk with a very understanding attorney or licensing agent who can answer all your questions and give you the licence or permission you're after. Based on our experience, however, even if you find this elusive attorney or agent, they're unlikely to be that co-operative. Unless you get a final refusal by the copyright owner, you need to keep digging. To find the copyright owner, first check the copyright notice on the work. You may also want to check with the Copyright Licensing Agency (www.cla.co.uk) who can provide info.

✔ If you're interested in a musical work, start with the record company. If you have no luck there, try to contact a licensing agency – a clearing house that a song writer or a music publishing company uses to license record companies. You may also want to contact the Mechanical Copyright Protection Society (www.mcps-prs-alliance.co.uk) for help.

✔ When dealing with a statue or other sculptural work, consult an art dealer if you can't decipher a recognisable name on the work. The dealer may be able to identify the author and the approximate date of distribution.

✔ Consult an IP attorney.

Part IV
Making Your Mark: Protecting Your Brand Identity

In this part . . .

Sure, you're probably familiar with that little ™ trade mark symbol. But did you know that several other types of marks, including trade names, product names, logos, and service marks are just sitting there waiting for you to put them into the game as well? All these marks have a common purpose – to put an exclusive (and hopefully favourable) brand on your goods and services, giving you an edge over your competition. We devote this part to helping you to understand which marks warrant trade mark protection, and how to go about ensuring that you protect your brand.

We also demonstrate (with plenty of examples) what makes an effective mark and what types you should avoid. And after you decide to draft one or more trade marks such as names or logos, you still need to make sure that they're the best pick. We lay out a game plan that walks you through the search for look-alikes (and sound-alikes) and outline how to register and use your trade mark or service mark.

Chapter 14

Solving Your Identity Crisis

. . . .

In This Chapter

▶ Understanding the roles and functions of trade marks

▶ Making the most of your trade name or trade mark

▶ Appraising the weight of a trade mark

▶ Striving for exclusive rights by using a distinctive brand identity

. . . .

A *trade mark*, such as your company name, the brand on your product, or the catchy tagline from your marketing campaign, is a goodwill ambassador, a herald, a promise – your trade mark is the first thing a customer sees or hears about your firm or your product. This first contact often determines the customer's attitude towards your business or product. Your trade marks are your prime marketing tools and help your potential customers choose between a range of similar products and services.

When you start a new business or introduce a new product or service, you have a chance to create value out of nothing. By selecting strong, protectable, and effective trade marks, you get inexpensive protection for your enterprise and the chance to catapult your products or services into a dominant market position. Yet the majority of business people don't give the selection process much thought.

In this chapter, we define some trade mark terms and lead you through the maze of business names, trade marks, and other commercial handles and signposts that make up your brand identity. We explain how trade marks play a key role in any business, and perhaps most importantly, give you some ideas on what constitutes a distinctive and legally protectable trade name and trade mark.

Hitting the Right Mark: Taking a Trade Mark Inventory

A trade mark protects any sign or symbol that allows your customers to tell you apart from your competitors. Your trade mark might be your business name, logo, or your key advertising slogan. You can even register shapes, colours, and sounds as trade marks. For example, Orange, the telecommunications company, has secured a particular orange Pantone for their products. Similarly T-Mobile have registered the colour magenta. The EasyGroup brands hold registrations for the colour orange within the aviation class (easyJet). When the easyGroup formed easyMobile, if they proceeded to trade in the telecommunications industry using the colour orange, they would have faced opposition from Orange.

To be registrable the trade mark you choose must fulfil a number of criteria. In this section we look at what makes a distinctive trade mark. You also can't use a mark that's similar or identical to someone else's mark for the same goods and services, regardless of whether or not they have registered their mark. Although registering your trade marks gives you an exclusive right to use them, unregistered marks have some protection through the laws of *passing-off*. These laws prevent someone from taking advantage of the goodwill and reputation another person or business has generated (in effect, hoodwinking the public into thinking that their goods or services to be in some way associated to the other person's goods or services).

So you may come up with an ingenious and catchy company name, but you need to be sure that you've considered the legal aspects of using that name before you bash on to generate your fancy stationery, have a name plate engraved, and get those all-important business cards printed.

Marking your product

A *trade mark* is any name, word, phrase, slogan, symbol, design, shape, or characteristic that, when associated with a product, distinguishes it from other similar products. For example, the word 'Kodak' is a trade mark. But any characteristic of a product or package can effectively act as a trade mark – so without reading the words on the package, you may know that a yellow package identifies Kodak film and a green box identifies Fuji film.

Distinctive shapes, colours, and ornamentations of products, packaging, and places of business can act as trade marks, making up the brand identity for that product. Some well-known examples of trade marks for different goods include:

- ✔ 'Dr Pepper', a mark identifying a soft drink
- ✔ 'I Can't Believe It's Not Butter', found on a range of margarine spread
- ✔ The Swoosh or Tick symbol on Nike sportswear and goods
- ✔ The harp symbol on a can of Guinness Irish stout

✔ The lemon shape of a Jif lemon juice container

✔ The colour turquoise for Heinz baked beans

✔ Four musical notes that accompany the mention of Intel processors

The list is endless. Anything that customers can associate with a product that influences buying decisions can qualify as a trade mark. We show an example in Figure 14-1.

Figure 14-1:
Shape as a
trade mark.

Identifying your service

The rules that we identify in the previous section on marking products also apply to trade marks for services. For example, the large yellow 'M' of a food service establishment identifies a McDonald's fast-food restaurant. A squat building with a red-lined, square-topped roof designates a Pizza Hut restaurant. Here are some other well-known trade marks for services:

✔ 'Kwik Fit' for an automotive tyre repair service

✔ 'Prudential' for financial services

✔ A red cross for the services of an international charitable organisation, The Red Cross

✔ The orange colour of an airline that tells you it's part of easyJet

✔ Internet domains such as lastminute.com

✔ The panda character of the WWF wildlife charity (see Figure 14-2)

As with trade marks for products, there's no limit to what you may use to singularise your business and catch the attention of the customer.

Figure 14-2:
WWF panda.

A *certification mark*, such as those we show in Figure 14-3, is a mark used to approve or certify the origin, quality, accuracy, safety, performance, or authenticity of another's product or service. A certification mark is used not by the proprietor of the mark but by authorised users who can demonstrate that their goods or services fulfil the required characteristics. Figure 14-3 shows some well-known certification marks:

- ✔ The BSI Kitemark of the British Standards Institute
- ✔ The 'Woolmark' logo to identify goods made from 100 per cent wool

A certification mark differs from any other type of mark because its owner can't use it to qualify its own goods or services, but only the products or services of others.

Figure 14-3:
Certification
marks.

Trade marks for goods and services fall under the same laws and regulations. Certification marks and Collective marks, however, are subject to additional special formalities and requirements, which we address in Chapter 17.

Naming your company

A brand identity, or *trade name*, identifies a company. Your brand identity takes a few different forms, depending on the context:

- ✔ **Legal name:** This mark appears on tax returns, judicial and administrative documents, and other official papers. Two well-known trade marks are 'The British Petroleum Company' and 'Marks and Spencer'.
- ✔ **Shortened version of official name:** For example, BP and M&S.
- ✔ **Logo:** BP, for example, can be identified by the distinctive yellow and green flower logo.

Putting Trade Marks to Work

A distinctive and appealing trade name advantageously positions your products or services on the market, giving you a greater degree of promotion, protection, and profit. Customers easily remember and recognise the name and, therefore, are motivated to patronise your business or buy your product.

An effective trade mark plays three roles in your business scheme:

- ✔ Promoting your products or services
- ✔ Protecting you against copycat imitations and other unfair appropriation of your reputation and goodwill
- ✔ Generating profit

The distinctiveness of your trade mark translates into legal clout, which in turn helps to protect your market position. (For more on this, see the section 'Testing the Legal Strength of Trade Marks' later in this chapter.) As your trade mark gathers strength and reputation, it becomes a valuable commodity that you can exploit financially, for example through sales and licences.

Promoting your product or service

A good trade mark motivates the person who sees or hears it to buy the product or service the trade mark identifies or to head towards the company that trades under the trade mark. Here are a couple of examples:

- ✔ The trade mark 'Evian', with its refreshing imagery of Alpine mountains under glittering dewdrops, suggests refreshment to the thirsty individual and motivates him or her to buy the pure bottled water it represents.

- ✔ A travelling businesswoman arrives in town after a long overnight flight. She has an important interview and needs to have her hair professionally done. In the phone book, she spots listings for Romance Stylists and Linda's Salon. The customer has no idea about the reputation of these two establishments, but she selects the glamorous-sounding listing and gives Linda the cold shoulder. The owner of Romance Stylists has gained another customer, thanks to the motivating trade mark.

When customers experience and appreciate the quality of a product sold under a particular mark, they naturally return to it whenever faced with a choice between the known brand and several similar products. They also tend to recommend the product to friends, who identify it by its label.

Products that are identified with an inspiring and motivating trade mark may promote themselves with little or no publicity. But if your trade mark isn't very stimulating, your products must rely on their own merits or on a well-orchestrated and costly advertising campaign.

When you launch a new product under a unique and inspiring handle, the product acquires an advantageous market position that may be impregnable if subsequent competitors can't use that identifier or a similar one. For example, there's no patent or other legal impediment keeping you from manufacturing and marketing hook-and-loop fabric fastener strips. But how can you make any inroad into the market without using or referring to the name 'Velcro', which confers a dominant market position to the pre-existing product, and contributes to the product's promotion and protection.

On the other hand, a mark such as 'Treadmill' on a line of treadmill exercisers is too generic to give you much marketing clout. Because you're not the only one making treadmills, your mark would also benefit your competition. And, if you later manufacture other exercise equipment, that mark won't fit.

Protecting your product or service

When we talk about protecting your product, the first thing you may think of is a patent. However, the percentage of products on the market that are protected by patents is relatively low compared to products that derive their exclusive or advantageous market position from a strong trade mark or brand identity.

Brand loyalty

An effective trade mark favourably positions a product on the market against the competition. And anybody who introduces a new product or service can give it a protected name or mark that nobody else can use or even come close to. If the mark is fitting and memorable, the public tends to associate the mark with that product. For instance, we bet you can't name a competing brand to 'Velcro'.

After a customer is used to referring to a particular product or service by an effective *proprietary name* (legal jargon for a name that can only be used by its owner), the customer tends to ignore similar products and services with less familiar or less inspiring designations.

The long arm of the law

After a product or service is favourably positioned on the market, a strong trade mark protects it against unfair competition. The misappropriation of a trade mark or using a confusingly similar one, is prohibited by law. Even if the trade mark has not been registered, the user of the mark is protected by the laws of passing-off. Such acts can be stopped by judicial orders, which are sometimes accompanied by seizure and destruction of the counterfeit goods or the closure of the offending establishment. See the section 'Testing the Legal Strength of Trade Marks' later in this chapter, for all the ins, outs, and upside-downs on trade marks and the law. If you choose not to register your trade mark, you can be vulnerable to anyone who registers a conflicting trade mark. Even though you may have been first to trade under that name, the other party might be able to rely on their registration to prevent your continued use.

The laws of passing-off provide some protection in the UK for unregistered trade marks (refer to the earlier section 'Hitting the Right Mark: Taking a Trade Mark Inventory'). The passing-off laws protect the goodwill in a business rather than the mark itself. Reasons to register your trade mark are:

- ✔ Proving that someone is infringing your trade mark is far easier than proving that he or she is trying to pass off as you.

- ✔ You can stop deceptively similar marks to your registered trade mark, whereas you can't rely on passing-off to prevent another party from trading under a similar name, unless your unregistered mark is distinctive of your goods and services and you've acquired sufficient goodwill.

- ✔ A registered trade mark gives you protection throughout the UK, allowing you to expand the business as you see fit. Relying on passing-off to prevent others from using a conflicting sign outside the locality within which you currently trade is tricky.

✔ If there's a risk of counterfeit goods within the market that you trade, misuse or infringement of a registered trade mark isn't only a civil wrong, but a criminal offence. HM Revenue & Customs have provisions in place to seize goods or packaging bearing signs that infringe registered UK or Community trade marks. In order to obtain this service you must register your trade mark details with them.

Creating a new source of income

In ancient Egypt people believed that names had their own existence, separate from the person or thing they designated. Trade marks have turned this belief into a reality – trade marks have their own existence and are worth a lot of money. When you sell your business, the value of your trade mark can be converted into cold, hard cash. However, you can even 'sell' your trade mark and still own it, if you exploit the trade mark in one of the following ways:

✔ **Franchising:** A *franchise* is a contractual arrangement authorising another firm to render services under your trade mark, such as Subway or Thornton's. Franchising often includes some transfer of know-how and technical assistance by the franchisor to insure the success, quality, and reputation of the products or services.

Choosing marks over patents

Entrepreneurs and companies attempting to introduce a new product on the market shouldn't underestimate the broad and easily enforceable protection they can get by using a strong trade mark in place of, or in addition to, the more costly patent protection. The legal community hasn't fully appreciated the protective role of distinctive trade names. It's no wonder that business and marketing people are, in general, unaware of the extent of protection that they can get from an effective moniker or a distinctive product configuration.

A fledgling company on a tight budget and needing effective protection for its new product should seriously consider adopting a good trade mark. A trade mark may be more appropriate and, in the long run, more effective at competitively positioning the product than a patent, which takes several years and large expenditures before the patent is granted and is difficult and expensive to enforce. A patent involves a public disclosure of the product's composition or manufacturing process and has a limited life. By contrast, a trade mark can be readily created, is valid as long as it's used, and can be expeditiously enforced, as we show you in Chapter 20.

Depending on your product, a trade mark is no substitute for a strong patent, but a good one may offer just the right degree of protection necessary to propel a product or service to a secure market position.

✔ **Licensing:** A *licensing arrangement* allows someone else to manufacture your product under your mark. For example, a product sold under the Disney trade mark may have been manufactured by a licensee of The Walt Disney Company.

✔ **Merchandising:** Under this method, you lease the use of your trade mark to others on a multitude of unrelated goods. For example, if you've played with Star Wars toys, you can see how The Force is with Lucasfilm.

In a licensing, merchandising, and franchising venture, the company that owns the underlying trade mark is responsible for the authenticity and safety of the products or services. That company must, by law, exercise effective quality control over the products or services. We discuss all these options in greater detail in Chapter 19.

Although trade marks aren't expressly bought and sold, they're indirectly the most traded commodity. Consider the following:

✔ When you buy a burger and fries from McDonald's, you're paying a few pence for the use of the famous name by the restaurant's owner, along with the pounds you're handing over for the meat and potatoes.

✔ If you sell a business, you sell not only your inventory and equipment but also your *goodwill* – the company's reputation and recognition in the marketplace – that's represented by the company's trade marks.

✔ When investors buy and sell stocks, investors are influenced by the value and performance of the company, represented by its trade mark. For example, Consolidated Foods changed its name to Sara Lee in order to increase the value of that company's stock. The strategy worked and was the prime factor in doubling the value of the company's shares within the following 12 months.

Testing the Legal Strength of Trade Marks

Every IP right is based on a number of subtle legal concepts, and trade marks are no different. Your right to the *exclusive* use of a trade mark and your ability to prevent imitations depend on two factors – the *distinctiveness* of your trade mark and the *likelihood of confusion* with other existing trade marks. The more unique the name or trade mark and the more dissimilar it is from trade marks already in use, the easier it is to get court orders against a competitor trying to confuse the public with names that look, sound, or even feel like yours.

Working towards distinctiveness

In the section 'Putting Trade Marks to Work' earlier in this chapter, we explain how distinctive marks can help you promote products and services and turn a profit. In this section, we concentrate on how distinctiveness affects your ability to legally protect your name and mark in court.

Trade marks have different degrees of distinctiveness. You can't protect a name or mark that exhibits no distinctiveness at all. A name for a product that merely conveys to consumers the intended purpose of the goods, with no additional features to render the sign distinctive, isn't a worthwhile trade mark, and isn't registrable. For example, The Phone Shop for a telecommunications company, Hair Cuts for a hairdressing service, or Spring Water for a bottled water brand. An indistinctive trade mark is completely useless anyway and can even jeopardise your legal rights, as we describe in Chapter 17.

As the level of distinctiveness of your trade mark increases, so does the legal strength of your brand identity. By 'legal strength', we mean your brand identity's clout – the ability to prevent others from using the same or a confusingly similar trade name or trade mark. Position your company or product on an impregnable pinnacle by selecting very distinctive trade marks. The distinctiveness of a mark (or lack of it) can be laid out on a four-part legal strength scale:

- Generic
- Descriptive
- Suggestive
- Arbitrary

We explain each of these identifiers in the sections that follow. Only suggestive and arbitrary identifiers are inherently distinctive. Descriptive names or marks can sometimes become distinctive over time. A generic term is a dud, incapable of identifying or protecting anything.

In case you're tempted, the law doesn't extend much protection to family names. The registration of family names as trade marks is subject to some restrictions. Check out Chapters 15 and 17 for the pitfalls of using your own name as a trade name.

Starting with the generic

Generic trade names and trade marks (also *commonly descriptive* names) have no legal strength at all because they're mere dictionary definitions that apply to all products or services of a kind no matter their sources, and the courts allow no one to monopolise the common language.

How about a simple example? Previously, we pointed out that using the trade mark 'Treadmill' for treadmill exercisers isn't very creative or effective from a marketing standpoint. It also brings other baggage:

- ✔ Somebody else is probably already using the same word as part of a trade name or trade mark for a similar product, which is likely to drag you into damaging conflicts, consumer confusion, and costly litigation.
- ✔ Legally, it would be impossible to register, and therefore difficult to enforce, such a generic label against future imitations.

Selecting that mark would be a pretty dumb move. Yet hundreds of entrepreneurs make this mistake every day when they name their companies or products.

One example of a company would be a bedroom- and bathroom-product retailer who chooses 'Bed & Bath' as a trade mark. They then get upset when a competitor comes up with 'Bed, Bath & Beyond', because the newcomer is likely to steal much of the goodwill already accumulated under the mark 'Bed & Bath'. However, the original retailer can't do anything about it because the only two terms appearing in both trade marks are common English words that name the type of products sold by these businesses.

Similar reasoning shows you that a shoe shop that operates under 'Discount Shoes' can't prevent another shoe shop from placing a 'Discount Shoes' sign over its door. Likewise, 'Imported Auto Parts', 'Discount Towing', and 'Auto Repair Specialists' are also ineffective marks.

Don't succumb to the temptation of picking a generic term for your company or product because it confers no distinctiveness to your trade name or trade mark. If you go generic, you're buying a heap of trouble.

Moving on to descriptive

One notch above a generic term is a descriptive trade name or trade mark. It's not quite the dictionary definition of your product or service, as a generic name often is, but a *descriptive* trade mark still only describes a common characteristic or function of the product or service without distinguishing it from similar names.

'Vision Centre' is a descriptive trade name for optometric services. It's not a common definition, but it tells you a lot about the services provided.

Although a descriptive name is a vast improvement over a generic one, it's not the best choice unless you can put up with a degree of risk.

The law recognises that a descriptive trade name or trade mark may eventually acquire some legal strength, and be considered distinctive, through continuous and exclusive use, extensive advertising, and the development of a reputation.

Eventually, the name takes on a *secondary meaning* that identifies a specific company, product, or service.

The following names have acquired secondary meanings:

✔ The slogan 'Have a Break' for a confectionary item is highly descriptive of any snack product. However, after many years of use, it's now a registered trade mark of Nestlé under their 'Kit-Kat' brand.

✔ About 100 years ago, Ford was just a family name. Now, it has become a very distinctive brand (trade mark) of automotive products.

Reaching distinctiveness

A distinctive name is so unique that it may have no relation to the product that it identifies, or it may merely hint at some characteristics of the product. A distinctive name gives you the biggest marketing advantage and the greatest degree of legal protection. Distinctive trade marks fall into two categories:

✔ **Suggestive:** A suggestive trade mark implies, rather than describes, a characteristic of the designated product or service:

- Arriva for transport services suggests that you'll reach your destination.

- Country Life for butter immediately brings to mind being down on the farm amongst butter churns and grazing cows.

✔ **Arbitrary:** An arbitrary or fanciful trade mark is either a known word or phrase that has been given a new meaning or one that's totally made up. Both types are unique, original, and unlikely to be accidentally used by another business:

- Kodak for photographic services and products

- Esso for petrol stations

- Cadbury's for confectionary

- Lego for sets of building blocks

Arbitrary trade marks have the most legal strength. They're protected against imitation from the outset. They can muster a very broad scope of protection that goes beyond strongly similar terms, and extends over marks that merely suggest a relationship with existing designations as shown in the following section.

Courting success (and failure): Distinctiveness on trial

The protection and legal clout a trade mark provides is proportional to its distinctiveness, as demonstrated by the following court decisions. Although the strength or weakness of the identifiers wasn't the only factor weighed by the courts, the verdicts pretty much followed the rule that a good, distinctive trade mark deserves a wide scope of protection, but a weak, descriptive one must endure close competition. Consider the following cautionary tales:

✔ The owner of the distinctive Lego trademark stopped a competitor from using the mark Mego.

✔ The well-known restaurant chain Wagamama opposed the opening of a restaurant under the name Rajamama, having gathered evidence of the public being confused by the similarity of the two marks.

Avoiding the likelihood of confusion

Another factor that affects the protection afforded to any trade mark is the likelihood of confusing it with pre-existing trade marks. Laws forbid the commercial use of any trade name or trade mark that's likely to cause confusion.

When you buy a yellow package of film, you expect to find a high-quality product manufactured by the Eastman Kodak Company without reading the name on the package. You rely on the yellow colour. You'd be very upset, with good reason, if you later discover that the product was made by some fly-by-night outfit.

Fortunately for you – and Kodak – that can't happen in the UK because the law gives the Eastman Kodak Company several very powerful means to weed out unscrupulous entrepreneurs who try to ride on a well-known mark's trade dress (the yellow colour of the package) to deceive unsuspecting consumers.

How far can a company go to prevent competitors from using copies or imitations of trade marks? Or, looking at it from the opposite perspective, how close can you get to an existing trade mark when you select a name or trade dress (without getting into trouble with the law)? The short answer is very simple: It depends. The full answer is more complex. You need to consider several critical factors to assess the likelihood of confusion between trade marks. The most important is the distinctiveness of the pre-existing trade name or trade mark. Other factors to consider include the similarity of the names or marks, the similarity of the goods or services, the respective channels of commerce through which the goods are marketed, the costs of the goods, and the sophistication of the typical buyer.

We address the issue of likelihood of confusion in more depth in Chapter 16. For now, just remember that the *likelihood of confusion* test in combination with the concept of *distinctiveness* determines how much protection your trade mark enjoys.

Chapter 15

Creating the Next Household Name

In This Chapter

▶ Dissecting some good trade marks

▶ Finding out the secrets of the branding trade

▶ Avoiding disastrous names

*F*ew good trade marks come to mind in a flash of inspiration or appear by accident. A good trade mark is built painstakingly from the ground up, piece by piece, keeping the legal and marketing ramifications in mind. You can't use arbitrary or subjective approaches to find an effective name – such methods prove very unreliable – you need to apply a structured methodology.

In this chapter we don't try to magically turn you into a professional name-smith, but we do spell out the basic steps of naming methodology so you can recognise a good trade mark and brand identity when you see one – and come up with your own. Just as importantly, we give you tips to avoid naming mistakes.

Laying out all the name-coining rules would take a dozen or so chapters. In this book we simply give you the basic principles behind coining effective names the same way that lawyers master law – by studying prior cases.

After defining the basics, we analyse a number of trade marks, some more desirable than others, before suggesting some practical naming techniques.

Marketing Muscle: The Components of Good Trade Marks

Trade marks should be evaluated under two distinct criteria – marketing power and legal clout. *Marketing power* is the ability to attract customers and favourably position the business, product, or service against the competition. *Legal clout* is the capability to prevent competitors using the same, similar, or even vaguely related marks.

In Chapter 14, we touch upon the legal aspects of trade marks. Legally speaking, a good trade mark must be:

- ✔ Distinctive
- ✔ Unlikely to be confused with another trade mark

A trade mark that meets these two legal factors also provides marketing power. It's one example of those rare cosmic events where the law is pretty much in sync with the real world. And the reverse is also true: A trade mark that packs a good marketing punch is also granted broad protection by the law.

Trade marks aren't limited to names. They also include graphics, logos, and three-dimensional shapes along with some more obscure registrations for sounds, colours, and even smells (although recent case law suggests it's highly unlikely that smells will be accepted). The same rules apply for all types of trade marks. If you use a drawing of a key to identify your key-cutting shop, you're using a generic designation that anybody is free to copy – and customers feel free to ignore. Instead, call your locksmiths something original and distinctive and use a graphic representation of keys or a lock as an icon to make your shop memorable and distinctive.

You may wonder how you can give marketing power to your business name or brand identity. In this section, we start you down the marketing motorway by outlining the three tasks a successful trade mark must accomplish and by discussing some case studies. In the later section 'Trying the Tricks of the Trade', we clue you in on tools you can use to build a strong brand identity or trade mark.

If you can foot the bill, we recommend working with a specialised marketing firm to develop your trade mark. Using the information in this chapter, you can be an informed client, take an active role in the process, and ensure that the trade mark and brand identity reflects your vision. If consulting an expert is just too costly, don't fear. This chapter shows you what to look for in a name and provides a number of hands-on methods you can employ to create a great trade mark on your own.

Meeting the ABCs of building a brand

Trade marks are your goodwill ambassadors and your best advertisements. Think about a radio or TV advertisement. Its purpose is to turn the customer on to a company, service, or product. A good and effective trade mark does the same thing by:

A Attracting the *attention* of the targeted customer.

B Establishing a *bond*, relationship, or common interest with the potential customer.

C Offering a *concrete* or abstract benefit to the customer.

In a TV advert, these three tasks are often done in 30 seconds of words and images. Your challenge in creating a trade mark is to perform all these tasks with a single word, a short phrase, a graphic image, or a unique package.

Dissecting success stories

In the following examples we show you how a number of successful commercial identifiers have mastered their ABCs.

Innocent: a UK beverages trade mark

A The mark shown in Figure 15-1 gets attention with its pure sound and its angelic word association.

B Their range of smoothies are as pure and fresh as they sound, being made from 100 per cent natural ingredients. The appeal is instant to all health-conscious individuals, and those trying to up their five-a-day fruit and vegetable count, as recommended by the government.

C The mark suggests: 'Drink me to look and feel healthy – no preservatives, no colourings, just pure, fresh juices and smoothies.'

Figure 15-1:
Innocent
trade mark
name and
logo
combination.

Apple Inc.: A computer and other electronic goods manufacturer

A Two wizards from Silicon Valley in the US broke through the clutter of minicomputer manufacturer names such as Control Data, Digital Equipment, and other quasi-generic, nerdy, techno-geek branding by selecting a fresh, somewhat incongruous, and pleasantly evocative name that immediately caught the attention of the newcomers and spurred a cult-like loyalty among many of them.

B The company initially targeted the educational market, of which the company still keeps a considerable share. What more endearing and enduring symbol of education than the legendary apple little Billy takes to his teacher?

C That bonding symbol is reinforced by a sharp logo of an apple with a bite taken out of it, as we show in Figure 15-2. It holds out a powerful invitation to take a bite of the good life the company's products can bring to you. The bitten apple has become so widely known, that Apple now use its apple trade mark as a logo, without the wording.

Figure 15-2:
Apple Inc.
logo.

Amazon.com: an Internet bookseller

A The name is arbitrary and consequently very distinctive (see Figure 15-3). It's at the beginning of the alphabet, quickly noticed, and very easy to remember.

B Amazon is a very simple, easily spelled word that triggers three friendly and fascinating impressions among potential customers. First, the reference to the Amazon River conjures adventure. Second, it subliminally suggests amazement. Third, the image of Amazon warriors suggests strength. The term is fluid and yet strong and reinforces the imagery of strength and adventurous discoveries. The word is the epitome of a customer-friendly name.

C The imagery of the longest river on earth with all its tributaries spread over an immense basin symbolises the many and vast resources of the company. It tells you that you can find anything you want on its site, from A to Z.

You can really see the strength and marketing power of Amazon when you note that the company survived while other dot-coms dropped like dot-flies. Compare the success of Amazon with the early collapse of companies with generic or highly descriptive domain names, such as pets.com, garden.com, furniture.com, and all the rest.

Figure 15-3:
The Amazon logo.

amazon.com

Trying the Tricks of the Trade

Name-smiths have a broad palette of elements and concepts they can draw on to paint powerful trade marks. In this section we cover some of the basic and most effective technical and artistic name-generating approaches.

Focusing too much on your company, product, or service and forgetting your target audience is a big mistake. By taking time to analyse your potential customers, you improve your chances of choosing a name that packs a powerful punch. A number of factors help to define your audience, including the following:

- ✔ **Age group:** Know who you want to attract and their demographics. The trade mark Polly Pocket is perfect for children and in particular little girls.

- ✔ **Educational level:** You don't have to be a rocket scientist to understand and respond to marks such as Mr Sheen, Pot Noodle, King of Shaves, and The Body Shop. By contrast, Arpeggio and Rejuvia address a more sophisticated audience. Microkeratome (for an eye surgery tool) speaks only to the highly educated specialist.

- ✔ **Geography:** Where are they located? Your choice of name may benefit from implying a connection to a certain geographic location. For instance mountain spring water would carry more clout with a reference to a mountainous region with fresh water springs. 'Highland Spring' appeals far more than 'Thames Spring'!

You can play with all sorts of factors, such as income level, aspirations and even political leanings to further focus your trade mark towards a specific group of customers.

Defining the message

When deciding what message you want your trade mark to convey to your targeted audience, try to think market and audience rather than product or service. Don't tell the domestic goddess that your vacuum cleaner has a high-tech motor-and-blower assembly with sound mufflers. Tell her that your product's quiet enough to use next to her sleeping infant. Forget features. Think results. In the 'Nytol' name, the message isn't about the therapeutic ingredients of the cough medicine but the promise of a good night's sleep.

Using your imagination

We're always amazed at how clever and entertaining entrepreneurs can be when naming their dogs and pleasure boats but how dull and boring they are when selecting their brand identity and trade marks. Some people are too close to their creations to look at the market and their target customers. We think that boring techies developed the brand names Digital Equipment and Control Data. On the other hand, people with vision devised the name Apple Computer.

Devising an advertisement

Your trade mark operates as an advert. A good start to your naming process is to practise writing a script for the best advert you can dream up for your company, product, or service.

Be serious about your advert. Analyse whether your ad conveys a basic concept or term around which you can coin a new name – exactly what professional name-smiths do. Ask your associates and marketing gurus to do the same. The process helps you get a consensus about what you can offer to the customer. After you agree on the message that the trade mark must convey, it's all downhill to the selection of that perfect name.

Playing the scale of name-coining options

Your trade mark can't simply define your company, product, or service, otherwise the name has no legal clout or protection (as we explain in Chapter 14). Don't make your trade mark too descriptive either – the more descriptive the trade mark, the less protection it carries. If you need help in coming up with a name, try some of our suggestions in the following sections.

What you can't say explicitly you can imply or suggest by a single word or phrase.

Coining a new term

Instead of using words from the English or any other language, try coining a brand-new word. Consider the following examples:

- ✔ **Abbreviate and then merge words:** Jazzercise (from jazz and exercise) for aerobic studios.
- ✔ **Clip the beginning or end of a word:** Fanta (from fantastic) on soda.
- ✔ **Fuse two words by sharing some letters:** Travelodge (travel and lodge) for roadside inns.
- ✔ **Imitate a common word:** Numberjack in the US (which imitates lumberjacks) for accounting services.
- ✔ **Join two or more words:** Kitchenaid on kitchen appliances, or Sunkist on citrus fruit.
- ✔ **Tack a prefix or suffix onto a word:** Microsoft for computer software and Vitalite on a margarine spread.

Making allusions

What you can't say directly, you can convey in a roundabout way. The following include what we consider to be good examples:

- ✔ **Evoke an image or sensation with a reference:** Iceland for a frozen food company, Cvit for a blackcurrant drink, or Regatta for sailing clothing.
- ✔ **Provide a role model:** Supercook for baking products, and Cover Girl on cosmetics.
- ✔ **Turn a common descriptive term into an attention-catching phrase:** Wok this Way is a far more distinctive way to advertise and promote a Chinese restaurant on the high street, and doesn't Kwik-Fit sound like a fast fitting exhaust company?
- ✔ **Use a symbol:** Greyhound suggests the speed of a bus service and Jaguar reflects the strength and agility yet sleekness of a sports car.

Personalising your mark

Using a fanciful character as a mark offers a good opportunity to devise clever adverts. The character mark turns into an effective and inexpensive advertising agent as people tend to bond with friendly cartoon characters. Some of our favourite examples are the Jolly Green Giant on canned vegetables, Mr Sheen on cleaning preparations, and Little Chef on roadside cafés.

Jazzing up the name

The aesthetic qualities of a trade mark have a great deal of impact on its powers of attraction and retention. *Aural impact,* the harshness or softness of a term, can help convey the right image. Regatta has associations with sailing. Jazz up a name with an *onomatopoeia* (a word whose sound imitates nature), such as jingle, splat, peck, and pop. For example, Cougar expresses the roar of a wild cat, and Cascade imitates the sound of falling water. Schweppes is almost the noise the can or bottle makes upon opening a fizzy drink.

Joking around

Humour is a great attention grabber – but don't overdo the jokes. Just the right amount of fun can impress your trade mark indelibly into the mind of your potential customer. Banana Republic as a US trade mark for clothing stores and Social Security for a cologne have just the right touch of witticism. Jogstrap on grips used to hold weights while running and No Deer Not Tonight on a wildlife-repellent spray may push the boundaries of good taste, but we reckon you won't forget them!

Heeding the muse

Don't be afraid to take a bit of poetic licence and give your trade mark flamboyance, but not pretension. Burberry and Rolls-Royce both combine smooth, melodious words. Fruit of the Loom is another pleasant brand identity. Try the following literary techniques:

- **Match sight and sound:** Use the coincidence of sound and image to emphasise your message. A great example is the trade mark Jaguar, where the harshness of the word combines with the image of the sleek yet ferocious wildcat to convey the power and strength of the sports car.

- **Think rhythm:** Put rhythm in your name, such as Coca-Cola, Burberry, or Dom Perignon.

- **Use alliteration:** Try the repetition of sounds in syllables, as in Cascade and Marmite, or Seven Seas for vitamins.

Avoiding the Deadly Branding Sins

Knowing how to avoid trade marks that can to lead you into a marketing fiasco, or an embarrassing situation, is essential. The cardinal sins of brand development are platitudes, pride, exaggeration, and plagiarism. But you also need to make sure that no skeletons lurk in the closet and no alternative meanings exist to the name you create.

Coca-Cola: The real story

Coca-Cola is probably the best-known trade mark in the world. For good or bad, Coca-Cola is an icon of American culture, and its trade mark is often cited as a model mark. But not so fast.

In 1886, the drink was originally touted as a medicinal elixir by its inventor, Dr John Styth Pemberton, for it contained a narcotic extract from coca leaves and a caffeine-loaded extract derived from kola nuts. Back then, people believed that those two extracts had therapeutic qualities (and they didn't need to take drug tests). With the product rather than the public in mind, the drink was named Coca-Cola. If you've read the rest of this chapter, you know that the mark merely described the ingredients of the drink and therefore was initially unprotectable.

After the use of the coca leaves extract was banned, the first half of the mark was no longer descriptive and became merely suggestive. In the meantime, 'cola', had become a generic name for a type of soft drink. Those guys at Coca-Cola Co. ended up with a mixed bag, but through extensive advertising, they boosted that mark to the pinnacle where it stands today.

However, the mark has its problems: Every time Coca-Cola is advertised, other brands such as Pepsi Cola and RC Cola derive at least half the promotion benefits. When Coca-Cola Co. opens a new market in an underdeveloped country, the other cola manufacturers take a free ride on its coat tails because the Coca-Cola Co. has already familiarised the new consumers with the term 'cola'. That wouldn't happen if the mark didn't contain a generic term.

We're not trying to denigrate the many aesthetic qualities of that mark. It's well-balanced, sonorous, and rhythmic because of its double alliteration and syncopated syllables. However, we personally prefer another type of bubbly – Dom Perignon, after the monk who put the fizz into champagne.

Platitudes

Using *platitudes* (trite commonplace words and phrases) to identify your business, product, or service is a no-no. A generic phrase such as 'The Builder's Yard' for a construction-material outlet, 'Discount Shoes' for a shoe shop, or 'Lite' (or 'Light') on a low-calorie lager identifies nothing because the phrase can't distinguish you from anyone else. Miller Brewing Company made the mistake of introducing the first low-calorie beer in the industry under the commonly descriptive (no better than generic) mark 'Lite' and spent a lot of dosh promoting the product. Within a few months, several of Miller's competitors marketed their own 'light' beers.

A platitude stems from the strong temptation to use a trade mark that tells people about your business or product. If you insist on using platitudes, do so with style and imagination by trying some of the tricks we suggest in earlier sections of this chapter. 'Rose-Coloured Glasses' for optometric services is merely suggestive and therefore quite distinctive. You may also add a generic term to a distinctive and fanciful one, as in Apple Computer.

If you need to be more specific, add an explanatory term or phrase to your distinctive trade mark, like that in Figure 15-4. These slogans or straplines can allow you to be far more elusive with the trade mark itself.

Figure 15-4:
Distinctive trade mark with explanatory phrase.

Many companies continue to be burdened with the surnames of long departed founders or a descriptive technical name that no longer fits its product line. In these situations, the management may resort to crunching the cumbersome corporate identity down to an acronym or a few initials. For example, Marks and Spencer is M&S these days, and the Minnesota Mining and Manufacturing is known as the 3M Company. However, because you've only 26 letters to play with, there's a high probability of conflicts with similar names. Furthermore, initials struggle to convey a message and therefore aren't typically distinctive, motivating, or memorable. Such examples include DKNY, WWF, KFC, and FCUK.

Pride

To be effective in the marketplace, a name should be distinctive and, if possible, unique. In most cases, there's nothing distinctive in a surname. The Yellow Pages directories are replete with Smith Brothers, Ltd, Smith Communication, Smith & Sons, and so on. But these are very common names, aren't they? Trust us on this one: Just about any surname you think isn't common probably is, and others have used it repeatedly.

Except in those instances where a personal name has already acquired notoriety, like George Foreman or Yves Saint Laurent, identifying a company product or service with a personal name is certainly a tricky one.

Using a name that describes an outstanding characteristic of your product is also a pit of personal pride. The developer of the Chemdry mark for carpet cleaning services may be very proud of their cleaning process, but the homeowner doesn't give a hoot how the carpet is cleaned, as long as it's cleaned. The term Chemdry is pretty descriptive and uninspiring. A competitor can closely imitate the name with impunity.

Exaggeration

Highly laudatory phrases, such as 'The Best Beer in Britain', is merely descriptive and neither registrable nor protectable. 'Probably the best lager in the world' has far more distinctiveness to it.

Plagiarism

You may be tempted to copy or imitate a successful trade mark in order to take a little ride on your competitor's coat tails. After the impressive commercial success of a chain of toy stores operating under the trade mark 'Toys 'R' Us', a plethora of 'Something 'R' Us' names appeared on the market. These copycat businesses soon had to change their names, at a great loss of goodwill and reputation – and in damages and attorneys' fees. In Chapter 20, we show you how easy it is to shoot down the imitator of a distinctive name. So don't fall into temptation and let the evil of plagiarism spoil your business venture.

The three main reasons for staying clear of names similar or too close to an existing name are:

- ✔ To protect yourself against accusations of infringement.

- ✔ To avoid restraining orders, injunctions, or seizure of your goods.

- ✔ To avoid being forced to change your commercial name after developing some goodwill and reputation under the infringing name.

Those closet skeletons

When selecting a trade mark, stay away from words that may have negative connotations. Terms that suggest death, suffering, and other painful implications may sometimes creep into a brand name. For example, the word 'pane' may be misunderstood as 'pain'.

Also, make sure that the name you choose doesn't have another meaning or connotation in a different language. If your product is destined for foreign distribution or a predominantly Asian market in your own country, verify that your trade mark doesn't evoke something morbid, ridiculous, or obscene in the foreign idiom:

- ✔ In Japanese, the word 'shi', which means four, has the same sound as the word for death. The Korean word 'sa' has a similar problem. Avoid both sounds when branding a product to be exported to Asia.

- ✔ The name 'Nova' for a car, with a shift of emphasis to the last syllable, means 'it won't go' in Spanish.

- ✔ In German, the word 'mist', as in the hair product trade mark Miracle Mist, means 'manure'.

- ✔ The French word 'camelote' means 'shoddy merchandise'.

- ✔ The Pschitt brand of Perrier water means 'fizz' in French. We probably don't have to tell you how the name is perceived in an English-speaking market.

- ✔ When the slogan used to promote Parker Pens 'It won't leak in your pocket and embarrass you' was translated into Spanish, it read: 'It won't leak into your pocket and make you pregnant.'

In view of the ever-increasing importance of global trade and the necessity for UK manufacturers to export their products, make sure that your new trade mark is compatible in any market where it may be introduced.

Chapter 16

Conducting an Availability Search

. . . .

In This Chapter

▶ Understanding reasons to search

▶ Limiting your search

▶ Combing through databases

▶ Interpreting your results

. . . .

*I*f you've just come up with the perfect name for a trade mark for your new business, you're probably very excited. But the chances of your name being up for grabs are pretty low: Finding an available trade mark on your first try is a bit like winning the lottery. Count on researching at least three options before you stumble upon an available name for your company.

In this chapter, we fill you in on what an availability search is and isn't and explain the purpose of the search. We describe what an appropriate availability search involves, outline a search strategy that you can use, and explain how to analyse your findings.

You can check the availability of a trade mark or service mark in the form of text or images on the UK-IPO website's search engine at `www.ipo.gov.uk/tm/t-find/ti-find-text/`. You can even conduct a text search that's a name search for part or the whole of a chosen name.

Practising Prudence

An *availability search* is a careful look at a whole range of trade marks that can be found on the World Wide Web and various business and legal databases (including the trade mark register through the UK-IPO Web site at `www.ipo.gov.uk`) to find out, as a first step, whether anyone else is already using your choice of trade mark.

After you uncover one or more prior uses, you need to answer two questions:

- ✔ Can you use your choice of trade mark without infringing the rights of the prior users?
- ✔ Can you obtain the benefits of registration (which we outline in Chapter 17)?

An availability search is essentially a legal process. Deciding what and where to search and analysing the results of the search require a good understanding of the legal-strength and likelihood-of-confusion concepts that we explain in Chapter 14. Although you can probably do some of the basic legwork, you may have to consult your IP attorney to decide whether your trade mark is available and registrable. (See 'Analysing the Results' later in the chapter for more on this.)

Seeing what an availability search is not

We can't overemphasise the need to conduct an appropriate availability search before you begin using a trade mark in the business community. (See Chapter 14 to review the types of trade mark you can use.)

Many people (business attorneys included) believe that the company registrar's office, whose role is to regulate company formations and limited liability companies, 'clears' a name before accepting it as a trade mark or brand identity. Working under this assumption, these chaps don't bother searching beyond the Companies House Web site.

But the registrar checks the name only for direct conflict with other names on the register – the registrar isn't interested in whether other laws prevent you from using that name. Reserving a business name through Companies House or having it accepted as a corporate identity doesn't necessarily mean that you can use the name commercially, whether locally or nationwide.

A renowned osteopathic hospital asked its corporate attorney to 'clear' the phrase 'Health Care Choice' to identify its health care insurance programme. The attorney checked with the registrar and confirmed that the company name was available. But this confirmation offered no defence to the frustrated directors of the hospital when a major health insurance provider sued them for infringement of its trade mark 'Choice'.

Understanding the reasons for an availability search

Just in case you're not quite convinced of the necessity of conducting an availability search, we list here a few of the legal and financial difficulties you may encounter if you don't do a search:

✔ **You can be sued:** Adopting a trade mark that copies or imitates one that's already used may be an actionable act of infringement.

✔ **Judges get angry:** If you're convicted of infringing the rights of a prior user and you carelessly neglected to conduct a search before using the trade mark, the court won't treat that as a show of bad faith, but may penalise you for your negligence by increasing the damages awarded to the plaintiff. However, if evidence exists that you had a prior warning or strong suspicion that the mark was already taken, the judge may consider your failure to do a thorough search as wilful and intentional infringement, and order you to pay the offended party's attorney and other court costs.

✔ **You may face a costly change of name:** If you launch your company or product under an infringing name, you'll soon have to change it. Think about the loss of goodwill that you'll incur and the cost of promoting a new name.

✔ **You may find yourself in bad company:** Assuming that you're a straight shooter – you took the time to buy and read this book – you probably want to do an availability search because you believe in your company, service, or product and you want it to stand on its own in the market. You don't need to piggyback on the goodwill developed by a similar trade mark, and you don't want the public to confuse your commercial identity with some organisation with a bad reputation.

✔ **Your application for registration may be denied:** The disappointment and financial losses associated with UK Intellectual Property Office (UK-IPO) denying your application for registration because your trade mark conflicts with an existing one are substantial. (We discuss registration in Chapter 17.)

Defining the Scope of Your Search

The extent of your search depends on the trade mark that you want to register. Before you get ready to search, make sure that you understand your own trade mark. You can then set search boundaries.

Assessing your choice of trade mark

The scope of your search and the interpretation of your search results (see the section 'Analysing the Results' later in this chapter) depend upon two factors:

- The legal strength of your trade mark.
- Your intended field and territory of use.

The *legal strength* of a trade mark is its ability to prevent other businesses from using the same or confusingly similar marks. Your first step in the great name search is to assess where your prospective trade mark falls on the *legal strength scale* – generic, descriptive, suggestive, or arbitrary – which we outline in Chapter 15.

Then you need to delineate the anticipated *field and territory of use*. In other words, you need to define the nature and utilisation, collectively referred to as the *definition*, of your goods or services and the geographical areas where they'll be marketed. Doing so is a three-step process:

1. **Write a concise definition of the nature, role, or function of the business, product, or service for which you want to use the prospective trade mark.**

   Here are some examples:

   - A business manufacturing automotive engine parts.
   - An engineering inspection and certification service for dwellings.
   - A single retail shop for high-end female fashion apparel.
   - A series of medical tomography scanners.
   - A nationwide fast-food restaurant chain.
   - An adult table game.

2. **Compare your product or service definition with those found in the International Trade Mark Classification.**

   By comparing, you determine which International Class (IC) you should search. The International Trade Mark Classification is a multinational system of grouping goods and services into different categories. You can read the definition of each IC through the UK-IPO Web site (www.ipo.gov.uk).

3. **Translate the territory of use into entities.**

   This refers to one or more countries, or where in the world you intend to trade and therefore use your trade mark.

The trade mark of any commercial activity that affects foreign commerce is considered as used in the entire country. This includes businesses serving tourists and travellers, such as hotels and restaurants.

Setting your boundaries

Good news! Unlike the patent search process that forces you to consider everything published anywhere in the world (see Chapter 6), UK trade mark law only makes you search for trade marks used within the UK and Europe. But that's a pretty big sea to swim in – so you need to narrow your search even further. Enter the legal-strength scale, which we talk about in detail in Chapter 15:

- ✔ **Distinctive:** If your trade mark is distinctive because it's suggestive or arbitrary, you must extend your search to practically all areas of commercial activities. The trade mark 'Kodak', for example, can refer to anything, so you'd need to look wider than the photographic industry and into every IC just in case. The search engine available through the UK-IPO Web site is particularly useful for this purpose.

   People who've come before you already have a tonne of legal protection for their distinctive marks. But the upshot is, after you clear your distinctive mark, you're afforded the same protection.

- ✔ **Descriptive:** If your trade mark is merely descriptive, you can limit your search to fields related to your own industry. If you're searching for the trade mark 'Bolton Brewers', you can limit it to the wine, beer, and spirits classes. The downside is that even if you find no one else using your mark, a descriptive mark offers very little protection against infringers.

- ✔ **Generic:** If your trade mark is generic, don't bother searching because anyone is free to use it.

Check out Table 16-1 for an idea on where to draw your search boundaries.

Table 16-1	Search Parameters for Sample One-Establishment Beauty Salon Names	
Position on Legal Strength Scale	*Mark*	*Search Boundaries*
Generic	Hair & Nails	No search necessary.
Descriptive	Permanent Waves Chester Care	Cosmetic products and personal care services found on the Web and trade mark registers.

(continued)

Table 16-1 *(continued)*

Position on Legal Strength Scale	Mark	Search Boundaries
Suggestive	A Cut Above Shear Delight Beauty and the Best	Cosmetics and toiletries goods and personal care services found on the Web and trade mark registers.
Arbitrary (existing word unrelated to goods or services)	Passion Flower Arabian Night Domani	Cosmetic and toiletries goods and personal care services found on the Web and trade mark registers.
Totally arbitrary (newly coined word)	Xokkox Capix Juvera	All categories of goods and services nationwide found on the Web trade mark registers.

Carrying Out Your Search

The number of trade marks in the UK and Europe amounts to millions, but only a quarter or so are actually registered with the UK-IPO. But even the hundreds of thousands of trade marks that aren't recorded in any readily searchable register are protected by the laws of passing-off. These laws prevent someone from getting away with implying that their goods or services are in some way associated with somebody else's. Therefore, an availability search can never provide you with 100 per cent assurance that your prospective identifier isn't already taken, but it can improve your odds.

In order of importance, we list four excellent places to search: the Internet, the UK-IPO database, private registers of trade marks, and foreign registers of trade marks. If you find the name you had in mind already taken on your first check, at least you've saved some time that you can devote to coming up with another name.

Investigating the Internet

The Internet is a bonanza for name searches. You need only type in a word and the search engine fetches hundreds – sometimes thousands – of references. Sometimes, the volume of information you retrieve is so overwhelming that you need to narrow it down by adding words to the search criteria. If that happens, you can request an advanced search, where you can search on a number of keywords or an exact combination of words. For example, if searching for

---

Trade marks: The world tour

Even when foreign companies or products have no commercial presence in the UK, their names can easily be recognised. Most people know that La Scala identifies an opera house in Milan, and that le Louvre is the name of a museum in Paris. A British person seeing an art print bearing the name 'le Louvre' probably thinks that the French museum sponsors the production and distribution of that print. In France, the word 'Champagne' doesn't designate just any old bubbly but the highly praised product of a small territory east of Paris. In fact, the generic use of the mark 'Champagne' in Europe and the US causes a lot of friction between commercial representatives and their indignant French counterparts who like to wash down their frogs legs and escargots with le vrai Champagne, sacré bleu!

Legislation is slowly catching up with the new global economy. Most industrial countries are moving toward standardisation of their trade mark laws through international treaties and conventions. Europe has the Community trade mark registration procedure to seek protection for the name in community member states, as we discuss in Chapter 18.

---

tornado as a mark for a drain cleaner, you get over three million references with one search engine. But if entering the combination *tornado* and *drain,* you get only around 27,000 results.

If you don't find your trade mark on the Internet, you've a pretty good chance that nobody is already using it. But unless you've coined a very unique term such as 'Kodak' or 'Xakkox', you're more likely to hit so many references that you have to sift through and then interpret them, as we explain in the section 'UK-IPO database,' below.

Unearthing the UK-IPO database

The UK-IPO maintains a comprehensive database of all marks that have been applied for, including those that were refused. The database also contains a record of all marks with current or expired registrations. You can access this database through the UK-IPO Web site at www.ipo.gov.uk. A registered UK trade mark lasts for ten years, and you can renew it for a further period of ten years. If the trade mark isn't renewed, it's shown as an expired registration. As we mention in Chapter 15, a key reason for having a trade mark is to protect the reputation of your name. Think twice before using a name that may already have a reputation in the eyes of the consumer.

The trade mark section of the UK-IPO Web site provides a very useful search tool for looking to see whether your newly created name has been used before for similar or identical goods and services The search engine now offers a way to search in a number of classes in one go, and also allows you to just enter part of the mark, like your distinctive ending.

Choose the 'Search' option under 'Trade Marks' to get started. Here you can enter a single word, a combination of words, or an exact phrase. Note that you can also search by registration number or owner.

If you get too many hits, refine your search by classifications, selecting just those that incorporate the goods and services for which you wish to use the mark.

You can also focus your search by specifying the exact product or service, such as 'Alibi' and 'bar' or 'Rubadubdub' and 'washcloth', using the Goods & Services category from the drop-down field box. Make sure that you try different definitions of your goods or services. For example, after you enter 'bar', try some synonyms, such as 'pub', 'tavern', 'inn', 'saloon', or 'lounge'. After plugging in 'washcloth', see whether terms such as 'towel', 'sponge', 'bathrobe', 'bathtub', or 'washbasin' return any results.

Trawling through trade mark registers

Many countries have their public records on the Internet so you can easily check the trade mark. Some private databases also provide access to specialised registers, as well as some business name records. To determine which registers you need to search, see the 'Setting your boundaries' section, earlier in the chapter.

An Internet search can prove just as valuable as a search of trade mark journals in establishing whether a mark is being used.

A few private companies provide trade mark search services or direct access to some name databases. You can conduct an in-depth search for a mark, including UK-IPO records and trade mark registers. If you want someone to do the search for you, take a look Chapter 24 for companies that offer such a service, or consult the Institute of Trade Mark Attorneys (ITMA), Web site www.itma.org.uk.

Ferreting through foreign registers

If you plan to export your products or services overseas, you may want to verify that your mark doesn't conflict with any mark used in the countries with which you may trade.

Most foreign trade mark registers aren't accessible online. Use a native trade mark agent to conduct this type of search. Most intellectual property (IP) attorneys have correspondents in major industrial countries whom they call upon for international inquiries.

The World Industrial Property Organization (WIPO) in Geneva, Switzerland, maintains databases of European trade mark applications. For trade mark information, look on the organisation's site, www.wipo.org, and work your way from the intellectual property section to the trade marks area. The organisation's Madrid Express Database (ipdl.wipo.int) provides anyone with a listing of trade mark applications. However, data about registered marks is available only to subscribers.

The laws pertaining to trade marks vary from country to country. In most parts of the world, you can only acquire exclusive rights by registration. We recommend that you consult an IP attorney before you spend time and resources checking foreign trade names and marks.

Analysing the Results

Remember, finding no reference to your prospective name in all the available sources of trade marks is no guarantee that your trade mark is available. Because so many trade marks are unregistered and unsearchable, the possibility of inadvertently infringing on some obscure yet protected trade name or trade mark is always there. On the other hand, finding out that your baby is already in use doesn't necessarily prevent you from using it.

If you do find that your trade mark (or something resembling it) is already in use, you have to consider the legal issue of whether using this mark is likely to cause confusion in the marketplace.

An IP specialist can give you a professional answer on this complex question, but even that would only be a best guess. Because the standards for determining the likelihood of confusion are so imprecise and dependent upon the circumstances of the case, many attorneys and law firms plainly refuse to issue a definitive opinion on the subject. Foolish would be the attorney who cleared a name of all risks of infringement.

Yet you have to make that judgement, unless you decide to drop any candidate name that's identical or vaguely similar to one already in use. Because of the sheer number of names and marks already used in commerce, you may have to change your selected name dozens of times before you stumble on that unblemished pearl nobody has seen before. The best we can do for you is to lay out the most common criteria that the courts use to decide on the issue of infringement of trade marks and give you a few examples.

Determining likelihood of confusion

Common sense is your best guide in analysing the likelihood of confusion between your trade mark and those you uncover during your search. Likelihood of confusion is hard to define. Courts try, without great success or consistency, to quantify likelihood of confusion. Quantification really boils down to a logical, honest, fair evaluation of all the circumstances.

 First, ask yourself earnestly, 'Am I trying to launch my product or business on the coat tails of a well-known one?' We've noticed that many people do just that without admitting it to themselves. We mention elsewhere that the trade mark TOYS 'R' US triggered a flurry of imitations. Then there was the 4U craze in the UK: Phones 4U, Loans 4U, Holidays 4U, and so on; and the Mate craze for products: Workmate, Paper Mate, Coffee Mate and a few others. Avoid this type of piggybacking if you want to steer clear of legal problems.

Although the various courts throughout the UK and Europe use slightly different standards to determine the likelihood of confusion between two trade marks, we describe the most used factors in the following sections.

Legal strength or weakness of the pre-existing trade mark

The protection afforded to a trade mark is proportional to its distinctiveness (see Chapter 14 for more on the appraisal of a trade mark). You can't apply an arbitrary term to any kind of product or service, no matter how your predecessor used it. The Eastman Kodak Company was able to prevent the use of its unique mark on watches and other products totally unrelated to photographic goods.

If the name you want is suggestive of your product or service, you may be able to use it – even if it's already used for a different type of product or service – because a suggestive term doesn't immediately make the customer think of a specific product or service. For instance, in order to make the connection between the trade mark 'Tour de France' and a bike shop, you have to know what the famous competition is about and then speculate that bicycles or bicycle-related goods or services may be involved. Finding that the mark has already been used in connection with clothing wouldn't, under normal circumstances, prevent you from using it for your bike shop.

If you settle for a descriptive term such as 'The Hair Palace' for your beauty shop, salons in other areas with the exact same name aren't likely to present a problem. The controlling issue here is the likelihood that some customer may frequent both establishments.

Quality of the prior goods

A mark used on high-quality goods is entitled to more protection than one used on average or low-quality merchandise. For example, if you plan to sell expensive, high-fashion dresses for full-figured women under the trade mark

'Strong & Striking', you may not be in conflict with the owner of the same trade mark who sells run-of-the-mill women's wear because there's little chance that your customer would patronise the other manufacturer. However being in the same class of goods or services may prevent the chance of registration.

Similarity of the two trade marks

The similarity in appearance, sound, and meaning of the two trade marks is taken into account. Obviously, the more your trade mark resembles the pre-existing one, the more likely the confusion amongst the customers.

The courts tend to give more importance to the sound of a mark than to its look, so you can't get away with misspelling an already established name. For example, 'Cauddac' won't differentiate your goods from 'Kodak', and 'Pleidow' won't distinguish your product from 'Playdoh'. That said, adding a distinctive logo may be enough to negate any likelihood of confusion, especially in the case of descriptive marks.

Similarity of the goods or services

You need to give considerable weight to the similarity of your goods or services to those of your predecessor. Again, a small difference between the marks or the goods may get you off the hook if you're dealing with a descriptive or generally weak mark, but you won't get away with imitating a suggestive or famous mark even if your goods or services aren't similar. For example, in the US, a toiletry manufacturer was allowed to use the mark 'Sport Stick' in connection with its deodorants, despite the fact that another party was already using the mark 'Sport-Stick' on a lip balm. The slightly descriptive or highly suggestive mark 'Sure' on an underarm antiperspirant didn't prevent another company from using 'Sure & Natural' on feminine protection products. However, you can't sell or do anything under the mark 'Playboy' because it's such a famous, and, therefore, strong name.

Likelihood of bridging the gap

You must also anticipate that the person already using your selected trade mark for different goods or services may one day bridge the gap by offering the same goods or services as yours. What's the likelihood that curriculum. com may offer a college transcript processing service in the future? If that's a possibility, you may be opening yourself up to infringement problems. Use your best judgement. Don't guess. If in doubt, err on the side of caution.

Marketing channels

Are your goods likely to appear next to those with the similar trade mark? Could your loan brokerage services and other services be offered by a bank or financial establishment with a similar mark? If so, that would cause customer confusion, so you must abandon the name. If the trade mark is descriptive, a slight difference in marketing channels may be sufficient to preclude likelihood of confusion.

Sophistication of the buyer

The likelihood of confusion increases when goods sold under similar marks are relatively inexpensive and subject to impulse buying. Confectionary and popular magazines fall into this category. More expensive and complex products, such as computers, are less subject to name confusion because they require more customer consideration of their functions and capabilities. Very expensive or customised equipment for discriminating buyers is almost immune to the likelihood of confusion.

Putting your search together

In the end, the only way to analyse the results of your search (especially if you found an identical or similar trade mark) is to look at *all* the criteria listed to determine whether your prospective mark is a good choice.

Imagine you're about to market a new type of CT scan machine to be sold for three-quarters of a million pounds to medical groups, hospitals, and health research centres. Your marketing group has coined the mark 'Novarad', but an availability search uncovers 'Novaray', which is used for X-ray equipment and is also marketed to the healthcare and medical research fields. Take a look at each of the factors for determining the likelihood of confusion that we outline in the previous sections and see where you come out:

- ✔ 'Novaray' is suggestive and deserves a broad scope of protection.

- ✔ The 'Novaray' X-ray equipment has been sold for many years and maintains a good reputation in the field.

- ✔ 'Ray' and 'rad' (short for radiation) are quasi-synonymous words, making the marks 'Novaray' and 'Novarad' very similar.

- ✔ The two brands of equipment are used in the same field, by the same people, for the purpose of looking into someone's anatomy.

- ✔ The manufacturer of the 'Novaray' device may someday expand its product line to CT scan equipment, as has already been done by companies such as General Electric and Siemens.

- ✔ The two machines are sold through the same channels of distribution.

Here you've already gone through six of the seven criteria mentioned above, and you've come up with six good reasons to send your marketing team back to the drawing board to coin another brand identity. However, the 'sophistication of the buyers' test saves the day and trumps all the other factors. Is there any chance that the people who purchase your equipment may be confused about the source and purpose of such an expensive piece of equipment? No way. Therefore, the first six negatives present no obstacle to using the 'Novarad' mark.

You may have realised that we offer no foolproof way to analyse the likelihood of confusion between two trade marks. Although some factors, such as the strong legal clout of the senior mark, carry more weight than others, a certain factor may override all the other factors, as in the 'Novarad' example above. Common sense must be your guide. If you follow that advice, you'll go a long way toward ensuring a good choice and an excellent chance of avoiding any legal difficulties.

Chapter 17

Establishing and Registering Your Trade Marks

. . . .

. . . .

*I*n the UK you acquire exclusive rights to your trade mark or service mark simply by making commercial use of your mark. However, you enhance your ability to prevent others from copying your trade mark when you register your marks on the Trade Marks Register, which also includes service marks.

This chapter covers the ins and outs of how to gain rights to your trade mark or service mark and how they can be registered. We take you through the application for registration process and also provide some info on the follow-up work you need to do after obtaining registration.

In this chapter we can't cover all the complex aspects of applying to register a mark. Filling out, filing, and processing your application for registration at the Trade Marks Office at the UK-IPO usually raises intricate legal issues and requires some tough choices on your part. Moreover, a trade mark examiner handles your application, and without the services of a competent IP attorney, who may be a trade mark attorney or a patent attorney, who also prosecutes trade mark applications, you may be at a great disadvantage. Even though the standard application forms are suitable in most cases where your application sails through the examination process, any prosecution difficulties require some legal massaging beyond what these forms are intended for. We suggest you don't dispense with the advice and services of a good IP professional if you want to avoid the many potholes on the road to successful registration.

Gaining Exclusive Rights to Your Trade Mark or Service Mark

In order to secure rights to use a mark you must do two things. First, you have to select a mark, as we describe in Chapter 16. Second, you have to use, or intend to use, that mark in connection with commercial activities. In addition to your exclusive mark, you may wish to use other marks. In the following list, we describe activities that qualify as commercial use for each type of mark:

- **Certification mark:** Used on a document or article to show compliance with certain certification requirements. For example, the membership of a trade association may be allowed to use a certification mark registered by the trade association as long as they comply with any terms and conditions relating to the certification mark. The Wool Mark is a very good example of a certification mark.

- **Collective mark:** Protected in the name of an association and used by members of the association in the same manner as a trademark or service mark or on cards, emblems, or other items carried or used by members.

- **Service mark:** Used on signs, business cards, letterheads, promotional materials, tenders for work, job estimates, and other documents. The service mark is that which signifies the service provided to customers; for example, a launderer and dry cleaner can register their marks in relation to the services they provide.

- **Trade mark:** Put on labels, tags, containers, point-of-sale displays, documents accompanying the product, and on the product itself. For example, the Levi trade mark on jeans and other clothing adorns products marketed by traders, including large high street stores.

Registering Your Mark

The most effective way to shore up the exclusive rights you've acquired through use of a mark is to register it as a mark with the UK-IPO.

The UK-IPO registers your mark on the Trade Marks Register and grants a registration certificate if your application survives a UK-IPO examiner's thorough examination and any eventual opposition by any interested party with a prior registered trade and/or service mark for the same or similar goods and/or services. We explain later in the section headed 'Important Changes in the Examination process' how an interested party is informed of a likely conflict between their mark and the mark for which you're seeking registration.

Trade mark registration isn't readily available for company names, especially company names that are common and widespread, such as Smith and Brown. The reason is that several companies can be dealing in similar commodities or providing similar services, leading to confusion in the mind of the customer. But you can often choose a company name that you can then alter slightly in order to register. Here are a couple of examples:

✔ You name your manufacturing company 'Ionic Scientific Manufacturing Company, Ltd.' Strip that name down to 'Ionic Scientific' and establish that name as a trade mark by applying it to your products. Then register the mark to protect and bolster both your mark and company name.

✔ You call your business 'Bean Brain Accounting Services Associates'. Highlight 'Bean Brain' on your business cards and put 'accounting services' under it as an explanatory legend. Then register 'Bean Brain' as a service mark for accounting services.

In general, registering your mark doesn't give you any ownership rights that you didn't already have, but it does give you a procedural advantage to stop an infringer. More specifically, your registration does the following:

✔ **Acts like the deed to your house:** Registration tells the world that the UK-IPO has investigated your mark, confirmed your ownership and concluded that your mark is valid and enforceable.

✔ **Allows you to place temporary restrictions on infringers:** Registration makes it easier to get an interim injunction, or seizure of counterfeit goods while awaiting trial. These temporary, but very effective, and often decisive, remedies stop infringers dead in their tracks.

✔ **Arms your IP attorney:** Registration is a really big stick to beat away someone trying to copy or imitate your mark.

✔ **Highlights your registration during an availability search:** Anyone as smart and as honest as you then keeps clear of your mark.

✔ **Shifts the burden of proof to the infringing defendant:** In a legal action, introducing your registration certificate shifts the burden of proof away from you. Without a registration, you'd have to prove in a Passing Off Action that you own the mark by introducing evidence that you used the mark first and that use by the alleged infringer caused loss and damage to your business. (Chapter 14 has more about passing off.)

✔ **Lets you obtain cancellation of domain names that conflict with your mark:** For example, with the creation and registration of domain names, some unscrupulous individuals registered famous names in the hope of cashing in by selling a company its own domain name. You can take action against these cybersquatters (see Chapter 20).

✔ **Makes international registration easier:** Registration makes it easier to register your mark abroad under many international treaties and conventions.

✔ **Stops the entry of infringing foreign goods:** HM Revenue & Customs can seize imported goods bearing your marks and eventually destroy them if the importer doesn't challenge the seizure.

Establishing eligibility

To qualify your mark for registration, you must use or intend to use your mark *in commerce*, that is, your goods or services must be available in the market place. Any mark that meets this criterion can be registered, except for a mark that:

✔ Contains immoral, deceptive, or scandalous material (this is the prerogative of the trade marks examiner!).

✔ Incorporates the flag, coat of arms, or other insignia of either the UK or any individual state, municipality, or foreign nation.

✔ Is a geographical indication of the origin of a wine or spirit.

✔ Disparages or falsely suggests a connection with any person, institution, belief, or national symbol.

✔ Uses a name, portrait, or signature that identifies a living individual without his or her written permission.

✔ Is generic, commonly descriptive, functional, or misleading.

✔ Is likely to cause confusion with a trade mark still in use by another.

✔ Is primarily a common surname. However, common surnames may be registered if, after a number of years, the reputation of the Mark has become recognised as the source of reliable products or services (such as Coleman for mustard and Patak for Indian sauces and chutneys).

About those symbols

Allow us to clear up some common misconceptions about the TM, SM, and ® characters you see next to some trade marks. TM (for *trade mark*) has absolutely no legal significance. It simply indicates that someone is claiming the rights to a mark. If the mark is distinctive and used properly, as we explain in this chapter, the status of the trade mark should be obvious without the symbol. If the mark is descriptive and weak, using such a symbol doesn't do much to improve its status. If, on the other hand, the mark is strong and you're seeking or are likely to seek trade mark registration, using the symbol TM to show that you regard the mark as your own does no harm!

The ® symbol is another matter. It's an international symbol indicating that the mark is registered at the UK-IPO or any other trade mark authority in the world.

Laws can often seem complicated and confusing and trade mark law is no different. UK trade mark law has so many hidden dangers that even IP attorneys and lawyers can get tangled in the web of trying to interpret precedents set by the trade marks registrar and the courts.

One way of avoiding becoming entangled in lengthy prosecution difficulties is to choose a distinctive mark that's unlikely to clash with a prior registered mark for similar goods or services. Use your imagination and invent a novel word that isn't descriptive of the goods or services that you're intending to provide.

Defining the owner

The trade mark and its registration must be owned by whoever, or whatever, stands behind the product or service. The trade mark carries an implication of warranty of quality and commercial fitness of the goods or services it identifies. If the product marketed under a mark fails, or is adulterated, the goodwill accruing to the mark may cause a loss of business to the owner. You may file the application on behalf of:

✔ Yourself, as an individual.

✔ A corporation.

✔ A general partnership.

✔ Another type of business entity, such as two or more individuals jointly, a trust, a limited partnership, or other limited liability company.

Defining the mark

Trade marks that incorporate graphics, shapes, colours, or other non-verbal characteristics require special attention. In the sections that follow, we provide some insight into graphic marks and get up – the way a mark is used on packaging and in trade literature – and we also provide form-specific instructions.

Your trade mark may consist solely of one or more colours applied to a particular object, such as a product, a packaging, a store sign, or a building. A colour mark, just like a product shape, isn't considered inherently distinctive until it has acquired *secondary meaning* – the mark becomes recognised as the source of good products or services over the passage of time, usually in excess of five years. Examples of colour marks are orange for telephone services and green for BP products.

Graphic marks

If your mark comprises verbal and design elements (including fanciful lettering), such as the one illustrated in Figure 17-1, you can file for:

- ✔ **The literal part (made of one or more typed standard characters):** The character, word, or phrase only. A mark that consists only of standard characters is commonly called a *word mark*, even if it consists of a single punctuation character.

- ✔ **The design part:** The graphics only, if they can stand alone and aren't part of the lettering.

- ✔ **The whole representation:** Both the characters and graphics of the mark.

To obtain the maximum coverage, register only the part that exhibits the greatest legal strength. For example:

- ✔ If you have a strong word mark, you can get broad coverage by filing for the literal part only. A person needs only to copy or imitate that part to create a likelihood of confusion among the public.

- ✔ If you have a non-descriptive and motivating design, you may want to obtain registration for that design only.

The odds that someone would copy both parts of the mark are relatively low. You can catch more flies with a limited form of the mark.

If you have a weak word mark, combining it with a graphic, even a fanciful one, won't save the mark from rejection by the UK-IPO examiner. For example, the surname 'Smith' is typical of a weak mark and is unlikely to be allowed onto the Trade Marks Register even if it's adorned with graphics.

Figure 17-1:
Combined
word and
design
mark.

Filing Your Trade or Service Mark Application

After you conclude your searches and feel satisfied that your choice of trade or service mark meets all the necessary criteria for registration and that you're happy with the Class and Specification of goods and/or services for which you require registration, the next step is to complete a Form TM3. To help you fill in the TM3, the UK-IPO provides excellent guidelines. In the meantime however, in this section we give you some pointers on processing your trade mark and/or service mark application.

The Class in which your trade mark application is made depends on the type of product or service you're going to provide under the mark (see the next section).The TM3 consists of Boxes 1–15. The numbers below correspond to those 15 boxes. You only have to fill in the boxes relating to the type of mark you intend to use.

1. **Personal reference:** Insert your personal reference here – it's used by the Trade Marks Registry whenever they communicate with you.

2. **Illustration of your mark:** You must provide an illustration of your mark or marks here. Use the international colour identification system if your mark has colour. If your mark does not fit in the box then use an additional A4 sheet.

3. **Is your mark in 3-D, or does it use a sound, or a repeating pattern?:** Indicate if any of these apply.

4. **If you've used a colour to illustrate your mark:** Indicate here if the colour is what you want or specify any differences.

5. **If you've used black-and-white to illustrate your mark:** Specify colours if you want them to be part of your mark.

6. **Series of marks:** If you're applying for a series of marks specify the number you're applying for.

7. **Does your application claim priority?:** Give details here if you claim priority from an earlier filed application in another country.

8. **Transforming a UK designation under an international registration into a UK application:** You need to give details including the transformation date and registration number.

9. **Goods and services on which you intend to use your mark:** You must indicate the Class number and list of goods and/or services here.

10. **Applying for a certification or collective mark:** Indicate here which type you want if applying for one of these.

11. **Limitations and disclaimers:** Indicate any disclaimers here, such as a territorial limitation, or any limitations designated in order to avoid conflict with a prior registered mark.

12. **Applicant's details:** Provide the name and full address of the applicant. If a company, include incorporation details of where it's incorporated. Also add the trade marks ADP number if you know it.

13. **Agent's details:** Full name and address of your IP Attorney if used.

14. **Declaration:** This section includes a declaration of 'use' or 'intended use' of the mark. You, or your IP Attorney, sign and date the form here.

15. **Day-to-day contact details:** They may be yours or any designated person.

Classifying and defining your goods or services

How you classify and define your goods or services not only influences the protection your mark gets, but also determines the types of prior marks that can be cited against your application.

Therefore, define the areas of commerce where your mark is used and then compare that definition with the International Classification listings, detailed on the UK-IPO Web site.

The International Classification listings separate products and services into easily managed areas so that searching, filing, and prosecution can proceed as smoothly as possible no matter where or when you file a trade mark or service mark application.

You can use the same mark on goods or services that fall into several classes. For example, if you're manufacturing leather articles, you may have to select all the following classes:

- ✔ Class 14 (Jewellery) for watch straps.
- ✔ Class 16 (Paper goods) for desk pads and chequebook holders.
- ✔ Class 18 (Leather goods) for handbags, briefcases, luggage, wallets, purses, and belts.
- ✔ Class 20 (Furniture) for jewellery cases.
- ✔ Class 25 (Clothing) for jackets, pants, shoes, and boots.
- ✔ Class 26 (Fancy goods) for leather belt buckles.
- ✔ Class 34 (Smokers' articles) for cigar and cigarette holders.

In the box for listing of goods and/or services on the TM3, enter a definition for each type of goods or services associated with your mark. Don't use a code, but find a description that's as close as possible to one found in the International Classification to identify the goods or services you want to use under the mark.

Prosecuting your application through the UK-IPO

Having decided to file an application for registration of your trade mark, you complete the Form TM3 and send it to the UK-IPO together with a Fee Sheet FS2 and your cheque for the £200, the application fee.

If you want to register your mark in more than one Class of Goods or Services, the application fee is £200 for the first Class and £50 for each additional Class. These fees are non-returnable in the event that your application is refused or abandoned by your own inactivity in response to an Official Action received from the UK-IPO examiner.

After posting your application, or completing the form online, you may think that your trade mark's well on its way to registration. Think again: The journey of an application through the UK-IPO may be 6–9 months or longer if your application meets with objections raised by the Trade Marks examiner (up to three or four years!). In this section, we explain how your application for registration is processed and what happens if your application is rejected.

Your trade mark application isn't confidential, which means anyone can see what you're up to. You can check the current status of any pending application or registration – including your own – online at www.ipo.gov.uk.

Passing (or failing) the examination

When your application arrives at the UK-IPO, an examiner is assigned to your case. Your first contact with the examiner, or the section of the Trade Marks Registry that's responsible for checking formalities, may be a request for corrections to some technical defects in your application, such as insufficient fees or missing information. Then, after the examiner completes a thorough availability search on your mark, you receive a first report on the status of your application, between three and six months from your filing date.

The examiner's report may include a combination of objections and refusals to register. The report always specifies the time (in most cases two months) within which you have to answer. Objections and refusals are never welcome, but they don't necessarily put an end to your application.

The report is in formal language and cites controlling authorities, such as sections of statutes, regulations, and court decisions. We suggest that you consult your IP attorney to help you understand the report.

You have to answer the report by filing an amendment with supporting arguments. An *amendment* is a legal document that answers every objection or ground for refusal and accepts, or contests, each of the examiner's findings and decisions. The name comes from the fact that it often includes a modification of the application. There's no fee required unless you have to split the goods or services into one or more additional classes, in which case you must pay the standard filing fee for each added class.

Promptly answer any communication from the examiner. Failing to do so may cause your application be declared abandoned. If your application has been declared abandoned because you failed to answer the examiner in a timely fashion, you may apply to revive it for no additional cost.

After a couple of exchanges with the examiner, you get a preliminary approval, or face a final refusal, to register the mark. After the preliminary approval comes the publication step, which we explain later in this chapter in 'Receiving the UK-IPO's seal of approval'. A final refusal leaves you with two options – appeal the decision or let the application lapse and pick another mark.

Dealing with examiner objections

The most common objections relate to improper listings of goods or services or a wrong classification. In most cases, the examiner suggests a new specification of goods or services and their appropriate classifications.

Don't blindly accept suggestions from the examiner without considering the impact of changes on the scope of your mark and the cost of the registration. You know your product or service better than the examiner. His suggestion may miss the mark (pardon the pun) and not give you the coverage you need. Also, each added classification raises the filing fee.

Finding the right lawyer

Any IP attorney may represent you before the UK-IPO during the examination and prosecution of your application. Although many lawyers who aren't IP specialists take mark-registration cases, you can't expect these occasional trade mark practitioners to give you the same quality of service as an IP professional who keeps up with the frequent changes in the laws pertaining to trade marks. Carefully investigate the qualifications of any professional before you hire him or her to advise and represent you. You can always contact the Institute of Trade Mark Attorneys for the contact details of a trade mark attorney in your area (www.itma.org.uk); or find one in the Yellow Pages.

The examiner may also ask you to disclaim a descriptive part of your mark and even suggest a wording for the disclaimer. In other words, you're asked to agree that you don't have any exclusive right to that portion of your mark. If you don't agree that that portion is merely descriptive, present a convincing argument against the need for a disclaimer.

Past experience with a rejection of an application was for the trade mark 'Farmhouse' in relation to roof tiles. The examiner stated that the mark was descriptive of the goods, namely roof tiles. The response to the rejection was that roof tiles, although used on farmhouses – and, indeed, on any dwelling – could not be said by any stretch of the imagination to look anything like a farmhouse. The argument succeeded and the mark was registered and is still in use today.

Facing rejection

If the examiner's report contains a refusal to register, all is not lost. You can also contest that decision. You must answer a refusal to register the mark with an amendment. There's no fee involved in answering a rejection, so the cost is the same, regardless of whether the examiner says yes first time round or says no a few times and eventually says yes.

The examiner may say that the mark isn't distinctive, but merely descriptive or primarily a surname. If registration is refused on the ground that the mark isn't distinctive, you can show evidence of the contrary in the form of intensive advertising campaigns, commentaries culled from newspapers and other publications, or written testimonials by competent individuals.

If you've used the mark in commerce for several years, you may establish secondary meaning by filing a statement, terminating with a declaration asserting that the mark has been in substantial, exclusive, and continuous use for several years and has become distinctive.

Receiving the UK-IPO's seal of approval

If you encounter no opposition, or an opposition is settled in your favour, your registration certificate is issued without further ado, about six weeks from the end of the opposition period.

After you receive your registration certificate you may place a notice of registered status next to the mark. The notice can consist of the legend *Registered* or the international symbol ® placed next to the upper-right corner of the mark when possible.

The symbol ® is an indication that a mark is a registered mark; however, unless you also indicate the country of registration, you may run into difficulties where a third party in any territory wrongly presumes that you have

Noting a change in the examination process

An important change was made to the examination process on 1 October 2007 that brought UK practice into line with that of the Office for Harmonization in the Internal Market (OHIM) which receives applications for Community trade mark applications in the European Union. The UK-IPO no longer refuses to register a new trade mark application because of an earlier conflicting registered trade mark, unless the owner of the earlier mark successfully opposes the new application.

The UK-IPO still searches the relevant registers as part of the examination process and sends the applicant the results, which may include conflicting marks already on the register.

The applicant may choose between continuing the application, restricting the list of goods or services in an attempt to avoid the conflict with the earlier mark, or withdrawing their application.

If the applicant decides to continue with the application, the UK-IPO writes to the owners of any earlier conflicting mark identified in the search when the application publishes in the *Trade Marks Journal*. The UK-IPO automatically informs the owners of earlier UK marks but EU mark owners will need to opt-in if they want to be informed of a likely conflict with a later filed mark.

When the mark is advertised in the *Trade Marks Journal*, the owners of any earlier marks or rights can oppose the application if they consider that use of the new mark infringes their earlier mark or right. If the opposition is successful, the applicant for the later mark could be liable for costs and may not be able to get their mark registered.

legal rights in that territory merely because of information contained on your Web site. This state of affairs is becoming very common with the degree of cover given to products and services and the marks they may be marketed under. We advise that you take great care when adding details concerning registered marks to a Web site, trade literature, and pamphlets. One good idea is to use the symbol ™, which may be described as indicating trade marks, registered or otherwise, and owned by you.

Renewing your registration

Your registration lasts as long as you use the mark in commerce providing it's renewed every ten years. During the ninth year of each renewal period, you must file a Form TM11 together with a Fee Sheet FS2 and your cheque for £200 for a first Class of Goods or Services and £50 for each additional Class. The mark is then renewed and an acknowledgement forwarded to you by the UK-IPO. Renewal fees change from time to time so check in with the UK-IPO Web site for the up-to-date fees when you need to renew your trade mark registration. You can download the Form TM11 and the Fee Sheet FS2 free of charge from the UK-IPO Web site at www.ipo.gov.uk/tm.htm.

Losing Your Trade Mark Registration

You can lose your exclusive rights to a trade mark under the following circumstances:

- **Authorising uncontrolled use:** The law protects exclusive use of a trade mark to give the public a reliable indication of quality. For example, you buy Kodak film because you know that it's a quality product. Authorising someone else to use your mark without controlling the quality of the products or services may lead to the cancellation of your mark.

- **Failing to use your trade mark:** If you don't use your trade mark for five years and show no intent to use it in the future, someone else can assume that you abandoned it and begin using it. To keep your trade mark rights, you must show credible evidence that you intend to use it and were prevented from doing so by circumstances beyond your control. Proving these circumstances is difficult, if not impossible. Use it or lose it.

- **Going generic:** If you're lucky enough to have a successful and profitable product marketed under a strong mark, the public may eventually adopt your mark as the generic term for that kind of product. The court may then declare your mark generic and unenforceable. It's a situation that's happened before – once upon a time, aspirin, linoleum, and cellophane were famous brand names.

- **Tolerating infringers:** If you fail to chase infringers of your trade mark, competitors may assume that you deserve a very narrow scope of protection. This clears the way for the copycats to use it. The longer you delay pursuing infringers, the less likely you'll be able to stop them.

- **Using the mark as more than a qualifier:** A mark must always qualify a product or service. Never use it as a noun or a verb, such as in 'Drink Schweppes' or 'You can Xerox any documents.' Your advertisement should say 'Drink Schweppes brand of lemonade' or 'You can duplicate any document on our Xerox copier.' If you don't treat your company name or mark as a valuable asset , others won't either. Your mark can lose its distinguishing character and become unenforceable.

  Always type a mark in bold, uppercase letters, or some other way that makes it stand out in text, followed by a generic term – for example, 'Our comfortable **TIPPYTOE®** slippers will keep your feet warm.'

  You can only use the ® symbol after obtaining registration for your trade mark.

- **Using the mark unfairly:** You can't take advantage of your strong trade mark to impose obligations that go beyond your exclusive rights. A common example of misconduct is when a fast-food franchisor insists that all franchisees buy their disposable tableware from them. Other abuses of a mark include forcing a trade mark licensee to also accept a license under a copyright or patent.

Part V

Exploiting and Enforcing Your IP Rights

'If he patents that, it'll mean the end
of falconry as we know it.'

In this part . . .

We talk about what you can do after you've acquired your British patent, registered design, or trade mark. If you're planning to do business abroad, your work isn't quite done yet. You need to know how to protect your IP overseas, so grab your passport, stow your carry-on case, and get ready for an IP overseas getaway.

And now that you've spent a load of time and money (or blood, sweat, and tears) to get that protection, find out how you can use your intellectual property to increase profits. Finally, we show you what to do if someone infringes on your IP rights (barricade not included).

Chapter 18

All Abroad: Protecting Your IP Rights in Other Countries

. . . .

. . . .

Acquiring foreign patents or registering your trade mark abroad can be extremely costly, complex, and time-consuming. In this chapter we ponder the pros and cons of obtaining foreign IP protection. We aim to help you chart a steady course before casting your money to wayward winds.

Pondering the Pros and Cons of International Patents

You may wonder whether you really want to go to all the trouble and expense of applying for international patents. Every case is different so before you plunge ahead or slink away, take a look at this section, where we give some reasons to file – and a reason to stay 'local'.

Counting the ways: Why file abroad?

If you have a good, solid invention with a reasonable potential of being used outside the UK, filing abroad can give you a real competitive edge by protecting you from infringers, increasing your licensing payoffs, and actually getting licensees.

Stopping foreign infringers

With few exceptions, a patent offers no protection beyond the borders of the country that granted it. Although your UK patent lets you sue anyone who makes, markets, or sells your patented gizmo anywhere in the UK, your British patent has no effect overseas. A foreign patent lets you exploit other potential markets in appropriate territories.

Considering the universal high cost and uncertainties of legal proceedings, you probably can't afford to sue abroad. But, this works both ways – few can afford to be sued. So you gamble that your foreign patents will deter potential infringers.

Leveraging your licensing revenue

A foreign patent increases your licensing clout and lets you collect royalties on the overseas activities of authorised parties. Consider the following example:

The good news is that you've been granted a solid UK patent and success-fully negotiated a lucrative, exclusive license with Titanic Tools, Ltd. (TTL), that agrees to pay you £1 for each of your two-handled fly swatters it makes or sells. The bad news – you didn't file for a patent abroad and now all appli-cation deadlines have elapsed. Don't be surprised if Titanic then has the swatters manufactured in China for sale all over the world. You're only enti-tled to royalties on units sold in the UK – nowhere else. The law forbids the use of your UK patent to extract royalties for your licensee's activities any-where you don't have patent coverage. However, if you had patent protection in China, TTL would have to pay you royalties on its entire production, and you could've asked for a higher royalty rate. The greater the territorial cover-age, the higher the royalty. Of course, the royalties secured depend upon the negotiating skill of yourself or your commercial agent, who, in exceptional circumstances, may also be your patent attorney.

Attracting licensees

Having overseas patent coverage makes you more attractive to potential licensees. Most large companies shy away from an invention if they can't secure a monopoly in most industrial countries. Ever-expanding globalisation of commerce discourages heavy investments in tooling, marketing, and other start-up costs for a product that competitors can freely copy outside the UK.

Adding up whether filing abroad is worth the money

The substantial cost of obtaining and maintaining foreign patents is often the factor that prevents you from implementing an overseas patent programme. Cost is a pretty major factor, because most inventors seldom seek only one patent. As the technology is improved, they file additional applications and often have to file for multiple patents in each foreign country.

As a rough estimate, plan to spend between £3,000 and £5,000 per patent per country – and you need to pay during the four years it takes to obtain the first generation of patents. So, getting patents in 12 countries can cost you between £36,000 and £60,000.

After you get your patent, add about £150 or more in maintenance fees per patent per country per year, for the next 16 years if you choose to maintain your patent for as long as possible. Obviously, if your patent isn't making any profits for you, or technology has moved on, you may allow your patent to lapse by stopping any further annual renewal fees. These figures are valid no matter which filing strategy you choose. (We discuss the different strategies in the 'Where to File Your Patent Application' section later in this chapter.) In some English-speaking countries, such as South Africa, Canada, Australia, and the US, the costs may be less because there aren't any translation costs to be met. However, in, say Japan, France, and Germany, the translation fees increase the costs considerably.

For example, if you file in the 12 major member nations of the European Union, plus South Africa, Australia, Japan, China, South Korea, and Mexico (a relatively modest programme), you need a piggy-bank holding between £50,000 and £60,000, the bulk of which you need up front.

You can't handle your foreign application yourself. Even your UK patent attorney must hire a patent attorney in each country you target. We included all these associates' fees and other charges in our estimates.

Don't think about starting an overseas application programme unless you're certain that you can finance it to completion. In our experience, many folks and small businesses abandon their applications halfway through the process for lack of funds. The large sums they've already spent (and can't recover) would've been better spent on research and design (R&D) or marketing.

Try to be creative, and let someone else pay the piper. If you can license your invention early, be a tough negotiator and insist that the big guy, your licensee, pays for the acquisition and maintenance of foreign patents. You can readily achieve this if your licence is for the exclusive rights to exploit your invention.

Making the decision

To decide whether to file abroad, ask yourself: Are the benefits that you and your business are likely to receive by filing abroad worth the cost? Only you can make this business decision. Your patent attorney can answer questions about the topic, but don't expect her to make the decision for you.

The simpler the technology of your product, the more foreign protection you need because other businesses are more likely to copy it.

In each country you consider, look at the revenue potentials of each patented product, the likely licence revenue, and the adverse consequences of not being covered. Add up your resources and try to work out whether patenting overseas is worthwhile for you.

Every business decision is a gamble. Filing for an overseas patent may be your biggest one.

Playing by the Rules of Foreign Patents

Before filing a patent application abroad, we suggest you consider our basic rules.

✔ **Keep your invention secret:** Under the provisions of the UK Patents Act 1977, and the novelty requirements of patent law in most other countries, you won't be able to obtain a valid patent if your invention was disclosed, without a confidentiality agreement, before you filed your patent application. Even just showing your prototype to your neighbour may constitute such a disclosure.

Treat your invention as a trade secret for as long as you can – and at least until you file your UK application. Don't discuss, show, or generally disclose your invention to anyone except your patent attorney. When you *do* disclose your invention to a third party, make sure that it's under strict conditions of confidentiality spelled out in a written agreement. You don't need a confidentiality agreement with your patent attorney. She's already under a legal obligation of strict confidentiality.

✔ **Filing an overseas application first:** As a UK citizen or legal resident, you can't file for a patent application or generally disclose your invention abroad before you obtain clearance to do so from the UK-IPO. Normally, when you file a patent application for whatever invention, if you don't receive a communication from the UK-IPO placing a secrecy order on your invention, you may assume that you're free to disclose your invention and to file an overseas application if you so wish. On the other hand, if you do file an overseas patent application, in the US for example, you may incur the wrath of the UK-IPO for doing so when you come to file a corresponding application claiming Convention Priority from the US application date. The reason for the requirement that you obtain clearance is perhaps somewhat archaic and reflects a time when the disclosure of inventions may have been of use to an enemy of the state. At the present, it's unlikely, but possible, that the UK-IPO would place a secrecy order on an invention for which a patent application is filed in the UK or when an applicant wishes to file overseas in the first instant. You may consider that the UK-IPO is being rather petty and that the likelihood of anyone devising a product that is of such import to the state that a secrecy order must be made is pretty remote. However, we've recently been party to receiving a disclosure from a retired electrical technologist who has devised a nuclear fusion device for generating electrical power in his garden shed. Not a problem you may think, but what if the invention had been for a nuclear fission device (a nuclear bomb), instead!

✔ **File your foreign patent application within one year from the filing date of your UK application:** This point is critical if you want to claim priority on an invention based on your UK filing date under the Paris Convention, as we explain in the section 'Filing separately under the Paris Convention'. If you don't take advantage of the Convention, you may lose your chance of getting foreign patents if your invention becomes known through publication of your UK application, or the issue of your patent.

The publication of an application or the grant of a patent constitutes a public disclosure of the invention. If this rule wasn't enforced, any unscrupulous individual who reads the published document could claim to be the inventor and file his or her own application.

As long as you keep your invention confidential you can file applications abroad more than one year after filing your UK application. But you don't get the advantage of an early priority date and may lose the patent to someone filing overseas just ahead of you. The absolute deadline occurs when your UK application is published, 18 months after its filing date or when your UK patent is granted, whichever comes first. To sum it all up: If you keep the invention secret, you have about 18 months to file abroad, but if you go public, you have only one year, under the provisions of the International Convention agreed between signatory countries in Paris in 1883. The agreement allows you twelve months from your UK filing date to file corresponding patent application(s) in any of the signatory countries and claiming the filing date of your UK application for your overseas applications.

Mark your calendar about ten months from your UK filing date to remind you that you only have two months left to start your overseas filing process, and also about five months thereafter to warn you of the publication deadline.

We'd like to add a fourth rule of our own: Let your patent attorney handle all your filing overseas through her own stable of foreign associates. Don't wait until the last month before any deadline. Your patent attorney and her associates may need time to prepare translations and obtain certified copies of assignments and other miscellaneous documents that may be necessary, particularly for applications in Latin American countries.

Working Out Where to File Your Patent Application

With the universal high cost of patents, few individuals or small businesses can afford a comprehensive foreign patent programme. Even huge multinationals carefully select the countries in which they apply for patent protection. These decisions can be difficult in the early stages of your business venture as you teeter between the need to conserve financial resources and your desire to secure a broad marketing territory for your invention.

In general, give priority to countries that offer a good potential market for your product over those that only have advanced manufacturing capabilities. If patent protection allows you to control the most important markets for your product then nobody else is going to be interested in making the product. For example, if your product relates to surfing equipment, you may seek protection in Western European countries as well as Australia, Brazil, the US, and Japan where products may be a commercial success. You can bypass Taiwan, South Korea, and China – although these last three countries are prime manufacturing candidates so include them in your filing programme if you have your products made in one or more of these countries. Such a move prevents the manufacturer from making your product for his own local market!

If the invention has worldwide applications, target the most prosperous countries rather than the most populous. The most popular choices include: Western Europe, Japan, Canada, Australia, Mexico, Hungary, Taiwan, New Zealand, Israel, South Africa, South Korea, the US, and Brazil. The nature of your invention dictates where you apply. Obviously, you can't sell many snowmobiles in Australia or surfboards in Hungary.

Research the population, average personal income, and manufacturing capabilities of the countries you consider. Don't rely on your patent attorney's recommendations, except in connection with expenses for each foreign application. Your patent attorney has a duty to help you obtain the maximum protection in as many countries as possible, but she's not a marketing expert. Most patent attorneys are reluctant to discourage you from filing in any particular country because that country may one day offer a lucrative market or be of particular interest to a potential licensee.

You can choose from two main strategies to get the patent coverage you need. You can file individual patent applications in each country you choose, or you can file in several countries at once under the *Patent Co-operation Treaty (PCT)*. We outline both options in this section and give you the pros and cons of each.

Filing separately under the Paris Convention

If you want to get a patent in only two or three countries or obtain a patent as quickly as possibly, you should apply directly with those countries. You must also apply directly with any country that isn't a member of a multinational patent-filing system, such as a number of South American nations.

Almost two hundred countries are members of the *Paris Convention for the Protection of Industrial Property* (Paris Convention of 1883), which outlines basic rules and IP protections. The Paris Convention gives you up to one year after the filing date of your first patent application in your own country to file a corresponding application in a member country and get the earlier filing date as your *Convention priority date* (often shortened to *priority date*).

That priority date defines both your priority of invention and filing. The Convention priority date is the best thing since the invention of the Swiss Army knife. If someone else has filed an application for the same invention in that country after your priority date and before your foreign application is filed, your application takes precedence over the later filed application. Also, if any document describing your invention is published during that interim period, it won't be cited against your foreign application. The priority date for trade marks and registered design under the same convention is limited to six months. The Convention priority date can be claimed in a single country application as well as in the multinational patent applications discussed in a moment.

A few countries haven't ratified the Paris Convention. For a list of the Convention signatories, go to `www.wipo.int/treaties/en/ShowResults.jsp?lang=en&treaty_id=2`. Taiwan is one exception, but don't fret! The UK and Taiwan have a separate arrangement that provides the same filing convenience to UK inventors.

In addition to providing a way to eliminate any interim patent application by another inventor, the Paris Convention makes it easy to meet two of the three basic rules in the section 'Playing by the Rules of Foreign Patents'. If you take advantage of the Paris Convention, you only need to keep your invention confidential up to the date of your UK filing. You can start selling your 'super-duper squabulators' the very next morning and file foreign applications, initiating them at home or abroad, up to 364 days later. That's because your foreign applications are considered to have been filed on the same date as the UK one. You must specifically claim the benefit of your UK filing date in each foreign application.

Make sure that your foreign patent attorney asks for this one-year convention-priority benefit when preparing your application, because the benefit's not automatically granted. However, this benefit has a price – government authorities extract a few more pounds from your pocket. Your attorney also wants her due reward for ticking the right box on the application cover letter. Then, you're also asked to provide a certified copy of your original UK application that the UK-IPO provides upon filing a Patents Form No. 23 plus a Fee Sheet FS2 and a payment of £20.00.

Hitting two or more birds with one stone: multinational patent applications

Some small, mostly developing countries, have established a common patent authority that can grant you a single multinational patent enforceable by the courts of all participant nations – a real bargain in terms of cost and time. These regional patent authorities include the following:

- ✔ **African Regional Industrial Property Organisation (ARIPO)** located in Harare, Zimbabwe, covers the former British possessions of Gambia, Ghana, Lesotho, Malawi, Mozambique, Sierra Leone, South Africa, Sudan, Swaziland, Uganda, United Republic of Tanzania, Zambia, and Zimbabwe. The ARIPO language is English. The ARIPO conducts a formal examination of the application before granting a patent.

- ✔ **Eurasian Patent Office (EAPO)** operating under the Eurasian Patent Convention (EAPC) in Moscow, Russia, gathers the former Soviet republics of Armenia, Azerbaijan, Belarus, Kazakhstan, Kyrgyzstan, Republic of Moldova, Russian Federation, Tajikistan, Turkmenistan, as well as Pakistan. Applications must be in Russian. The EAPO conducts a substantive examination only upon request. You must enter this request when you file your application.

- ✔ **Office Africaine de la Propriété Industrielle (OAPI)** with headquarters in Yaoundé, Cameroon, groups the former French colonies of Benin, Burkina Faso, Cameroon, Central African Republic, Chad, Congo, Côte d'Ivoire, Equatorial Guinea, Gabon, Guinea, Guinea-Bissau, Mali, Mauritania, Niger, Senegal, and Togo. The OAIP accepts patent applications in English and French.

  Currently, the OAPI doesn't conduct any substantive examinations. An OAPI patent that's enforceable in all the member nations is granted without warranty of validity. The patent validity issue remains to be resolved at the time of trial when you sue an infringer.

Filing under the European system

The members of the European Union (EU) and a few candidate nations have instituted a well-rounded patent system, administered by the European Patent Office (EPO) located in Munich, Germany, and in The Hague, Netherlands.

The contracting states are Austria, Belgium, Bulgaria, Cyprus, Czech Republic, Denmark, Estonia, Finland, France, Germany, Greece, Hungary, Ireland, Italy, Latvia, Lithuania, Luxembourg, Malta, Netherlands, Poland, Portugal, Romania, Slovak Republic, Slovenia, Spain, Sweden, and the UK. This list grows as other nations join the EU. For a nominal fee, an EPO application can be extended to candidate nations including Albania and Macedonia, in anticipation of their future admission.

The EPO accepts patent applications in English, French, or German. After the application has been approved in one of the three official languages, it must be translated into the other two. The patent can then be filed in any one of the designated countries to be issued by the local patent authority. Only the claims of a patent have to be translated into a local language where a patent is maintained in a non-English, -French, or -German language EU country.

After your patent application has been approved by the EPO, you must hire patent attorneys in member countries you selected on your application. At this point, you've paid your UK patent attorney, and her associates in some other designated nations. Also, you need to pay a plethora of government charges, and don't forget the translations of the claims – two more reasons to keep your application short and simple, especially if you require protection in countries where translation charges are very costly.

Filing under the Patent Co-operation Treaty

Under the *Patent Co-operation Treaty* (PCT), over 135 nations operate a common, uniform process for the filing of patent applications. The PCT lets you submit a single patent application in your own domestic patent office whilst reserving the right to file that application in any contracting nation. Moreover, the PCT integrates the Paris Convention of 1883, and counts among its members the EPO and the four multinational patent authorities listed in the previous section 'Hitting two or more birds with one stone: multinational patent applications'.

By filing a PCT application in English with the UK-IPO, you can postpone entering your application abroad for about 30 months from the priority date of your initial UK application. The World Intellectual Property Organisation (WIPO), headquartered in Geneva, Switzerland, administers the PCT.

This system allows you to postpone the heavy cost of filing overseas, giving you time to test-market your invention. By the 30th month you should know whether you're going to get a worthwhile patent. By then, you either have your UK patent, or you've undergone a fairly complete examination. (See Chapters 4 through 10 for the whole patent story.) If it looks as if you're not getting a good patent, you can abandon your foreign filing and avoid unnecessary expense.

Membership in the PCT changes constantly. You can download a comprehensive list of contracting nations at `www.wipo.int/treaties/en/Show Results.jsp?lang=en&treaty_id=6`

A PCT application goes through four processing stages: the filing stage, the international stage, the regional stage, where a bloc of territories are bound by an agreed protocol, and finally, the national stage.

PCT procedures, regulations, and fees are in a constant state of flux. What we write today may change by the time you read this. Check the WIPO Web site frequently for the latest rules and forms.

Filling out the filing stage

You begin by filing your PCT application with the UK-IPO, which serves as the receiving office. See Chapter 7 for information on patent applications.

1. **Find the forms you need to fill out.** You need a:

   - Request form

   - Transmittal Letter form

   - Power of Attorney form (when applicable)

   You can view and download all the necessary forms from the WIPO Web site at `www.wipo.int/pct/en/forms`.

2. **Fill out the Transmittal Letter and Power of Attorney forms.** These forms are self-explanatory.

3. **Complete the Request form.** It comes with ample instructions, but here are some pointers:

   - Follow the instructions to the letter or your application may be rejected.

   - Claim the filing date of your prior UK application – so long as it was filed no more than a year before the PCT application – in order to establish the earliest possible priority date.

- Sit down before you tackle the Fee Calculation Sheet, which is part of the Request form. The total often exceeds €1,800 just for filing the application.

- Keep in mind when selecting the countries to apply in that you never have to pay for more than ten designated countries. Most applicants designate all members of the PCT on the Request form, and then, before entering the regional and national stages, drop the ones they don't want or can't afford.

4. **Send in your application.**

   You may mail your application, but you get a discount off the filing fee when you file electronically. Check out the *PCT Applicant's Guide* on the WIPO Web site.

5. **The UK-IPO, acting as a receiving office, verifies that your application conforms to all applicable regulations and that you paid the necessary fees.**

   You also get some time to provide any necessary corrections or additions before the application is forwarded to the *International Bureau* at WIPO for the second stage of the procedure.

Going through the international stage

The International Bureau deals only with the multinational aspect of the application, which is the International Stage. Because the PCT was approved in two separate parts, the treaty is divided into two chapters. Member countries can observe the limited provisions of Chapter I, which includes an anticipation search but no examination of the merits of the invention, or adhere to the whole treaty, including Chapter II, which includes an examination of the claims based on the findings of the Chapter I search. Both chapters are processed during the International Stage. Currently, all PCT nations are bound by both chapters. Some future members may limit their participation to Chapter I. Check the WIPO Web site at `www.wipo.int` for the current members' status.

Form-filling, European style

The PCT administration is essentially European in style and mentality. Every form must be filled out exactly as prescribed. Your last name must be entered first and your first name last. Your country of residence can't be listed as *UK* or the *United Kingdom*. It must be *GB* with no full-stops. And so it goes, with a multitude of meticulous rules that, just because they're so detailed, must be constantly updated. Fortunately, the good people in the UK-IPO are most willing to help you comply with all these PCT procedures. Most of the time, they graciously correct your minor mistakes, instead of returning the whole application.

In Chapter I, a few months after your application reaches the International Bureau, your claims are subject to an anticipation search, better known as the *International Search,* which is conducted in your receiving office, in your case the UK-IPO, or the *International Searching Authority* at the International Bureau.

After you review the *International Search Report,* you have the opportunity to amend your claims. Exactly 18 months from the priority date, the application, search report – and any amendments – are published for the entire world to read.

Before the end of the 19th month from your priority date, you can initiate the Chapter II phase by filing a 'Demand for International Preliminary Examination' of your application. The Demand form *must* include your final list of the designated countries.

Rules are forever changing among the members of the PCT. The list of countries that still observe the 'Demand for International Preliminary Examination' requirement has shrunk to a point where many applicants don't bother filing the Demand. They accept filing of the application in their respective patent offices up to 31 months from the priority date. You can file your application in any of these countries that you elected in your Request. Consult your patent attorney to decide which way to go. You may not be interested in a patent in some of the designated countries.

If you file a Demand, you should receive a report on the International Preliminary Examination a few months after you submit the Demand. You then have another opportunity to amend your claims before entering the regional and national stages.

Upon entering Chapter II with a Demand, you also have until 30 or 31 months from your priority date to file applications in the countries or groups of countries that adhere to Chapter II.

You must file your application before the expiration of the 19th month from your priority date in the countries that don't adhere to Chapter II.

Entering the regional stage

After the International Publication of your PCT application, you can move on to getting the actual patents by filing your PCT application with one of the three regional patent authorities mentioned earlier in this chapter: OAIP, ARIPO, and EAPO. These applications must be filed within the same time period as applications into individual countries. You can also file your application in the EPO under the same time constraints.

The EPO conducts a fully fledged examination and then issues a patent that can be entered in any designated country in the group. In most EPO countries, after the patent is issued, it only needs to be translated into the national language before it becomes locally enforceable.

During the regional phase, your patent attorney's associate deals with the multinational organisations on your behalf. The office reports are sent to your patent attorney for your review and instructions on how to answer any objection or rejection. Don't be surprised if the process drags out over a year or two.

Entering the national phase

Some countries, including the US, Australia, Canada, China, and Mexico, don't belong to a regional group. You must send your PCT application to each one separately through your attorney's associate. Your PCT application may be subject to a complete new examination, just as any domestic (non-PCT) examination. Some countries skip the new examination if you agree to accept the results of the Preliminary International Examination (if you haven't amended your claims after that examination).

You must have a local patent attorney (in most cases a foreign associate of your UK patent attorney) at each level and pay local fees. This makes the whole process quite expensive, but cheaper than filing directly in the patent office of each country.

Filing a PCT application after a basic UK patent application

After you file a patent application in the UK, within one year you can file a PCT application and applications in non-PCT countries as illustrated in Figure 18-1. This approach postpones the big expenses associated with regional and national filings for up to 31 months, and expedites the grant of your UK patent.

The time line of Figure 18-1 indicates the set periods within which you need to take necessary action to prevent your application from lapsing. For example, you can't file a PCT application after twelve months and claim the priority date of your UK application on which it may otherwise be based. However, after filing your UK application, you may file your PCT application at any time within the twelve-month period.

You may, of course, file a PCT application in the first instant, especially if you wish to speed up the prosecution to grant or issue of a patent in countries of prime interest.

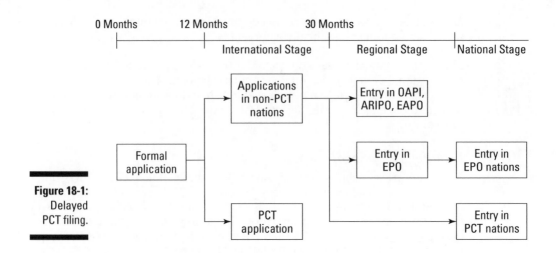

Figure 18-1:
Delayed
PCT filing.

Filing for Design Protection Abroad

In Chapter 11 we offer extensive information and guidance for filing applications to protect your design. In that chapter, we explain that the European Union provides *Community Design* protection for a new appearance of a product that exhibits 'individual character'. The Community Design protection has a term of five years from the deposit of a graphic representation of the design, and can be renewed four times for a total span of 25 years.

Applications to register a Community Design are processed by the Office for Harmonization in the Internal Market (OHIM) located in Alicante, Spain. Download information about the OHIM registration process from their Web site at http://oami.europa.eu. After the registration is granted, it's enforceable in all member nations of the EU without having to obtain a separate registration in each country.

The Community Design protection is typical of what's available in most industrialised countries. You can register industrial designs in Africa with the OAPI and the ARIPO (see the section 'Entering the regional stage,' earlier in this chapter, for more info on these regional patent authorities). The conditions and procedures are similar to applying with the OHIM. These applications have to be handled by the local associates of your patent attorney.

You may also want to check out the *International Deposit of Industrial Designs Agreement* (The Hague Agreement). About 30 nations adhere to this agreement, which offers basically the same type of protection as the Community Design. Check the WIPO site or ask your attorney.

Any type of application for design protection abroad can claim a priority date upon a design patent application filed in the UK-IPO no more than six months before filing abroad, instead of one year for a patent.

Have a local IP attorney handle your filing or deposit. Most UK patent attorneys maintain a network of foreign associates upon whom they rely for that kind of filing. Requirements vary widely from country to country. A design doesn't usually disclose any kind of technological breakthrough and consequently isn't subject to the foreign filing consent that is required for patent applications.

Looking After Your Trade Mark Abroad

In Chapter 17, we set out the procedure to be followed in order to secure a Registered Trade Mark in the UK. If your business interests are widespread and you're actively involved in marketing your design, or you're taking steps to market your design in one or more European countries, it may be to your advantage to seek Trade Mark Registration with OHIM in Alicante. OHIM is the European Community's Office for Harmonization in the Internal Market. You may also have business interests in some African territories, in which case you may make use of the provisions provided by the OAPI and the ARIPO in Africa to get a registration enforceable in all their member states.

The European Union, which currently consists of 27 member states, including the UK, may be a market for your designs. Therefore, if your business interests are in France, Germany, Italy, or Spain, you should consider filing a trade mark application at OHIM.

The application may be filed direct to OHIM in Alicante, Spain or to the UK-IPO by fax, mail, or electronically. The electronic application form to OHIM, is on their Web site at oami.europa.eu/en/design/form.htm.

You may fill in the application form in any of the languages of the European Union. You must also choose a second language from Spanish, German, English, French, or Italian.

The UK-IPO has produced a booklet entitled 'How to apply for a Community Trade Mark'. The booklet contains full details of how to fill in the requisite application form, the mailing addresses of OHIM and the UK-IPO, and full details of the information required. The booklet also sets out the fees due with the application and, in the case of applications made to the UK-IPO, the handling fee that must be paid.

Considering Copyright Overseas

International conventions and treaties, subscribed to by almost every country, mandate that each nation gives non-residents the same copyright protection it extends to its own citizens and legal residents, with no registration or other formality. So, in principle, there's no compelling reason to register your copyright abroad. However, some countries, including the US, grant special procedural rights to owners of registered copyrights.

If you're concerned about infringement of your copyright in a particular country, ask your patent attorney to look at the copyright regulations in that jurisdiction to see if you can benefit from a local registration.

Because of the complexity of the laws of copyright in the UK and elsewhere, your patent attorney may have to seek the advice a lawyer who specialises in the law of copyright. Even so, the lawyer may also need the help of associates in other countries.

For example, if products were being copied in the US, although you may own the copyright that was being infringed, you have to register your copyright with the US Copyright Office before you can enter an infringement action in the US.

Always seek expert opinion before embarking upon a course that may prove to be very expensive and may not be resolved in your favour.

Chapter 19

Making 'em Pay: Licensing Your IP Rights

- -

In This Chapter

▶ Exploiting your IP rights – licensing

▶ Considering assigning

▶ Avoiding tax and competition problems

▶ Maximising the income from your musical works

- -

*I*f you have vision, you develop your intellectual property (IP) assets with an eye towards letting these assets, and your IP rights to them, work like a lucrative investment. The royalties your IP assets generate, just like dividends and interest, can keep your wallet bulging – without having to lift a finger except to hoist that frosty piña colada off the table by your poolside lounge chair. That dream has become reality for many astute entrepreneurs who took advantage of licensing opportunities that rewarded their creativity. You can license your invention, know-how, an original work of authorship, or brand as long as it's protected by a patent, trade secret, copyright, or trade mark. In this chapter, we explore the different kinds of licences and the legal requirements you need to comply with. We also touch on developing a licensing plan and dealing with the quirks of the music business.

The specific legal language of licensing contracts is very important. The language used in this chapter's examples, although based on legal agreements, may or may not be appropriate for your industry, field, and/or invention. Get good legal counsel when setting up a licensing agreement.

Considering Different Types of Licence

A *licence* is a contract between two parties. The *licensor* is the owner of an IP asset and its corresponding IP rights. The *licensee* is an individual or company that wants to use the IP assets in exchange for the payment of royalties or other valuable considerations. For example, if the IP asset is an invention and the IP right a patent, the licensee can practice the invention without being sued for infringement by the licensor.

A licence doesn't actually transfer an asset or right – rather, a licence gives the licensee permission to use the IP asset backed by the licensor's promise not to cancel that authorisation as long as the licensee keeps up his or her end of the bargain by making the required payments.

A licence is like the lease of a house, where the landlord gives the tenant permission to live there as long as the tenant pays the rent on time. If you evict a tenant or they leave, you're free to re-let your house.

If you cancel the licensee's authorisation to make, use, and sell your invention, you may seek other licensees so that you can continue to have an income from your invention.

An *assignment*, which is an outright transfer of an IP asset or right, is like *selling* a house. By agreeing to assign your IPRs to an individual or a company, you accept the payment for the assignment, which is normally paid in full when you and the assignee (the other party), sign on the dotted line. At the same time you hand over the certificate of grant for the patent (and any documents relating to registered design, trade marks, and so on).

If the settlement's big enough you can now retire to the south of France, and forget all about the tiresome business of remembering to pay renewal fees for maintenance of the patent!

Be aware that having assigned all rights in your IPRs, you can't continue to make, use, and sell your invention. However, you can continue with your research and development of your next invention, which you can assign (sell) in due course.

We list here six types of licence, which vary according to the underlying type of IP right:

- ✔ **Combination licence:** In a combination licence, several IP assets and rights are bundled together, such as when a manufacturer is authorised to produce and sell a patented article under the licensor's mark and package it with copyrighted graphics.

- ✔ **Copyright licence:** A copyright licence allows the licensee to enjoy the copyright in a work. For example, if you've designed a new shape for a wheelbarrow or a car, the design drawings for the wheelbarrow and car enjoy copyright protection from the date they're created. Therefore, you may give any interested party permission by way of a copyright licence to make, use, and sell the wheelbarrow or cars made to your design.

- ✔ **Merchandising licence:** This is a copyright or trade mark licence, or a combination of both, where the range of goods upon which the mark or the copyright work is used goes beyond its original purpose. Certain marks are so strong, recognised, and widely accepted that they can be rented out for use on a wide variety of goods. For instance, a movie studio may license the use of a cartoon character on a variety of children's products from toys to school satchels.

Merchandising is pure name exploitation that depends on the value of the mark itself and the impression it conveys, and not the quality or reputation of the products or services originally provided under the mark. For example, the 'Dior' mark appears on a multitude of products, from garments and perfumes to sporting goods.

✔ **Patent licence:** This licence permits use of a technological breakthrough, such as a new type of mousetrap. In a licence or other legal document, your technological breakthrough is modestly referred to as an *improvement*, not an invention.

You can license your asset before you get your patent, because a licence is a contract that stands independently from the patent. Courts recognise that when a manufacturer takes a licence from an inventor, the former is buying insurance (with the royalties as the premium) against being sued for infringement when the patent is granted. After the licence agreement is signed, it doesn't matter whether the patent is granted. The manufacturer may have to pay royalties for the duration of the agreement unless agreed otherwise.

✔ **Trade or service mark licence:** This licence authorises someone else to operate under one or more of your marks. The law requires that you keep some quality control over the activities of your licensee so that the customers who relied on the quality of your goods or services in the past won't be deceived.

Nowadays, many products aren't made by their original manufacturers but by firms that use the trade mark under licence from the original manufacturer and strict quality control conditions. For example, a Marks & Spencer dressing gown may have been manufactured by one of many domestic and foreign licensees of M&S.

In the UK, you automatically create rights in your mark by using it in business. For example, if you make and sell 'exceedingly good cakes', there's no legal requirement to register it first (although we recommend that you do so). However, in some countries the person or company who registers the mark first is recognised as the legal owner of the mark.

✔ **Trade-secret licence:** A trade-secret licence is a contract to have the licensor disclose proprietary and confidential information to the licensee in exchange for a payment and a promise to keep the information under wraps. This is common in the chemical field where it's relatively easy to keep formulae and processes secret, and is more practical than getting a patent (see Chapter 5).

A *franchise* is a trade mark or service mark licence with rules about how the licensee (or *franchisee*) shall conduct the business according to a method imposed by the licensor, called the *franchisor*. Franchising is a type of contractual relationship that includes some transfer of know-how and technical assistance by the franchisor (coupled with a hefty down payment by the franchisee). Fast-food franchises are a familiar example, where a franchisee acquires a restaurant carrying the franchisor's trade mark or service mark and prepares and serves food under a set method and under strict quality control.

Inspecting the Basic Elements of a Licence

Before you can negotiate any type of licence agreement, you need to understand the important parts of an agreement and the specific legal clauses that you may want to include. We give some examples here from a patent licence to give you some legal speak to chew on. These clauses can be adapted to cover licences for other types of IP assets and rights.

The outline of the basic clauses in a licence agreement that we offer here isn't exhaustive. Like any contract, the licence agreement must include a number of additional clauses relative to future improvements, technical assistance, warranties, legal action against infringers, termination, notices and arbitration, just to name a few. Our goal is to make you aware of the key issues you should address when exploiting your IP assets. We strongly recommend that you seek the assistance of a competent IP attorney for negotiating and drafting the licence agreement.

Defining IP assets and rights

You must first clearly define the IP asset or right you're licensing:

> *The licensor is the sole owner of an improvement in an auto-focusing mechanism for cameras (The 'Improvement'), disclosed in a pending UK Patent Application No. GB0765432.1 entitled Auto-focusing Mechanism for Outdoor Surveillance Video Camera (the 'Application') from which a number of domestic and foreign patents are expected to be granted and/or issued (the 'Patents').*

> *The licensee wishes to obtain the right to manufacture and sell several types of cameras using the Improvement.*

Granting permission to use your IP

The clause granting permission defines the scope of the permitted activities and is the most important part of the licence agreement because it spells out the different scope of the types of licence and the rights granted to the licensee and those retained by the licensor.

Exclusivity

The *exclusivity clause* states who gets to use the invention.

- **Exclusive:** The licensor waives any right to practise the invention or to authorise anybody else to do so.

- **Non-exclusive:** The licensor reserves the right to practise the invention and can also license third parties in competition with the licensee.

- **Sole:** The licensor reserves the right to practise the invention, but agrees not to license anyone but the licensee.

The exclusivity clause determines other terms of the agreement, such as the amount of royalties, and the legal rights of the parties. For instance, an exclusive licence carries higher royalties than a sole or non-exclusive licence. Only an exclusive licensee can file legal actions against infringers.

The clause must be very specific in order to avoid future disputes. For the sake of illustration, the following licence contains multiple exclusivity provisions. Most licences have a single exclusivity clause.

> The licensor grants the licensee:
>
> a) an exclusive licence and permission to manufacture, offer for sale, sell, and use digital still cameras incorporating the Improvement with the right to grant a sublicence to others to do the same,
>
> b) a sole licence and permission to manufacture, offer for sale, sell, and use analogue and digital video cameras incorporating the Improvement without the right to grant a sublicence to others to do the same; and
>
> c) a non-exclusive licence and permission to manufacture, offer for sale, sell, and use analogue still cameras incorporating the Improvement without the right to grant a licence to others to do the same.
>
> The licensor reserves the right to manufacture, offer for sale, sell, and use said analogue and digital video cameras, without the right to grant a licence to others, and to manufacture, offer for sale, sell, and use said analogue still cameras with the right to grant a licence to others to do the same.
>
> The licensor shall not use any IP right he/she may acquire over the Improvement to exclude the licensee from doing the acts authorised by this clause so long as the licensee complies with all the terms and conditions of this agreement.

Territory and field of use

An owner of any type of IP asset and rights can divide and parcel the geographical areas and commercial fields where the invention can be practised or applied. In the illustration below, each licence has a distinct territory:

> *Said exclusive licence shall be limited to the consumer market in the United Kingdom and Ireland and shall not extend to cameras primarily intended for professional or industrial use.*

> *Said sole licence shall be limited to the United Kingdom and Ireland in any field of use except geographical mapping and law enforcement surveillance cameras.*

> *Said non-exclusive licence shall apply worldwide without any field of use limitations.*

Duration

To avoid allegations of abusive conduct, the duration of the licence must be no more than the life of the patent or any other applicable IP right. A patent licence agreement should specify that if no patent is granted or issued, the duration should be no more than 20 years (the maximum life of a patent).

> *The term of the above licences and the obligations imposed on the licensee in this agreement shall not last beyond the expiration of the last of the patents. In any territory where no patent has been granted or issued within ten years from the effective date of this agreement, said licence and obligations shall expire on the tenth anniversary of said date.*

Where 'secret know-how' is included in a licence agreement, it's not unusual for the licence to be maintained after any patent is refused or found invalid but on a reduced royalty rate.

Getting paid

The law allows great flexibility in setting up the payment for the licence. Payment may comprise:

- One or more lump sums.
- Royalties based on net proceeds, number of items made or sold, costs of goods, or any other readily verifiable parameter.
- A combination of the above.

Advances against royalties, delayed payments, stepped-up or stepped-down royalty rates based on sale proceeds or number of items sold, and guaranteed remittances can be used to fine-tune the agreement to the circumstances:

The licensee shall pay the licensor each of the following:

A non-refundable lump sum of £5,000 on each anniversary of the effective date of this agreement.

During the first 10 years of the term of this agreement, royalties at the rate of £10 per camera manufactured under said exclusive and co-exclusive licences, and at the rate of £3 per camera manufactured under said non-exclusive licence; plus 1 per cent of the net proceeds from the sales of all types of cameras. After the 10th anniversary of the effective date of this agreement, said royalty rates shall be reduced by one half.

A royalty advance of £25,000 upon execution of this agreement by all parties. The licensee shall not apply more than £5,000 per month out of said advance payment against royalties payable to the licensor.

Business circumstances usually dictate the details of the remuneration clause – issues such as the financial status and marketing expertise of the licensor, the anticipated sales, the required investment in tooling and marketing, and so on.

A minimum performance clause should always be included in an exclusive licence because you depend entirely upon the licensee's performance to exploit your IP asset. Such a clause may use a sliding scale to keep the licensed company on its best behaviour. For example:

The licensor shall have the right to terminate this agreement by thirty day written notice to the licensee in the event that the total amount of monetary remuneration received by the licensor does not exceed:

£50,000 during the first full calendar year,

£100,000 during the second calendar year,

£150,000 or one half of the total monetary remuneration received by the licensor during the preceding calendar year in any subsequent calendar year, whichever is the greater.

Reporting on royalties due to the Licensor

Except when licence fees are fully paid up front or by a fixed payment schedule, the licensee should be required to periodically report its sales and pay the applicable royalties:

Within thirty days from the end of each quarter the licensee shall provide the licensor with a report of the number of cameras manufactured under each of said licences and of net proceeds collected by the licensee during said quarter and shall tender payment of royalties applicable to said number and proceeds. The quarters are usually set to end on 31st March, 30th June, 30th September, and 31st December in any one calendar year.

Controlling the use of a trade mark

If the licence authorises the licensee to use or operate under your trade mark or service mark, you must include a clause allowing you to control the quality of the goods or services provided to the customer under your trade mark or service mark.

> *Goods manufactured under this agreement shall conform with all applicable standards and shall maintain a level of quality and merchantability equal to or better than the goods currently being manufactured and sold by the licensor. The licensor shall have the right to enter the licensee's manufacturing and storage facilities on any working day during regular business hours without prior notice to inspect said goods for compliance with this clause.*

As owner of the trade mark or service mark, you're liable for any losses suffered by the consumer as a result of any defect or failure of the product or inadequate service. This is why any trade or service mark licence includes conditions relating to the quality and standard of products or services provided under the marks. You set the quality and standards and you're responsible for periodically monitoring them. Neglecting to keep an eye on your licensee's activities may cost you dearly in having to meet the financial losses suffered by anyone buying your licensed products or services from your licensee. With pharmaceutical products, you risk having to meet large awards for damages if anyone suffers physical impairment by using a product that didn't meet the quality and standards set down by you before it was placed on the market.

In a patent licence agreement, the licensor usually won't make any warranty that the invention is worth anything, that it'll work as expected, or that the product or process made under it is effective and safe. No legal obligation is imposed on the licensor to exert any degree of quality control over the activities of the licensee, making the licensor immune to liability for any of the licensee's failures or misdeeds. It's up to the licensor to make sure that the patented invention he makes, uses, and sells under licence is fit for purpose.

Assigning Rather Than Licensing

Under certain circumstances, and for sundry reasons (such as tax considerations, wanting no further entanglement with the licensee, or because your prospective licensee wants it), you may decide to sell your IP asset and IP rights, under a written document called an *assignment*. Just like a grant deed on a piece of property. The assignment is signed by the parties and, for good measure you, the assignee, can register the assignment at the UK-IPO.

If you reside abroad, the assignment must be notarised (acknowledged before a UK consular officer) to be readily admissible in court. This type of legal paper can be quite short and to the point, like our example.

For good and valid consideration, hereby acknowledged, I, John Brown, the owner of UK Patent No. GB9,999,999 for an improvement in motorcycle helmet, hereby assign and transfer my entire interest in said improvement and patent to John Smith, a UK citizen residing in Halifax, Yorkshire.

The same wording can be used to transfer a copyright or mark. Just make sure that the description of what's being transferred is complete and readily identifiable (attach a copy or photograph if necessary). To be on the safe side, draft a more comprehensive document, preferably drawn up by your IP attorney.

If (based on the example above) you're John Smith, you want to record the assignment as soon as possible at the UK-IPO, or any other appropriate agency. In general, recording stops the transferor from assigning the same asset or right to another person and for renewal, notification purposes. If you don't record a patent or patent application assignment any subsequent assignment takes precedence over yours when it's recorded. Your sole remedy is to sue that weasel John Brown and try to get some compensation for your losses.

Whether you license or assign doesn't necessarily dictate how you get your money – you can use a lump sum payment or royalty programme for either method. However, a royalty programme should include an agreement with all the payment and reporting clauses usually found in a licence agreement.

Recording your document

In general, licence agreements don't require filing or registration with government regulatory agencies. However, you can record (don't confuse recording with registering) a patent or trade mark licence with the UK-IPO, just as you'd record an assignment or other transfer of title. An exclusive licensee wants to record the licence to deter infringers and to prevent the licensor from granting a similar licence to someone else.

Considering tax advantages

The government wants a chunk out of most exchanges of money. So although we're not tax experts, we'd like to alert you to the tax consequences of licensing your IP assets and rights – versus assigning them.

For tax purposes, proceeds from a licence are usually considered ordinary income. Proceeds from an assignment of assets are treated as capital gains. HM Revenue and Customs may treat some exclusive patent licences like assignments.

If you become involved in the transfer in or out of any intellectual property rights (IPR), you should consult with your accountant or tax adviser for the most advantageous way of scheduling payments for any monies paid to you or paid by you to a third party. The transfer of IPRs can attract large up-front payments to HM Revenue and Customs based on a notional value of future royalties. Therefore make sure that you take every step to ensure that you're not burdened with crippling tax liabilities before you begin to enjoy the rewards that are due to you as an inventor or designer.

Avoiding illegal entanglements

To a certain degree, patents, registered designs, copyright, and trade marks are monopolies and exceptions to many unfair competition and antitrust regulations. Therefore, the courts and government agencies monitor their use to prevent any coercive practices (such as tie ins, which we explain in a moment) by IP rights owners. We summarise here some basic rules to help keep you out of trouble: Don't leverage your IP rights to obtain advantages not directly related to those rights.

The most common faux pas committed by licensors are:

- ✔ **Bundlings:** Bundling occurs when you compel someone to take licences based on several patents or other IP rights or when you bundle different IP assets or rights in a single licence or in related ones. The practice of bundling is questionable rather than outright illegal because the nature of the wrongful conduct depends upon the circumstances.

    In the camera example, if you have a patent on a lens design and force the licensee to take a licence for the lens along with the auto-focusing mechanism that he or she wants, and other sources of lens technology exist, the licence may be held invalid. However, if the licensee requests a licence to make your lens because of its superior design, you're off the hook.

    It's also a no-no to obligate your patent licensee to also use your trade mark, but if the licensee likes your trade mark and asks you to license it along with your patent, no harm is done.

- ✔ **Tie-ins:** An illegal tie-in obligates a licensee to buy something from you that lies beyond the scope of your IP rights. For instance, in the camera example we use in this chapter, you can't obligate the licensee to buy his or her lenses from you, because your patent doesn't cover the lenses.

The main reason to avoid anti-trust or anti-competition clauses in your license agreement is that your licensee may have grounds to attack the agreement in any future dispute, and sue you for redress of any damage caused to him or her.

Adopting a Licensing Strategy

Many inventors and other developers of IP assets and rights don't have a clue about how to find a licensee to bring their creations to the market. They often fall victim to unscrupulous invention development companies (see our comments about these guys in Chapter 3). No magic formula works for everybody, but the best way is to plan your licensing strategy before you pursue IP rights. If you haven't planned your licensing strategy in advance, all is not lost. If you understand your market, you can develop an effective and lucrative strategy.

The first step to developing a good licensing strategy is to understand market realities. We give here a few of our personal observations based on many years of service to fledgling entrepreneurs:

- ✔ The more you develop your project, the more you get for it. Generally you can't sell an idea or concept. A patented but unproven invention may sometimes be sold or licensed, but not for much. An ongoing business, built around a product, process, or method protected by IP rights can be readily and lucratively sold.

- ✔ Few large companies respond to an unsolicited licence offer or proposal.

- ✔ Some large companies don't accept the disclosure of your device or concept in confidence, perhaps because they don't want to take the risk of compromising any ongoing research and development. Don't disclose your invention outside a non-disclosure agreement unless you have a granted patent. In addition, if you only have a pending patent application we would still advise you to disclose your invention within the added safety of a non-disclosure agreement. Check the small print in any so-called non-disclosure agreement offered by a manufacturer. You'll find plenty of escape clauses that render any promise of confidentiality meaningless.

- ✔ Manufacturing companies that can directly benefit from your product or process are your most promising licensing candidates. Don't bother with firms that promise to market anything to anybody.

- ✔ Don't spend your resources on a product that carries a substantial risk of personal injury without making sure that you or your eventual licensee can obtain product liability insurance at a reasonable cost. Product liability insurance is especially important for medicinal products (especially those to be taken internally), infant toys, baby carriers, and power tools.

Making Beautiful Music

The recording, sale, and performance of musical works is a huge, complex industry that relies heavily on copyright law to regulate most of its activities and large-scale licensing of copyright to distribute its creations.

As a copyright owner, you control and can license reproductions of your song on sheet music or recordings under a *mechanical licence*, and its public performance under a *performing licence*. You can also authorise a motion-picture studio to use your creation as background music under a *synchronisation licence*.

You can't possibly enter into licensing agreements with all the record companies, theatres, radio and TV stations, and other organisations that you hope are going to record, perform, and broadcast your music. Instead, associations of songwriters, music publishers, and recording companies have established complex but very efficient systems to transfer the copyright and channel a small part of the mechanical and performing royalties back to you.

Performing licence and royalties

The bulk of the money you get for your musical creation is from performance licence and royalties. Songwriter and author organisations collect your royalties every time a musical work is publicly performed or broadcast live or by recording. In the UK, the bodies that collect revenue, pay songwriters, and promote their business interests include:

- British Music Rights Organisation (BMR)
- Mechanical Copyright Protection Society (MCPS)
- Music Publishers Association (MPA)
- Performing Rights Society (PRS)
- Welsh Music Foundation (WMF)

Each of the preceding organisations maintains a list of all the works created by its members. They enter into licence agreements with theatres and broadcasting companies to monitor, report, and pay performing royalties, which they then distribute to the authors and music publishers.

Your first step as a songwriter is to join one of our listed organisations and give it a list of your songs. If your song is popular, a trickle of royalty payments flows in during the first few quarters as radio stations and DJs play your creations. More recently, bands place their music on the Internet and rely on downloads for their reward. Radiohead and other well-known groups have placed their latest releases on the Web with a proviso that anyone downloading their tracks merely pays what they consider is just. Where this leaves ongoing royalty payments for music and lyrics is still developing and may impact on the way in which songwriters benefit from their work.

Meeting mechanical licences and royalties

Mechanical licences allow a company to publish or record your music. Mechanical licences fall into two categories:

- A standard, *voluntary licence* is a licence that you willingly negotiate and grant on your own to a specific music publishing or record company. Little negotiation is involved because the royalty rates and modes of payment are pretty standard throughout the industry.

- A *compulsory licence* can be claimed by any recording company, without your consent, after you authorise a company to produce and sell a recording of your work (see Chapter 12).

Most music publishing or recording companies have standard licence agreements that don't give you much elbowroom to negotiate terms and conditions. They offer you a pittance for each record or piece of sheet music sold, because they have to pay a royalty to the recording artist, pay for the musicians and recording studio time, and assume other expenses associated with the packaging and sale of the recordings. Songwriters, in general, derive the bulk of their income from performing royalties and, to a lesser extent, from synchronisation royalties for the chosen few who are lucky enough to have their music selected by a movie producer (see 'Sounding out synchronisation licences' later for more info).

Your challenge is to maximise the performing royalties you receive. The music publishing company already collects your performing royalties – you as the author get your agreed share. This arrangement may be a bit unfair, because the company already receives revenue from the sale of sheet music and recordings. To level the playing field, many songwriters create their own music publishing companies that only deal with real music publishing and record companies. In turn, these other companies agree to give your own music publishing company an equal share of the performing royalties The net result is that you get 75 per cent in total of the royalties received, made up by 50 per cent from the real music publishing and recording company and your paper company's 25 per cent.

Sounding out synchronisation licences

A *synchronisation licence* allows the licensee to use a musical work as background music in a movie, play, video production, or other performance. The name comes from the fact that the music score has to be synchronised with the images and other sounds on the film or other recording medium.

If the job is substantial (an entire movie score), or if there's an existing relationship between the copyright holder and the producer, or if the holder is a famous composer or songwriter, the copyright holder and the producer may enter into a negotiated licence agreement. In other, more anonymous relationships, or when only a few minutes of music are at stake, the producer simply contacts a mechanical licence organisation and gets a standard licence at a standard rate.

Copyright in the electronic age

Periodically, the Copyright, Designs and Patents Act (1988) is revised to keep up with, among other things, advances in the music business. The changes being sought and thereafter being made aren't necessarily in response to the needs of the songwriters, but to the whims of the big players – the recording and movie companies and the major broadcasters.

However, that system is becoming obsolete. The Internet and music-sharing software threaten the recording industry with near extinction. Peer-to-peer music sharing is a blatant violation . You can be sure that a solution will soon be devised, not by facilitating copyright enforcement, but by amending the law to legitimise electronic music sharing and compensating the record companies with royalties from taxes paid by computer equipment manufacturers and transmission service providers. At that point, we'll rewrite this chapter!

Chapter 20

Nailing the Bad Guys
(The Infringers)

• •

In This Chapter

▶ Understanding the concept of infringement

▶ Enforcing your IP rights

▶ Checking out a remedy through the courts

▶ Negotiating your way out of a problem

• •

From a legal point of view, your patent, registered design, trade or service mark, or copyright, does nothing more than give you permission to exclude others from doing something only you can legally do. However, such permission has many limits and restrictions. You can't take things into your own hands and go shoot the meddler. You can't seize counterfeit merchandise made by your competitors. If you can't substantiate your allegations in court, you'll find yourself on the pillory being pelted with malodorous accusations of unfair practices, in the poorhouse, or both.

Our goal in this chapter isn't to discourage you from asserting your IP rights but to explain some of the procedures particular to IP litigations and to point you towards the most expeditious and least expensive approaches.

Determining Infringement

Determining whether an IP right has been infringed requires a careful legal analysis of all circumstances. Working through each IP right, we describe their respective infringement tests and how to apply them.

Violating a copyright

A copyright may be infringed by copying or making adaptations of the protected work, distributing or displaying copies or adaptations, publicly performing a musical or dramatic work, or transmitting and, in certain cases, defacing the work (see Chapter 12).

The act of copying requires special analysis, but all other instances of infringement are simply based on cold facts. For example, a recording of your song was either played over the radio or it was not. The test for infringement by copying is relatively simple and requires only a review of the facts and a bit of legal analysis. The infringement test can be summarised in three words: access, expression, and substantial similarity. Ask the following three questions:

✔ Did the alleged infringer have access to your copyright work?

✔ What part of your work constitutes a protected expression rather than a pure idea or material already in the public domain?

✔ If the answer to the first question is positive, do the similarities between that part of your work containing protected expression and the infringer's work indicate that partial or whole copying occurred?

If only part of the work was copied, make sure that the copied portion was protected by copyright and isn't in the public domain. Here's an example: You design home furnishings and create an elegant pedestal made of a long, fluted Greek column with a Corinthian capital, capped by a square plateau. One of your competitors comes out with a coffee table supported by a single foot in the shape of a squat and fluted Greek column with the same Corinthian capital as yours. You can prove that your competitor visited your showroom, but you can't prove infringement. What your competitor copied was the idea of a Greek column and the Corinthian capital used to support a piece of furniture. The concept of using an architectural column in a piece of furniture isn't protected by copyright. Corinthian capitals have been around since Alexander the Great was in nappies some 2,400 years ago. The copyrighted portion of your pedestal – its overall harmonious proportions – hasn't been copied.

For the infringement test of a computer program and other more complex works, check out Chapter 12.

Finally, you must make certain that the suspected infringement doesn't fall under one of the exemptions or exceptions listed in Chapter 12.

Imitating a trade mark or service mark

Determining whether your trade mark, or service mark, is being infringed is a bit more complex than assessing infringement of a copyright. The test is whether there's a likelihood of confusion between your mark and the alleged infringer's. *Likelihood* doesn't mean possibility but a reasonable expectation that the public can be confused, based on court-defined parameters.

Most courts use the tests we go over in Chapter 16 (do the marks look or sound alike); an additional factor is whether there have been instances of actual confusion. To document instances of actual confusion between the marks, keep records of any mistaken calls or enquiries you receive that were meant for the alleged infringer. Also, note any instances where one of your customers ordered or bought goods or services from the alleged infringer, thinking he or she was buying from you.

Establishing likelihood of confusion is fairly easy, and the penalties are severe and include costs incurred by the proprietor of an infringed mark and any damages that may be awarded by the court. Add to that the fact that you'll have to re-brand your products and pay for new packaging and advertisements. That's why imitating another's trade or service mark is a very risky choice.

Infringing a patent

Determining patent infringement requires very complex and costly legal analysis. We wouldn't expect you to conduct such an analysis – it's conducted by your IP attorney or even an IP lawyer – but we outline the gist of it here.

Don't worry if all the legal mumbo-jumbo is a bit difficult to understand. To determine patent infringement, you still need to shell out a few thousand pounds for an infringement analysis and obtain written opinion from a patent attorney or a lawyer specialising in IP law, or a Queen's Counsel.

A patent is infringed if the alleged infringer's device or process includes all the elements (or a substantial equivalent) listed in any one claim – in other words, the accused device doesn't have to infringe on all the claims, just one in its entirety (because each claim defines a different, distinct area of protected technology). The first step in determining patent infringement is getting the scope or coverage of your patent claims nailed down. The scope of a claim is strictly limited by its language. Language is, of course, open to interpretation, so both you and the alleged infringer propose your own interpretations of the claims to a judge, who decides the scope of each claim in a trial.

If the claim language is ambiguous, the description or the drawing (and sometimes both) are used to interpret the claim. Or the judge can receive expert testimony to interpret the meaning of a claim.

During the prosecution of a patent – that is, the actual official procedure before the UK-IPO – the inventor or his attorney may make concessions, such as restricting the meaning of a term, to avoid rejection because of a prior disclosure. For instance, the phrase 'tubular sleeve' may be restricted to tubular elements that are open at both ends, and exclude tubular sleeves that are closed at one or both ends. This kind of concession can only be discovered by careful examination of the prosecution file.

A patent claim that addresses a combination of two or more elements or components can be infringed if one of the elements or components is offered, sold, or imported in the UK with the intent to infringe a patent. Note that even assembly of elements or components outside the UK and imported into the UK may constitute an infringement.

Stopping Infringement Cold

If you've done your homework and are convinced that Tom is copying your poster that is protected by copyright, or Dick is using the *Kitty Love* trade mark on toastable tarts in derogation of your registered *Puppy Love* fast-food restaurant service mark, or Harry is making, importing, and selling cameras that incorporate your patented auto-focusing mechanism, you can take one of the following paths:

- ✔ Take the high road and file an infringement action. Don't forget to bring your chequebook!

- ✔ Look for a way, for example, mediation or arbitration, in order to reach an agreed settlement short of fullyfledged litigation.

- ✔ Send a *cease and desist notice* threatening the infringer with a lawsuit if the unlawful activities aren't promptly stopped. Be aware, however, that you must follow such a threat by an action for infringement, otherwise, you may be countersued in a threats action entered by the alleged infringer, especially if the alleged infringer considers that he has a cast-iron defence.

- ✔ If possible, negotiate a friendly face-to-face meeting with the alleged infringer and reach a settlement that accommodates the interests of both parties.

Taking the high road and going for broke

Suing the infringer is the most effective way to stop an infringement. However, suing can be a very expensive business and may drag out over two or more years, especially if a patent is involved.

Taking the litigation route in order to remedy a situation where your business interests are compromised by an infringement of your patent is not to be taken lightly. However, if there is no other way of dealing with the matter you should take full advantage of the expert advice and opinion of your patent attorney, your IP lawyer, and Queen's Council. Only then should you proceed on a path that may be rewarding but can't always be guaranteed. The proceedings can be broken into the stages we explain in the following sections.

The Patents Court

Almost all actions in the UK for patent infringement, or a declaration of non-infringement, and most cases for revocation of a patent, come before the English Patents Court, which is a specialised part of the Chancery Division of the High Court and is based in London.

Disputes that centre around technically simple issues are usually brought before the Patents County Court by small business enterprises. The Patents County Court is becoming more popular of late because of the speed with which it resolves disputes and the acceptable costs involved.

Starting the infringement action

A patent action in the High Court is commenced by issuing and serving a claim form (this used to be a writ). The claim form lists the claimant and the defendant as well as the patents and any other cause to be resolved such as copyright infringement, and other infringements of rights.

Stages in the action

A patent infringement action in the Patents Court usually takes about 12 months from service of the claim form to trial and judgement.

- In the first stage the parties exchange documents called statements of case (or pleadings) defining their respective allegations – those that are admitted and those that are to be resolved.

- The second stage (disclosure or discovery) principally involves collecting and disclosing to the opposite party all relevant documents and may also involve experiments by either party or both. For example, if the patent is for a chemical composition for effecting a particular result, each party is obliged to provide the other party and the court with the details of any experiment conducted to prove or disprove any allegation of infringement.

- The third stage involves the parties preparing and exchanging their written evidence for trial, which consists of experts' reports, witness statements, and selected documentary evidence from either sides' disclosure documents or other sources.

- The fourth and final stage consists of final preparation and the trial itself. The trial takes the form of a hearing in open court before a judge sitting without a jury. A patent action is almost always heard by one of the specialist Patent Court judges. Once a trial is started it normally proceeds continuously until the judge reserves judgement, which is usually given several weeks later.

You may have guessed, from reading these brief notes on the four main stages of a patent infringement action, that the use of IP professionals is of paramount importance if you're to stand any chance of success. It may transpire that you lose and are refused leave to appeal. That, unfortunately, is the end of the matter except for paying your legal team, paying the damages and costs awarded to the defendant if you're the plaintiff, and suffering loss of business. In certain cases, the trial judge or the Court of Appeal grants leave for an appeal to the Court of Appeal where you can raise points that may have been wrongly decided in the lower court. After that there's only the House of Lords, provided that the issues concern points of law with significant general public importance.

Praying for paying remedies

Your goal in a lawsuit is a court order that ends the infringing activities. Depending upon the type of action, and the statute under which you filed your complaint, you may ask for and recover your losses due to the infringer's activities; you may also ask to recover the infringer's profit, your attorney's fees, and the court costs.

What's the cost?

Here's our very rough estimate of the average cost to litigate or defend an infringement action all the way through trial, but short of appeal:

- ✔ Copyright: £100,000 to £200,000

- ✔ Trade secret: £100,000 to £200,000

- ✔ Trade or service mark: £100,000 to £250,000

- ✔ Registered design: £100,000 to £200,000

- ✔ Patent: £500,000 to £1,500,000

The infringer doesn't have to pay all of these costs but a proportion set by the court.

Use the preceding average figures for budgetary purposes, but bear in mind that actual costs can deviate substantially from these estimates. In some complex and dragged-out patent cases, courts have awarded very large damages and costs to the successful party. If the defendant doesn't have the resources to fight, he or she will cave in very early. Even large companies try to avoid the cost and the drain of human resources caused by IP litigation. That's why, in a large majority of patent cases, settlement is reached before trial. The parties may agree to a licence arrangement or the alleged infringer may decide to stop the infringing activity. In any case, the parties don't incur the high costs of paying for the services of a legal team made up of IP attorneys, IP lawyers, and Queen's Counsel.

We were involved in the preparation of one infringement action that went as far as visiting the court for the beginning of a trial, only for the parties to agree a settlement minutes before the scheduled start of the trial. Although the settlement was in the interests of both parties, the preparation had taken some 18 months and the cost to both parties, not including the time of the company executives spent in many conferences, was in excess of £300,000 for each party!

Insuring against litigation

If you just read the list of costs in the previous section, you're probably thinking, 'I can never afford to sue someone for infringing. Should I really even bother applying for a patent (or some other IP right)?' Good question. For a reasonable premium, you can purchase a policy that pays the cost of defending a claim of infringement brought against you or your company and also pays your attorney to pursue infringers of your intellectual property right (IPR). Refer to Chapter 24 for a source of litigation insurance information. The premium for that kind of insurance depends on many factors and is a matter for negotiation with the insurer.

Taking advantage of special remedies

Because of the high cost of fully-fledged litigation, in this section we cover some alternative and cheaper ways to stop copycats.

Criminal statutes

The following laws provide criminal penalties for some infringements of IP rights:

- ✔ Anti-piracy law provides for punishment of copyright infringement for commercial advantage or private financial gain, as well as the reproduction of recordings, the trafficking in counterfeit recordings, computer programs, and motion pictures. The penalties can be a term of imprisonment and a fine.

- ✔ The penalties for trafficking in counterfeit goods or services (using a counterfeit mark) can be a term of imprisonment and a fine.

Ask your patent attorney whether you can take advantage of these criminal statutes in order to fully protect your IPRs.

Anti-cybersquatting

If you find a domain name on the World Wide Web that's confusingly similar to your trade or service mark, you may make use of the World Intellectual Property Organisation's (WIPO's) Arbitration and Mediation Centre that deals with domain name disputes to get the offending name cancelled. You must prove that the name was selected and used in bad faith, which means that the infringer knew about your mark and intended to profit from or disparage your mark.

One well-known young man was recognised as a potential celebrity by a cybersquatter who registered the domain names www.waynerooney.com and www.waynerooney.co.uk when the budding football star was only sixteen years old. After Wayne Rooney scored his first Premiership goal as the youngest player, his fame as a footballing celebrity was established.

Wayne Rooney and his management secured registration of the words 'Wayne Rooney' in August 2004 and subsequently sought redress of the situation by filing an action under the WIPO Uniform Domain Name Dispute Resolution Policy (UDRP).

Although the cybersquatter claimed that his intent was to set up a fan club site, it was decided by Mr Tony Willoughby, an IP practitioner, that the domain name be transferred to Wayne Rooney and his management team.

If you discover a domain name that is confusingly similar to your registered mark, don't sit back and allow the cybersquatter to benefit, through use of your registered mark, from the goodwill you may have established. We suggest you seek the advice of an IP practitioner with experience in this complex area of IP theft.

Getting help from HM Revenue and Customs

HM Revenue and Customs can seize counterfeit merchandise that violates your registered trade or service mark or bears your company trade name. If you suspect an unlawful importation, you can notify HM Revenue and Customs of your registered mark so that they can seize the targeted goods. You can find contact details for HMRC at www.hmrc.gov.uk.

Acting swiftly with the help of HM Revenue and Customs is a much more efficient – and less expensive method – to stop counterfeit imported goods being sold on the UK market than waiting until they appear and then suing the UK distributor in a court of law.

Threatening litigation

Rather than making a beeline for the court as soon as you find out someone is infringing your rights, ask your attorney to send a letter to the infringer, identifying you as the registered proprietor of a patent or trade mark. What happens next can run from a great disappointment to a big surprise. The infringer may:

✔ Ignore your letter (the most frequent occurrence). If this happens, we suggest you move to the section 'Taking the high road and going for broke' earlier in this chapter.

✔ Contact you to seek an amicable solution, where you forego the payment of damages and the infringer agrees to cease all infringing activities.

✔ Drag you to court and defend an action for infringement, dragging you back into the litigation circus. In such an action, the alleged infringer may ask for a judgment on the grounds that he or she isn't infringing your IP right, or that your IP right is invalid because, for example, prior art anticipates the claims included in your patent thereby rendering your patent invalid. Likewise, in an action for infringement of a registered design, you may be able to show that the features allegedly copied contain no more than normal trade features found on similar products made and sold before the date of the registered design.

Negotiating a compromise

In most situations, your most sensible approach to resolving an infringement issue is through skilful negotiations. That's where attorneys excel. The result may be the grant of a very narrow non-exclusive licence to the infringer. In the case of a trade mark infringement, you may perhaps offer concurrent use of the mark in distinct territories or markets. Trust your IP attorney to balance all the legal and business aspects of the case and guide you to some safe haven, free of tempestuous litigation.

Covering yourself

Accusing somebody of infringing your IP rights on your own judgement without obtaining a written opinion from a knowledgeable attorney is reckless. Never consider entering an action for infringement of your IPRs without jumping through the infringement analysis hoop – and obtaining the opinion of a qualified IP attorney and, if a lot is at stake, the opinion of a Queen's Counsel.

Part VI
The Part of Tens

'So, you would like a career designing
trade marks when you leave school, Darren.'

In this part . . .

This part contains some great information, even if we do say so ourselves, in easily accessible and digestible lists. Want to know the most common mistakes people make when doing the patent thing? You can check them out here, along with other useful info like frequently asked copyright questions, the ten worst ways to go about naming a company or product, and additional resources that you can use when entering the IP jungle.

Chapter 21

Ten Patent Application Pitfalls

In This Chapter
▶ Avoiding common mistakes in preparing and filing
▶ Choosing the right approach

*I*n this chapter we describe the most common and most damaging errors committed by inventors. Because of these mistakes, many great inventions never make it to the market. Over the years, we've seen many inventors torpedo their own patent applications or get into serious legal trouble when a grain or two of knowledge and a bit of caution may have saved the day. Forewarned is forearmed – by reading this book, you can understand how to avoid these problems.

Choosing Patent Protection When Other Methods Fit the Bill

A patent takes lots of time and money to obtain and even more to enforce against an infringer. Sometimes, you can adequately protect many IP assets by less costly IP rights, such as a registered design, copyright, trade secret, or trade mark. Check out Chapter 5 for information on when and why another type of IP protection may be right for you.

Concealing the Past

Too many patents are declared invalid during an infringement trial because the inventor failed to tell the patent examiner everything he or she knew about the background and history of the invention, including prior technology that may be relevant to the issue of patentability. Even if the invention seems entirely new and non-obvious, you have a duty to disclose everything you know. See Chapter 7 for the information you need to disclose to your IP attorney.

Disclosing Too Little

You must describe your invention with enough detail to allow a person who's skilled in the art to practise (implement) it without undue experimentation. That's called the *enabling disclosure requirement*. You must also describe what you believe is the best way to actually use the invention, not necessarily the way you built your original prototype. Failure to disclose a critical element of the invention, can be fatal. For example, if you think that your new sander works best with a diamond powder coating, but you only described it using a cheaper glass powder coating, you aren't disclosing the best way to practise the invention.

Disclosing Too Much

Some applicants, fearful of failing the *enabling disclosure* requirement (see Chapter 7) because they didn't provide enough information, go overboard and describe everything including the kitchen appliances. Anything that a person skilled in the field of the invention can figure out on his or her own is nonessential. We're not talking about the person of ordinary skill defined in Chapter 7, but about a sophisticated expert in the field who understands the technology, is familiar with all the common acronyms, and knows how to anneal a metal, reduce a chemical solution, or modulate a carrier with a waveform without further explanation.

 Adding superfluous descriptions and drawings to your application ends up costing a lot when you file corresponding applications abroad because in some countries, you pay according to the number of pages and the number of drawings in your application, not to mention the translation costs.

Filing When You Haven't Got the Cash

We've seen plenty of inventors abandon their patent application mid-stream for lack of funds. Take a good look at the overall cost (check out Chapter 3 for some handy cost estimates) *before* you prepare the application. If you're not sure where the money will come from, and you're not planning to sell your invention, think twice before filing a patent. You can of course compile it yourself, and file a description of your invention and a diagram or two with the UK-IPO. Doing so allows you to put 'patent pending' on the product, which can give it some clout and ward off the odd infringer, and won't cost you a penny for the first year. You can use your limited resources to develop an effective marketing programme, including a blockbuster of a trade mark, and look at an alternate and cheaper form of IP protection. We outline the options for protection in Chapter 5.

Giving It Away

You must keep your idea confidential before you apply for a patent. You won't be able to gain patent protection for your idea if you tell other people about it (called 'putting your idea into the public domain'), who aren't bound by confidentiality. If you do have to tell other people about your idea, make sure that you have a confidentiality agreement in place. It's essential to have a confidentiality agreement in place if you're looking to file a patent application later. Putting your idea into the public domain includes using your new lawnmower invention in your garden, overlooked by other dwellings, regardless of whether anyone was actually looking at the time! So keep it under wraps. Keep even Great Uncle Alfred in the dark until you have protection in place.

Going It Alone

Unless you have special legal training, don't think that you can file and pursue a patent application without help from a patent attorney – what you end up with probably isn't worth the paper it's printed on. The worst part is that you won't even know that you've messed up on the application until you try to sue someone for infringement.

Reading this book is an excellent first step, but it's not going to replace a competent patent attorney. What it does is provide you with a basic knowledge base from which you can confidently communicate with the experts, make informed decisions, evaluate the commercial potential of an idea, work with others to protect your businesses IP rights, and do much of the IP legwork, such as gathering a complete background file for your invention and laying out a sensible IP protection strategy. Most importantly, you'll know to avoid some very damaging faux pas. In certain uncomplicated cases, you may be able to conduct preliminary patent and trade mark searches and obtain copyright registrations on your own.

Naming a Non-Inventor

Purposely listing someone who didn't contribute to the invention as an inventor is a misrepresentation that can invalidate a patent. The same goes for failing to name a bona fide inventor. Some inventors feel obligated to name their spouses as co-inventors on the mistaken belief that by doing so it makes them equal owners of the invention. An employer wants to be listed as an inventor because the employee who came up with the invention was working on their behalf and using their facilities, therefore automatically making the employer a contributor. An employee sometimes names the supervisor just to score some brownie points. Some believe that the technician who built the prototype is automatically a co-inventor, although that technician didn't contribute anything beyond standard engineering knowledge. If you faithfully provide your IP attorney with all the information listed in Chapter 8, he then knows how to identify the correct inventors.

Publish and Be Damned

In the UK, you must file your patent application before you make the invention public, unlike the US where you have a year in which to exploit your invention before you need to file a patent application (known as a *grace period*). See Chapter 8 for all the important deadlines to filing a patent application.

Be careful – making an invention public doesn't take much. Bragging about it to your neighbour Dave may be enough of a public disclosure to blow you out of the game. So get on the ball and file your application as soon as possible – in the meantime, keep your invention under wraps. As we explain in Chapter 2 you need to treat your invention as a trade secret, as long as you possibly can, and at least until you have a complete patent application on file.

Don't Rush It

Preparing a patent application takes time. Consulting your IP attorney close to a filing deadline may result in the drafting of the application being rushed at the expense of completeness and accuracy. Attorneys aren't magicians – give them a few weeks to do the job right. It's all to your benefit.

Chapter 22

Ten Common Copyright Questions

In This Chapter

▶ Clearing up common copyright misconceptions

▶ Addressing what you can and can't borrow

*P*eople come up with the same misconceptions about copyright all the time, such as thinking that copying less than 30 per cent of a copyrighted work is legal (it's not) and believing using a recording as background music for an aerobics class because they bought and paid for it is fine (it's not). In this chapter we cover the questions our clients ask most often about copyright.

Can I Copy a Page from a Book and Give the Copies to My Students?

Yes. Copying a work for students is one of the *fair-use limitations* to copyright, meaning exactly what it implies. See Chapter 11 for a list of fair-use limitations. These limitations set out certain actions that may be carried out, but would normally be regarded as an infringement of the work in question. The principle effectively allows commentary, parody, research, news reporting, and education of copyrighted works without the author's permission. So a teacher wanting to provide copies of a work for the students is within the fair-use limitations.

Can I Copyright My Campaign Slogan for the Next Election?

Probably not. Names, titles, slogans, and short phrases typically aren't considered substantial enough to deserve copyright protection. A limerick or short poem, a single original bar of music, and a simple line drawing may all have enough substance to pass the threshold. It depends on whether your slogan contain sufficient authorship or amount of artistic merit. If you create a product name or slogan for your business, don't forget to check out trade marks.

Can I Protect Software with a Patent?

No, not in the UK. However, a recent court decision means that claims for computer software will be allowed if, but only if, the program implements a patentable invention. Copyright protects software in the UK and Europe, however in the US computer programs can be protected by a patent. While you're at it, you can keep a good part of the program instructions confidential and protect them as a trade secret. (Find out how to preserve the trade secret in a computer program in Chapter 13.) You may also give a distinctive name to your software and get some trade mark protection. (Check out Chapter 15 for tips on creating distinctive names.) Seek advice if you're looking at selling your software into other territories such as the US, where you may need to file a patent application to achieve suitable protection.

Can I Use a Popular Song in a Video Clip of My Dog to Send to a TV Show?

No. Copying a song from a CD to your videotape would be your first count of copyright infringement. Then every time your tape is played in public or broadcast constitutes another act of infringement. We can hear you thinking that everyone does it, and you may be right. Check Chapter 11 for exceptions and exemptions.

Can I Use Graphics Copied from a Magazine for My Web Site?

Yes, but watch out for the catch: You need to get permission from the copyright owner of the material you borrow. Check out Chapter 12 to find out how and where to get the permission that you need. No permission, no use. This applies to photographs, images, clipart, logos, and all other graphical material.

How Do I Copyright My Idea for a TV Show?

Sorry, but you can't. You can't copyright ideas, concepts, systems, procedures, principles, methods, or discoveries. Copyright protects only the original *expression* of an idea and not the idea itself, so you have to at least commit the script to paper in order to get copyright. Check out Chapter 11, where we talk about the copyright golden rule.

How Do I Register Copyright for My Children's Story?

You don't need to. Like all authors, you automatically enjoy copyright when you write down your story or dictate it into a recording machine. You don't need to register under the laws of copyright for your story. Just mark your work with the copyright symbol © followed by your name and the year of creation – for example, © Z X Smith 2007.

How Much of a Copyrighted Work Can I Copy Without Infringing the Copyright?

None. Unless you get permission to use the work from the copyright owner, or unless you fall within the fair-use limitations (that we list in Chapter 11), any copying is infringing. You can't copy a little bit any more than you can copy the whole thing. However, with proper permission, you can even modify and adapt the pre-existing copyrighted material.

How Long Does Copyright Last?

It depends. Copyright duration in a work depends on when the copyrighted work was first published or registered. The safe rule is 70 years beyond the death of the author.

Where Can I Get Permission to Copy a Protected Work?

You can seek permission from the author, or owner, of a particular work. You need to determine whether copyright is still enforceable for the work, because the term may have expired. Read about investigating the status of a copyright in Chapter 12. If you're talking about a musical recording, read about the music business in Chapter 19.

Chapter 23

Ten Naming Blunders to Avoid

*I*n our opinion, the most popular ways people use to select a company or brand name are usually the worst approaches, and they often spell disaster. We think that the best way to choose your brand is to follow the methodical approach that we outline in Chapter 15. You probably want to coin a motivating, memorable brand identity that nobody can copy or imitate – a name that gains you a loyal customer base and may even give you a new and independent source of income. In other words, we suggest you avoid the routes for selecting a trade mark that we outline in this chapter.

Choosing Availability over Exclusivity

Just because a name's not already registered doesn't necessarily make it a good candidate for your product or company. If the name isn't strongly enforceable in court, you'll soon be copied and lose goodwill and market share, to the despair of your investors. (Check out Chapter 14 for more info on making your name hold up in court.) Go for the gold, not the tinfoil of an ordinary trade mark.

Creating Technical Jargon

Cold and unpronounceable combinations of Zs and Xs, or meaningless and pseudo-scientific marks like MicroChloraseptic and Hybrinetics just don't communicate. The minor technical gloss doesn't make up for the lost opportunity to carry a high-impact message to the market several times a day.

Describing Your Product or Service

Description is the most frequent and serious mistake. Do you want to name your company Digital Products (among dozens of Digital This and Digital That) or would you rather display uniqueness, brilliance, and creativity with a name like Apple? Should your beer be known as Lite and lose its identity to a gaggle of imitators or sport a shining tiara like Corona? A trade mark must be unique and distinctive, and not a mere description of your product that can apply to other similar products.

A descriptive name is a ticket to the courthouse and to endless, expensive, and time-consuming litigation because it's bound to be imitated eventually by your competitors. The courts have determined that you can't monopolise any part of the language. You can create a new word out of nothing, such as Kodak, or give a totally new meaning to an existing word, such as Crest for toothpaste. See Chapter 14 for more info on descriptive versus distinctive names.

Having Brainstorming Sessions

Brainstorming monopolises expensive management time and generates more arguments than deciding on the merits of chocolate versus vanilla ice cream. The result is a predictably colourless compromise that lacks the marketing punch and legal clout you need.

Group interaction in naming has its place, but such endeavours need method, structure, and common goals to be effective.

Holding a Naming Contest

Holding a public or employee contest to coin a name makes as much sense as practicing medicine by popular vote. It's haphazard at best. And a contest requires a winner, even if the best entry is unsuitable. Save your money and have a company picnic instead.

Ignoring the Customer

Insiders can be too close to the product and its history to be open-minded. A brand identity that's effective in the marketplace looks outward; it speaks the customer's language, not the engineer's or designer's. It should motivate your prospect, catch his or her fancy, and be long remembered. Don't focus on your achievement. Consider what will attract the public. Here is where a naming consultant or brand identity specialist may be of some use.

Leaving Your Mark Unprotected

Registration is your most powerful weapon and should be your top priority. Chapter 17 tells you everything you ever wanted to know about registering your mark.

Mimicking Another Company's Brand

Imitation may be the sincerest form of flattery, but why flatter your competitor? Worse, there's liability for infringing upon brand identity. Copying is stealing, and penalties can include a seizure of your goods and a court order to change your counterfeit brand name. Copying is the lazy way to avoid the discipline of naming. Be unique. Move to the head of your industry, rather than dissolve in the crowd.

Relying on the Logo

A creative ad and a snazzy logo help the customer remember your brand. When he or she decides to buy a widget, your name pops out first. A logo should enhance the impact of a name, but great graphics won't save a weak name. Do your best when coining your trade name and *then* take it to the graphic artist.

Using Your Family Name

Family pride may drive you to name your new enterprise the Jones Company, but doing so limits you in many ways. A surname isn't easy to register as a trade mark or to protect against copycats, unless it has some alternative meaning (for example, if you're a scooter manufacturer with the name Dash). Unless your name is unique and memorable, it contains minimal promotional value, and the valuation and transfer of the name upon the sale of the business is often problematic. Some companies have been about for decades that have managed to use a surname to great effect, such as Sainsbury's, Kellogg's, and Cadbury, although another Smith & Sons for a building company is unlikely to carry much clout in the marketplace.

Chapter 24

Ten Great IP Resources

In This Chapter

▶ Finding out where to get more information

▶ Diving into Web sites about IP rights

Although this book is full of useful information, the subject of intellectual property rights can fill thousands of printed volumes and millions of Web pages. In this chapter we point you in the direction of additional sources of information, resources, and forms, which you can use to find out more about the various topics that we discuss in this book.

UK Intellectual Property Office (UK-IPO)

The UK-IPO (www.ipo.gov.uk; UK-IPO Concept House, Cardiff Road, Newport NP10 8QQ; tel. 0845 9 500 505) can give you general information and answer your enquiries about patents, registered designs, copyright, and trade marks. We recommend you take a look at their information booklets, available online or by ordering over the phone or by post.

World Intellectual Property Organisation (WIPO)

The World Intellectual Property Organisation is an agency of the United Nations dedicated to promoting the protection of IP throughout the world. You can file a single application to protect your patent, design, or trade mark that is valid in multiple countries. WIPO has an Arbitration and Mediation facility providing mediation in IP disputes. Visit the World Intellectual Property Organisation Web site (www.wipo.int).

EU Office for Harmonization in the Internal Market (OHIM)

Check out the European Union's Office for Harmonization in the Internal Market Web site at http://oami.europa.eu/ for a huge amount of information on trade mark and design protection. The FAQ section of the site is particularly useful.

British Library Business and Intellectual Property Centre

The British Library Business and Intellectual Property Centre is a useful resource for all budding entrepreneurs, and the information is all available for free. You can gain market data, trawl through their patents library, and speak to one of their experts about how to find out about the right stuff for your invention. Check out the Web site at www.bl.uk/bipc.

Federation Against Copyright Theft (FACT)

FACT is the UK's leading trade organisation established to protect and represent the interests of the film and broadcasting industry against copyright and trade mark infringements. Take a look at their Web site at www.fact-uk.org.uk.

Patent Information Centres (PATLIBS UK)

Patent Information Centres are easy-to-access patent and other IP information sources, providing a free basic information service to the general public, and helping you to make the best use of patent databases so you can assess whether your invention is new. To find your nearest centre, take a look at the British Library Web site `http://www.bl.uk/collections/patents/patentsnetwork.html`.

Department for Business Enterprise and Regulatory Reform (BERR)

BERR summarises legislation and gives practical information for companies on the subject of innovation. `www.innovation.gov.uk`.

Trevor Baylis Brands plc (TBB) is a team of IP experts and attorneys who can help you to achieve the best result for your invention with a range of professional services. TBB is just one of the organisations out there that can help you to conduct an IP search. `www.trevorbaylisbrands.com`.

Useful Books

Of course, this book gives you heaps of information and advice, but if you want to take things a step further, dip into the following:

- *A Better Mousetrap: The Business of Invention* by Graham Barker and Peter Bissell (only available from `www.abettermousetrap.co.uk`). A great guide to inventing and how to avoid the mistakes along the way, including the IP pitfalls.

- *Inventing For Dummies* by Peter Jackson and Philip Robinson (Wiley). If you have an invention and need more information about the commercial side to IP, this is a great resource to start you on your merry way to making your invention successful.

- *James Dyson's History of Great Inventions* edited by Robert Uhlig (Constable and Robinson). Sir James Dyson, one of Britain's best-known engineers, provides a fascinating reference book taking a closer look at inventions and inventors that have shaped our civilisation.

- *Gowers Review of Intellectual Property (UK).* An extensive report that's the result of an independent review of the UK IP framework commissioned by the Chancellor of the Exchequer and carried out by Andrew Gowers. Downloadable free-of-charge from HM Treasury Web site at `www.hm-treasury.gov.uk/independent_reviews/gowers_review_intellectual_property/gowersreview_index.cfm`.

Networking and Lobbying

Try these resources for networking and lobbying:

- **Intellectual Property Awareness Network (IPAN):** An informal group of professional and business organisations with a shared interest in improving awareness and understanding of patents, trade marks, designs, copyright, and other IPRs. (www.ipaware.net.)

- **Ideas 21:** An innovation network devoted to the successful exploitation of ideas and intellectual property. (www.ideas21.co.uk.)

- **Institute of Patentees and Inventors:** A chance to contact like-minded inventors, and discuss IP issues amongst other things. (www.invent.org.uk.)

- **Anti Copying in Design (ACID):** An action group committed to fighting copyright theft. (www.acid.uk.com.)

Getting Legal Help

Check out these organisations for legal help:

- **The Law Society:** This organisation is the representative body for solicitors in England and Wales, and offers access to high quality legal services to the public. (www.lawsociety.org.uk.)

- **The Licensing Executives Society Britain and Ireland (LES):** The society for professionals interested in the licensing of IPRs and technology transfer. (www.les-bi.org.)

- **Institute of Trade Mark Attorneys (ITMA):** For guidance with trade marks and to find a trade mark attorney that can help you secure protection for your brand or name, ITMA is the place to contact. (www.itma.org.uk.)

- **Chartered Institute of Patent Attorneys (CIPA):** The Institute can provide you with a list of Chartered Patent Attorneys that may be able to assist you, and offer advice on patent issues. They also offer a free 30-minute clinic for you to have a one-to-one with a Patent Attorney. (www.cipa.org.uk.)

Appendix

Sample Patent Applications

● ●

(12) UK Patent   (19) GB   (11) 2 433 914   (13) B

(45) Date of publication: **28.11.2007**

(54) Title of the invention: Book binding

(51) INT CL: *B42B 5/10* (2006.01)

(21) Application No:	0612612.2	(72)	Inventor(s): **Beverley James Pyke**
(22) Date of Filing:	27.06.2006		
(43) Date A Publication:	11.07.2007	(73)	Proprietor(s): **Beverley James Pyke** 22 Victoria Street, ALDERNEY, Guernsey, GY9 3TA, United Kingdom

(52) UK CL (Edition X):
NOT CLASSIFIED

David William Stanley
1 Mare Jean Bott, ALDERNEY, Guernsey,
GY9 3TX, United Kingdom

(56) Documents Cited:
WO 2004/076200 A2   **US 2178887 A**

(74) Agent and/or Address for Service:
Stanleys
PO Box 62, ALDERNEY, GY9 3JU,
United Kingdom

(58) Field of Search:
As for published application 2433914 A *viz*:
UK CL (Edition X) **B6A**
INT CL **B42B, B42D, B42F**
Other
EPODOC, WPI, TXTE.
updated as appropriate

- 1 -

BOOK BINDING

The present invention relates to book binding.

Books have been bound for hundreds of years. The traditional
hardback book comprises sewn sections that are assembled together in a cover.
5 This is a relatively time-consuming and expensive process. In cheaper paperback
books, the pages are typically held together by an adhesive -- for example, using
the so-called perfect binding method.

Various binding systems are available for custom bindings, ranging from
one-off office reports to low-volume specialist publications. Plastic comb
10 bindings engage rectangular apertures in assembled pages of a book. A spiral
wire binding engages circular apertures in assembled pages of a book. A twin-
looped coil binding makes tongue shapes out of wire to engage rectangular
apertures in assembled pages of a book, rather like the plastic comb binding but
stronger. Modern wire bindings typically use a metal wire with a tough plastics
15 coating. Plastic comb and wire bindings will be very well known to the skilled
reader and therefore are not further described in great detail here. For
convenience, all such bindings are referred to in the context of this specification
as "coil" bindings, made from "coil members".

Hardback and paperback book binding methods lend themselves well to
20 mass production. However, they have a distinct practical disadvantage in that
the books have to be held by hand or placed on some kind of stand in order that
they may be held open. They do not naturally lie flat and open. They can
sometimes be made to lie flat at a particular page by applying excessive force to
the binding. However, this tends to break down the spine and eventually the
25 book may come to pieces.

- 2 -

A well-known advantage of coil bindings is that, in general, they allow a book to be opened flat. Readers of workshop manuals, reference books and recipe books have long recognised this advantage. However, readers of books more generally will also find it much more convenient if books could easily be
5   opened and laid flat.

A disadvantage of coil bindings is that they may be rather weak, as compared to a well-made hardback or paperback book. Another disadvantage is that the coil binding generally affords little opportunity to display a title. Therefore, it becomes very difficult to locate a desired volume on a bookshelf.

10   US 4,596,482 (Salzer) shows a backing for affixing a title label to a comb binding. However, this provides no strengthening within the comb binding and may interfere with the easy opening and laying flat of the book. US 7,052,045 (Park) shows another way to label a book with a coil binding. This comprises a small title clip that attaches to the coil binding. However, rather than adding
15   strength to the coil binding, the title clip relies upon the coil binding to support it.

Preferred embodiments of the present invention aim to provide book binding systems that may be generally improved in the foregoing respects.

According to one aspect of the present invention, there is provided a
20   book binding system comprising:

an elongate coil member adapted to engage apertures at the edges of pages of a book, thereby to bind the pages;

an elongate outer spine member extending between the ends of said coil member, externally thereof; and

- 3 -

an inner spine member extending between the ends of said coil member, internally thereof:

such that the coil member is reinforced by the inner and outer spine members engaged about the coil member and said outer spine member presents
5   an outer surface to display a title.

Preferably, said inner and outer spine members are joined directly together.

Preferably, said inner and outer spine members are joined together as a snap-fit.

10   Preferably, said inner and outer spine members are joined together at a plurality of positions along their lengths.

Preferably, said inner and outer spine members are joined together at their respective ends.

Preferably, said inner spine member is of cylindrical cross-section.

15   Preferably, said inner spine member is of circular cross-section.

Preferably, said outer spine member is of a generally flat shape.

Preferably, said coil member is of spiral configuration.

Preferably, said coil member defines tongues adapted to engage in rectangular holes of respective book pages.

- 4 -

Preferably, said coil member comprises a wire.

Preferably, said coil member comprises a plastics material.

Preferably, said coil member is of substantially circular cross-section.

Preferably, said coil member has a flattened outer face against which
5   said outer spine member abuts.

Preferably, said inner and outer spine members extend for substantially
the full length of said coil member.

Preferably, said inner and outer spine members extend beyond the ends
of said coil member.

10   Said inner and outer spine members may extend for less than the full
length of said coil member.

The invention extends to a book that has been bound by a book
binding system according to any of the preceding aspects of the invention.

Preferably, a space is defined between said inner spine member and
15   opposing edges of the book pages.

Preferably, a title is printed on said outer spine member.

For a better understanding of the invention and to show how
embodiments of the same may be carried into effect, reference will now be
made, by way of example, to the accompanying diagrammatic drawings, in
20   which:

- 5 -

Figure 1 illustrates one example of an embodiment of a book binding system, in side elevation;

Figure 2 shows the binding system of Figure 1 in top plan view;

Figure 3 shows the binding system of Figures 1 and 2 in end elevation;

5   Figure 4 shows an inner face of an outer spine member of the binding system of Figures 1 to 3, together with a plastics rod;

Figure 5 is a first detailed perspective view of the top of the binding system shown in Figures 1 to 4; and

Figure 6 is a second detailed perspective view of the top of the binding
10   system shown in Figures 1 to 5

In the figures, like references denote like or corresponding parts.

The book binding system 1 illustrated in Figures 1 to 6 comprises an outer spine member 2 and an inner spine member 3 that snap-engage with one another about a twin-looped wire coil binding 4 that is otherwise of
15   conventional design and engages rectangular apertures 5 formed at the edges 61 of pages 6 of a book, thereby to bind the pages.

The outer spine member 2 is in the form of a generally flat title strip of plastics material, formed at each end with respective bosses 21 that fit alongside the end loops of the coil binding 4. In this example, the outer face 22 of the title
20   strip 2 is slightly convex, but alternatively, it may be completely flat. The inner face 23 of the title strip 2 is formed with projections in the form of nipples 24 that engage the coil binding 4 to restrict movement of the coil binding 4 with

- 6 -

respect to the title strip 2. This may be to restrict such movement longitudinally of the title strip 2 or to restrict angular movement of the coil binding 4 – or both of these. The nipples 24 may engage the ends of loops of the coil binding 4.

5   The inner spine member 3 is in the form of a plastics rod having ends that snap-engage within the bosses 21 of the title strip 2. As may be seen in Figure 2, a gap is provided between the rod 3 and the edges 61 of the book pages 6, to facilitate the turning of the pages 6 in the coil binding 4 and to allow the pages 6 of the book to be opened flat.

10   It may be appreciated that the illustrated book binding system 1 may be implemented very cheaply, simply and effectively. The book may be bound with the coil binding 4 in a conventional manner. Then, in order to provide a title strip and spine, the title strip 2 is placed against the outer face of the coil binding 4, and one end of the plastics rod 3 is inserted through one end the coil binding 4 and a respective one of the bosses 21 until it reaches the other of the bosses

15   21, where one or each end of the plastics rod 3 is snap-engaged in its respective boss 21. The assembly of the title strip 2 and rod 3 about the coil binding 4 together provide significant reinforcement to the coil binding 4.

Various resilient snap-engagement means may be provided between the rod 3 and title strip 4, and/or alternative securing means (e.g. friction-fit) may be

20   provided. As another example, the title strip 2 may be provided on its inner face 23 with resilient jaws configured to snap-engage about the rod 3.

For large runs, the title strip 2 may be pre-printed with title information. For custom bindings, one may write directly on the title strip 2 or apply a printed label to it. Thus, one may readily locate the book on a bookshelf and pull it

25   from the shelf without damaging the coil binding 4.

- 7 -

Books come in various sizes. However, experience shows that they tend to be of standard heights -- for example, A4 and A5 sizes in Europe. A few standard diameters of coil bindings 4 have been found sufficient to accommodate most needs. Therefore, title strips such as 2 and rods such as 3

5   may be provided in just a few standard sizes to accommodate most needs.

By way of example, the coil binding 4 in Figure 1 may have a diameter of 14 mm, the title strip 2 may have a width of 14 mm, the rod 3 may have a diameter of 3 mm and the bosses an outer diameter of 6 mm. In an alternative example, the coil binding 4 may have a diameter of 9 mm, the title strip may

10   have a width of 9 mm, the rod 3 may have a diameter of 3 mm and the bosses an outer diameter of 6 mm.

Although, in the illustrated embodiment, the title strip 2 and the rod 3 are of plastics materials, they may be made of other materials. Although a twin-looped coil binding 4 is illustrated, other coil bindings may be used.

15   The coil binding 4 may be provided with a substantially flat face adjacent the title strip2, which may therefore fit more closely against the coil binding 4. The rod 3 may conveniently be of circular cross-section but may alternatively be of any other suitable cross-sectional shape, cylindrical or otherwise.

The title strip 2 may be provided with, for example, a ridged portion to

20   assist gripping the book to pull it from a bookshelf.

It is found convenient for the title strip 2 and rod 3 to interengage at the ends of the title strip 2. However, they may interengage at other positions. Although it is practical for the title strip 2 and rod 3 to interengage at at least

- 8 -

two positions, it is conceivable that they may be attached together at only one point.

It is found convenient for the title strip 2 and rod 3 to be of substantially the same length and extend for substantially the full height of the
5   book pages 6. However, they may be of shorter lengths – e.g. at least 50%, 60%, 70%, 80% or 90% of the height of the book or its pages 6.

In this specification, the verb "comprise" has its normal dictionary meaning, to denote non-exclusive inclusion. That is, use of the word "comprise" (or any of its derivatives) to include one feature or more, does not exclude the
10   possibility of also including further features.

- 9 -

CLAIMS

1.   A book binding system comprising:

   a.   an elongate coil member adapted to engage apertures at the edges
   of pages of a book, thereby to bind the pages;

5   b.   an elongate outer spine member extending between the ends of
   said coil member, externally thereof; and

   c.   an inner spine member extending between the ends of said coil
   member, internally thereof:

   such that the coil member is reinforced by the inner and outer spine

10   members engaged about the coil member and said outer spine member presents
   an outer surface to display a title.

2.   A book binding system according to claim 1, wherein said inner and
outer spine members are joined directly together.

3.   A book binding system according to claim 2, wherein said inner and

15   outer spine members are joined together as a snap-fit.

4.   A book binding system according to claim 1, 2 or 3, wherein said inner
and outer spine members are joined together at a plurality of positions along
their lengths.

5.   A book binding system according to claim 4, wherein said inner and

20   outer spine members are joined together at their respective ends.

- 10 -

6.   A book binding system according to any of the preceding claims, wherein said inner spine member is of cylindrical cross-section.

7.   A book binding system according to claim 6, wherein said inner spine member is of circular cross-section.

5   8.   A book binding system according to any of the preceding claims, wherein said outer spine member is of a generally flat shape.

9.   A book binding system according to any of the preceding claims, wherein said coil member is of spiral configuration.

10.   A book binding system according to any of the preceding claims,
10   wherein said coil member defines tongues adapted to engage in rectangular holes of respective book pages.

11.   A book binding system according to any of the preceding claims, wherein said coil member comprises a wire.

12.   A book binding system according to any of the preceding claims,
15   wherein said coil member comprises a plastics material.

13.   A book binding system according to any of the preceding claims, wherein said coil member is of substantially circular cross-section.

14.   A book binding system according to any of the preceding claims, wherein said coil member has a flattened outer face against which said outer
20   spine member abuts.

- 11 -

15.   A book binding system according to any of the preceding claims, wherein said inner and outer spine members extend for substantially the full length of said coil member.

16.   A book binding system according to any of the preceding claims, 5   wherein said inner and outer spine members extend beyond the ends of said coil member.

17.   A book binding system according to any of claims 1 to 14, wherein said inner and outer spine members extend for less than the full length of said coil member.

10   18.   A book binding system substantially as hereinbefore described with reference to the accompanying drawings.

19.   A book that has been bound by a book binding system according to any of the preceding claims.

20.   A book according to claim 19, wherein a space is defined between said 15   inner spine member and opposing edges of the book pages.

21.   A book according to claim 19 or 20, wherein a title is printed on said outer spine member.

22.   A bound book substantially as hereinbefore described with reference to the accompanying drawings.

1 / 1

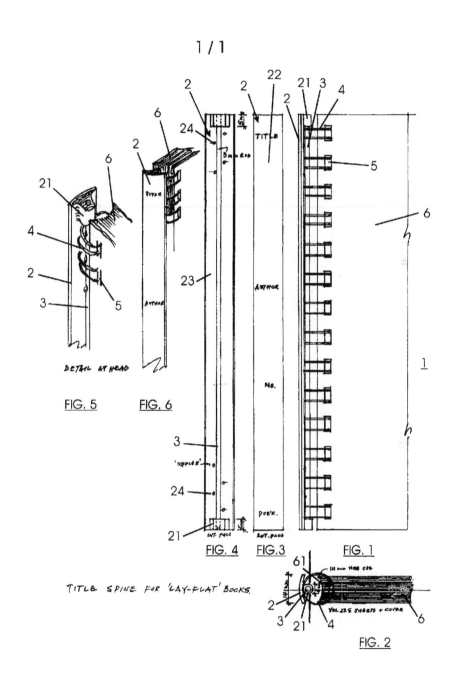

DETAIL AT HEAD

FIG. 5   FIG. 6

FIG. 4   FIG.3   FIG. 1

TITLE SPINE FOR 'LAY-FLAT' BOOKS.

FIG. 2

PCT

WORLD INTELLECTUAL PROPERTY ORGANIZATION
International Bureau

INTERNATIONAL APPLICATION PUBLISHED UNDER THE PATENT COOPERATION TREATY (PCT)

(51) International Patent Classification ⁶ : B63C 9/06	A1	(11) International Publication Number: **WO 98/55358**
		(43) International Publication Date: 10 December 1998 (10.12.98)

(21) International Application Number: PCT/GB98/01642

(22) International Filing Date: 4 June 1998 (04.06.98)

(30) Priority Data:
9711531.5   5 June 1997 (05.06.97)   GB

(71) Applicant *(for all designated States except US)*: WARDLE STOREYS (SAFETY & SURVIVAL EQUIPMENT) LIMITED [GB/GB]; Grove Mill, Earby, Barnoldswick BB18 6UT (GB).

(72) Inventor; and
(75) Inventor/Applicant *(for US only)*: MARTIN, Michael [GB/GB]; 7 Richmond Drive, Lymm, Cheshire WA13 9HE (GB).

(74) Agent: MATHISEN MACARA & CO.; The Coach House, 6–8 Swakeleys Road, Ickenham, Uxbridge, Middlesex UB10 8BZ (GB).

(81) Designated States: AU, CA, GB, JP, US, European patent (AT, BE, CH, CY, DE, DK, ES, FI, FR, GB, GR, IE, IT, LU, MC, NL, PT, SE).

Published
With international search report.

(54) Title: LIFERAFT

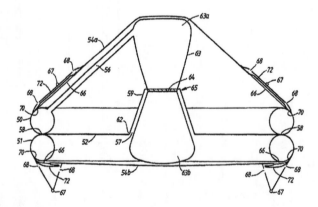

(57) Abstract

A liferaft has a floor (52) surrounded by one or more inflatable tubes (50, 51). Two canopies (54a, 54b) are provided, one (54a) covering one side of the floor (52) and the other (54b) covering the other side of the floor (52). When the liferaft is deployed on water, support means, which may be an inflatable column (63), erect the canopy (54a) that is above the water. The other canopy (54b) is unerected and lies in the water. The system of weights (67) and elastic ropes (66) forms the canopy in the water into stabilizing means in the form of water pockets. Similar means are provided on the deployed canopy (54a) but, when the canopy (54a) is erected, they lie flush with the canopy surface and so do not interfere with the operation of the liferaft.

Index

• T •

Notes

Notes

FOR DUMMIES®

Do Anything. Just Add Dummies

UK editions

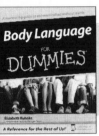

FOR DUMMIES®

Do Anything. Just Add Dummies

HOBBIES

Poker
FOR DUMMIES

978-0-7645-5232-8

Knitting
FOR DUMMIES

978-0-7645-5395-0

Drawing
FOR DUMMIES

978-0-7645-5476-6

Also available:

Art For Dummies
(978-0-7645-5104-8)

Aromatherapy For Dummies
(978-0-7645-5171-0)

Bridge For Dummies
(978-0-471-92426-5)

Card Games For Dummies
(978-0-7645-9910-1)

Chess For Dummies
(978-0-7645-8404-6)

Improving Your Memory
For Dummies
(978-0-7645-5435-3)

Massage For Dummies
(978-0-7645-5172-7)

Meditation For Dummies
(978-0-471-77774-8)

Photography For Dummies
(978-0-7645-4116-2)

Quilting For Dummies
(978-0-7645-9799-2)

EDUCATION

Psychology
FOR DUMMIES

978-0-7645-5434-6

The Koran
FOR DUMMIES

978-0-7645-5581-7

Anatomy
& Physiology
FOR DUMMIES

978-0-7645-5422-3

Also available:

Algebra For Dummies
(978-0-7645-5325-7)

Astronomy For Dummies
(978-0-7645-8465-7)

Buddhism For Dummies
(978-0-7645-5359-2)

Calculus For Dummies
(978-0-7645-2498-1)

Cooking Basics For Dummies
(978-0-7645-7206-7)

Forensics For Dummies
(978-0-7645-5580-0)

Islam For Dummies
(978-0-7645-5503-9)

Philosophy For Dummies
(978-0-7645-5153-6)

Religion For Dummies
(978-0-7645-5264-9)

Trigonometry For Dummies
(978-0-7645-6903-6)

PETS

Puppies
FOR DUMMIES

978-0-470-03717-1

Dog Training
FOR DUMMIES

978-0-7645-8418-3

Cats
FOR DUMMIES

978-0-7645-5275-5

Also available:

Labrador Retrievers
For Dummies
(978-0-7645-5281-6)

Aquariums For Dummies
(978-0-7645-5156-7)

Birds For Dummies
(978-0-7645-5139-0)

Dogs For Dummies
(978-0-7645-5274-8)

Ferrets For Dummies
(978-0-7645-5259-5)

Golden Retrievers
For Dummies
(978-0-7645-5267-0)

Horses For Dummies
(978-0-7645-9797-8)

Jack Russell Terriers
For Dummies
(978-0-7645-5268-7)

Puppies Raising & Training
Diary For Dummies
(978-0-7645-0876-9)

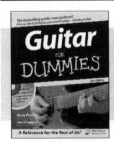

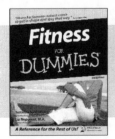
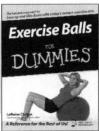

FOR DUMMIES®

Helping you expand your horizons and achieve your potential

INTERNET

978-0-470-12174-0

978-0-471-97998-2

978-0-470-08030-6

Also available:

Blogging For Dummies
For Dummies, 2nd Edition
(978-0-470-23017-6)

Building a Web Site For
Dummies, 3rd Edition
(978-0-470-14928-7)

Creating Web Pages
All-in-One Desk Reference
For Dummies, 3rd Edition
(978-0-470-09629-1)

eBay.co.uk
For Dummies
(978-0-7645-7059-9)

Video Blogging FD
(978-0-471-97177-1)

Web Analysis For Dummies
(978-0-470-09824-0)

Web Design For Dummies,
2nd Edition
(978-0-471-78117-2)

DIGITAL MEDIA

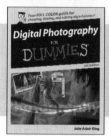

978-0-7645-9802-9

978-0-470-17474-6

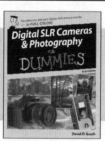

978-0-470-14927-0

Also available:

BlackBerry For Dummies,
2nd Edition
(978-0-470-18079-2)

Digital Photography
All-In-One Desk Reference
For Dummies
(978-0-470-03743-0)

Digital Photo Projects
For Dummies
(978-0-470-12101-6)

iPhone For Dummies
(978-0-470-17469-2)

Photoshop CS3 For Dummies
(978-0-470-11193-2)

Podcasting
For Dummies
(978-0-471-74898-4)

COMPUTER BASICS

978-0-470-13728-4

978-0-470-05432-1

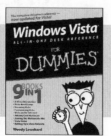

978-0-471-74941-7

Also available:

Macs For Dummies,
9th Edition
(978-0-470-04849-8)

Office 2007 All-in-One Desk
Reference For Dummies
(978-0-471-78279-7)

PCs All-in-One Desk
Reference For Dummies,
4th Edition
(978-0-470-22338-3)

Upgrading & Fixing PCs
For Dummies, 7th Edition
(978-0-470-12102-3)

Windows XP For Dummies,
2nd Edition
(978-0-7645-7326-2)

Printed and bound in the UK by
CPI Antony Rowe, Eastbourne